Best Wishes,
Franklin Foster

BORDERING ON GREATNESS

A History of Lloydminster's First Century

1903 - 2003

by

Franklin Lloyd Foster

B.Ed., B.A., M.A., Ph.D.

and

Alan Grant Griffith

B.Ed.

Foster Learning Inc.
Lloydminster, Alberta
© 2001

Editor/Author:
Franklin Lloyd Foster

Co-Editor/Co-Author:
Alan Grant Griffith

LDCCA Fund Raising:
Lynn Manners

Photographer:
Don Whiting Photography

Layout and Design:
Alan Griffith, Foster Learning Inc.

Printed and bound by:
The Print Stop Inc., Edmonton, Alberta

National Library of Canada Cataloguing in Publication Data:

Foster, Franklin Lloyd, 1945-
Bordering on greatness:

Includes index.
ISBN 0-9689193-0-8
1. Lloydminster (Sask. and Alta.)--History. 2. Lloydminster (Sask. and Alta)--Pictorial works. I. Griffith, Alan Grant, 1972- II. Title
FC3549.L59F67 2001   971.24'2   C2001-910918-0
F1074.5.L55F67 2001

Researchers:

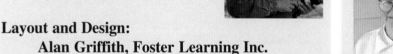

Sheila Bennett   Dorothy Foster   Ian Goodwillie

Heather Gray   Alan Hagen   Jean Henry

Penny Manners   Cindy Trigg   Heather Yuzik

Linda Nykolaychuk   Denise Ramsay-McKenzie

Cover by Alan Griffith, Foster Learning Inc.

With photos courtesy of the following contributors:

Don Whiting Photography
Professional Touch Photography
BayVan Photography
Lloydminster Regional Archives
Saskatchewan Archives Board
Glenbow Archives
Marjorie Brooks
Bob Hayes
Foster Learning Inc.

2000
Canada

SHARING THE MEMORY   DES SOUVENIRS À PARTAGER
SHAPING THE DREAM   DES RÊVES À FAÇONNER

Bordering On Greatness: A History of Lloydminster's First Century 1903 - 2003
is proud to have been selected as a
Canada Millennium Partnership Project
and gratefully acknowledges the
financial contribution received to complete this project.

Produced for the

Lloydminster and District Centennial Commemorative Association Inc.
www.lloydminster.net

Produced by:
Foster Learning Inc.
www.fosterlearning.com

The opinions expressed in this publication are those of Foster Learning Inc.
and do not necessarily reflect the official views of the Government of Canada.

In addition to the Canada Millenium Partnership Program, the following
Proud Partners
provided financial support for this project:

Alberta Lottery Fund/Lloydminster Community Grant Society #76
ATCO Electric
City of Lloydminster
Foster Learning Inc.
Husky Oil Operations Ltd.
Lloydminster Agricultural Exhibition Association
Lloydminster and District Centennial Commemorative Association
Lloydminster and District Co-operative Ltd.
Lloydminster Community Futures
Lloydminster Public Library Foundation
Nelson Lumber Foundation
OTS Heavy Oil Science Centre
Rotary Club of Lloydminster
Saskatchewan Heritage Foundation

Donors:
Ann and Vic Juba
George and Kathleen Matheson

Donations In Memory Of:
Aston and Springford Pioneers, 1903
George Franklin Baynton, 1912-1983 and Dorothy Evelyn (Willard) Baynton, 1910-1996
Dr. G. L. (George) Cooke, 1887-1984 and wife Florence B. (Wert) Cooke, 1892-1960
Dr. Frank Creech, 1914-1999
E. Harold Davies, Sr., 1883-1971 and May (Martha Evans) Davies, 1883-1965
Roger Price Jones, 1896-1962 and Margaret E. (Ames) Jones, 1907-1996
Richard Larsen, 1906-1994 and Jane (Holman) Larsen, 1912-1992
George Gwynne Mann, 1877-1938, telegraph operator and lineman, and
Ethel Mary (Burgess) Mann, 1882-1958, Barr Colonist
Headley James Manners, 1895-1982 and Florence Mary (Lampitt) Manners, 1898-1990
A.F. (Art) Shortell, 1919-1976
Ken Stanley, 1946-1994

Foreword

Come on along, come on along
Let me take you by the hand
We'll sing a song; we'll sing a song
About a place that's really grand!
When you hit Lloydminster
Well the place is a buzzin' -
Come on along, come on along,
Lloydminster's really grand!

These were the lyrics of a bouncy radio jingle that introduced the "Lloydminster Show" on CJCA Edmonton in the early 1950's, before we had our own radio station. It captures something of the pride in place that has so often found expression in our history. That pride appears in the numerous first hand accounts of the Barr Colonists. Some are humorous, one or two are bitter, but all are filled with a sense that the original settling of Lloydminster and District was a tale of epic proportions. The excitement continued with the Board of Trade pamphlets of the 1920's, which kept up a chorus of boosterism. The sense of achievement and celebration was alive and well in the elaborate and sustained celebrations of our Diamond Jubilee in 1963.

Now we come to the celebration of our community's Centennial. The year 2003 will provide us with a full century of experiences to review and reflect upon. It is our hope that this book will provide something of an introduction to those first 100 years. History is the way we keep track of who we are, by recalling where we have been. History gives us our identity, individually and communally. Lloydminster's history is the synergistic result of the intertwining of thousands of individual histories over our first 100 years. Each story is part of the fabric – sometimes easily overlooked and forgotten, sometimes boldly front and centre. All individual stories contribute to the one community story – the community story provides the context and meaning to the individual stories.

What follows is the first comprehensive history of Lloydminster. However, despite the assistance and generous support of many, time and resources allowed only a sampling of some of the stories that need to be told. We hope that others will build on the framework we have provided. We believe that any careful reader will gain a better appreciation of our rich and unique history. We hope that time and resources will allow us to continue to develop the companion web site for this book at www.lloydminster.net. There we could have the room to record what space in this book did not allow. There we could update and correct and develop a truly comprehensive and useful resource of our local history. We hope, most fervently, that the growing interest in our history will bring about City support for the staffing of our Archives with a qualified, full-time archivist. So much of our history has already been lost. So much is even now passing away.

This book, then, is a salute, by way of words and photos, to the individuals who comprised Lloydminster's first century. Our work is also a gift to those who will make the history of Lloydminster's second century.

Thank you for supporting, in word and deed, the preservation and celebration of our local history.

Franklin Foster and Alan Griffith
in Lloydminster
Summer 2001.

Contents

Top: Dominion Day 1903 - the Colonists celebrate with picnics, softball and impromptu horseraces. Photo courtesy of Doug Aston Collection

Bottom: Canada Day 2000 - the Citizens celebrate with picnics, entertainment and slow tractor races. Photo courtesy of Doreen Plant

Chapter One

Settlement

Research by Cindy Trigg

At the beginning of the 20th Century, Lloydminster did not exist. The area on which the original townsite grew was a slight depression of grassland interspersed with shallow, boggy sloughs. Periodic prairie fires swept the area, cleaning out any trees that might bravely start to multiply. All that remained were clumps of silver wolf willow and small red willows clinging to the margins of the sometimes watery, always muddy slough bottoms. To the immediate north, west and south, the land rose slightly, culminating in what locals would come to call hills although the overwhelming impression of first arrivals throughout our first century has been that Lloydminster is incredibly flat. It would be on the higher elevations, especially to the southwest, that the city would grow and expand in its second half century.

Photo courtesy of Provincial Archives of Alberta B2369

This 1904 photo shows some of Lloydminster's earliest homes and also illustrates the landscape. Note the fringe of willows on the right.

Some Barr Colonists, and other early settlers, came down the North Saskatchewan River and off loaded supplies at places such as Hewitt's Landing. There still remained over 20 miles of hauling to reach the new townsite.

Photo courtesy of Provincial Archives of Alberta B5625

There had been nothing to attract human settlement to our specific location. Aboriginal people may have passed by but there was no reliable food source to hold them. There were no trees to shelter game, the water bodies were too small and unreliable to host much in the way of waterfowl and the great herds of buffalo had preferred the higher plains around present day Kitscoty and Marwayne, the northern edge of their North American range. Survey crews had worked the area in 1883, marking section lines and staking township corners for expected waves of settlers who did not come. Traders and travellers used either of the distant rivers or the trails that skirted along their banks: one to the south of the Battle River and the other on the north side of the North Saskatchewan.

In fact it was the very emptiness of this area on the map which, in 1902, attracted the eye of one Rev. Isaac Montgomery Barr and convinced the Canadian Government to agree to his plan for a group settlement in the area. What made that project seem somewhat sensible was that the Canadian Northern Railway had just surveyed a right-of-way through the heart of this "empty quarter", on a direct line between Battleford and Edmonton. The government agreed to reserve for Barr the exclusive right to file "homesteads" on even numbered sections in a tract of some 16 townships (576 square miles) along this proposed rail line. So it was that Isaac Barr hastened back to Britain to recruit settlers for his grand scheme of planting firm in the middle of Western Canada a colony of truly British folk.

The Barr Colony

In 1902, the Boer War was ending and British pride in their world encircling empire was high. Talk was rife in all parts of the British Isles of making new lives in the greater opportunities afforded in the "Colonies" or the "States". Many had already been in India or South Africa or had thought of emigrating to such places as Australia or Kansas. In September of that year, Rev. Barr produced a pamphlet promoting settlement in Canada's northwest. At the same time, Rev. George Lloyd wrote a letter to a London newspaper recommending the opportunities available in Canada. The two men would join in an unlikely and ultimately acrimonious partnership – Barr as the organizer and administrator of the expedition and Lloyd as the chaplain.

Photo courtesy of Glenbow Archives - NA-118-27

Above: Barr Colonists in Saskatoon had to scramble to find wagons to complete their epic journey. Below: Rev. Lloyd offers words of encouragement to apprehensive travelers along the trail.

The Canadian government had agreed to reserve Barr's lands only until April 15, 1903 so speed was necessary. By Christmas, Barr published a second pamphlet detailing his success to date and specific plans for the colony. He had originally thought of a colony of 500 British subjects. However, response was so overwhelming that soon the potential colonists numbered well over 3,000.

Special rates were obtained on the Elder Dempster Shipping Line. They were scheduled to sail on March 25, 1903 which, Barr calculated, would give them just enough time to reach their homesteads by mid-April. However, the shipping line delayed the sailing to March 31st. Colonists who were to sail even later on the Lake Simcoe and Montrose were advised by Barr that they should take berths on the S.S. Lake Manitoba. As a result, over 2,000 people (over 3 times the ship's rated accommodation) embarked.

They arrived at St. John, New Brunswick on Good Friday, April 10, 1903. Because of the holiday, passengers were forced to wait anxiously aboard ship until Sunday. They then clambered onto four chartered trains.

Photo courtesy of Saskatchewan Archives Board

Rev. Isaac Montgomery Barr

Isaac Barr was born March 2, 1847 near Hornby, in what is now Ontario. His father, William, a Presbyterian minister, and mother, Catherine, the daughter of a Presbyterian minister, emigrated from Ireland in 1846.

Barr's early career with the Church of England was tumultuous, moving quickly from parish to parish. In 1875, he went to Prince Albert, N.W.T. but returned to Ontario within weeks due to his daughter's ill health.

Soon after, his personal views almost resulted in his loss of ordination. When confronted about his opinions, Barr "reacted as he was to react again and again in his life. When the going became difficult, he backed away from a confrontation" writes his biographer, Helen Reid in <u>All Silent, All Damned</u>. Next, Barr took a parish in the U. S. and even applied for American citizenship.

Photo courtesy of Saskatchewan Archives Board

Above: a rare photo of Barr (closest to horse) and Lloyd together, taken in April 1903, at Saskatoon. On the threshold of achieving success for his mammoth scheme, he would be rejected as leader.

However, Barr maintained his interest in the expansion of the British Empire, following closely the career of Cecil Rhodes. In December 1901, Barr resigned his pastoral charge, intending to go to South Africa and work with Rhodes. These plans ended when Rhodes died three months later. Barr then turned to establishing a British colony in Canada's Northwest. His trip to Prince Albert, he claimed, had shown him the area's potential.

Barr was a planner and schemer with big dreams. He wrote pamphlets promoting a British settlement and promising a variety of amenities such as co-operatives to supply everything from groceries to farm equipment. He even set up a hospitalization plan. "Men of capital" were invited to invest in these programs.

Many have said that Barr was only out to make money. The evidence is contradictory. Barr was not wealthy. Publishing his promotional pamphlets took almost all his funds. He did receive a per capita commission from the Elder Dempster Steamship Company for those who travelled on its ships and he acted as an agent for the CPR. He also expected compensation from the Government of Canada but nothing came of that.

Some of the problems which erupted stemmed from the overwhelming numbers who responded to Barr's idea and from the colonists' unrealistic expectations. As well, several episodes along the way cast a shadow on Barr. For example, according to Rev. Lloyd, just before the S.S. Lake Manitoba docked at St. John, Barr bought all the ship's flour and had the cooks bake bread for sale to the colonists at 10 cents a loaf. When advised this was twice the cost in town, Barr lowered the price to 5 cents but the damage had been done.

As the colonists travelled to the reserved lands, dissatisfaction with Barr mounted. On May 16, 1903 at a meeting of 140 colonists, Barr was rejected as leader and a resolution passed to drop all mention of his name in connection with their "Britannia Colony".

Despite this, Barr's role in the settlement of Lloydminster has been recognized. Thus we have Barr Colony School, Barr Crescent and the Barr Colony Heritage Cultural Centre. Barr made some poor decisions, but he did succeed in bringing about the largest group settlement in Canadian history and planted them in a land of opportunities in which they began our community.

After leaving the colony, Barr returned to Ontario where he married his secretary, Christina Helberg, his fourth wife. They settled in the United States, and later emigrated to Australia as part of yet another group settlement scheme. He died in Australia in 1937 just days before his 90th birthday.

Rev. George Exton Lloyd

George Lloyd was born in London, England in 1861, coming to Canada in 1881. He was just graduating from Trinity College in Toronto when soldiers were hastily recruited to deal with the 1885 Rebellion in Saskatchewan. Lloyd joined up and received a campaign medal for bravery under fire while rescuing a downed companion. Later, in Toronto, he was ordained and married. For some years, he was principal of a boys residential school in New Brunswick. He returned to England in 1901 as assistant secretary to Canon Hurst, Colonial and Continental Church Society (CCCS). Although he had no intention of returning to Canada, he wrote a letter to the London Times suggesting he could advise people thinking of emigrating. The volume of response was incredible, including one from Rev. Isaac Barr telling of his plans for a British colony in Western Canada.

Above: Rev. Lloyd (right) and Mrs. Lloyd who holds the first baby Christened in Lloydminster. Spring 1904.

Lloyd became actively involved in that project, filling in when Barr was away, often conducting personal interviews and answering queries. A number of prospective colonists asked how the people's religious needs would be met. Lloyd suggested a chaplain with Canadian experience be recruited. No suitable candidate applied. Five weeks before sailing Lloyd enrolled himself, his wife and their five children in the adventure. The CCCS agreed to maintain him for three years.

Lloyd and family sailed with the largest group of colonists, on the S.S. Lake Manitoba. He recorded the number of passengers as 2,684 souls. While on board, he held daily question and answer sessions for the colonists. "Lloyd developed a good rapport with the colonists; he was tactful, he was clear, he was forthright. He projected the image of a leader and it imprinted itself," Lynne Bowen writes in Muddling Through: The Remarkable Story of the Barr Colonists.

Relations between Lloyd and Barr quickly soured. Lloyd, an outstanding example of Protestant zeal and rectitude, was appalled by Barr's disorganization and disgusted by his drinking. Almost 40 years later in his memoir, Lloyd still icily referred to Barr, never as Rev. or Isaac but always as I. M. Barr and related such tales as the blanket incident. Blankets had been stashed deep in the ship's hold but the people needed them on the trains. Lloyd began distributing them. Suddenly, a voice over his shoulder yelled, "What are you doing with my blankets?" He turned and saw "I. M. Barr with a very white face and fierce eyes looking just like a spirit drunk man. I was angry and said, 'Why were you not here to look after this yourself?' ... and off I went in an angry mood." (G. E. Lloyd, The Trail of 1903)

When Barr was dropped and his name removed from the expedition, Lloyd officially took over. When some wanted to name the new town after him, Lloyd demured and insisted on recognition of the central role of the church. The compromise was "Lloydminster", the "minster" being the "mother church".

An active prohibitionist and staunchly pro-British, Lloyd spoke against "foreign immigration" into Western Canada for the next thirty years of his life. However, the Colonists would gratefully remember his leadership and the legacies he left to his community. Beyond establishing St. John's Minster Anglican Church, he also secured a post office for "Lloydminster" and provided the original townsite by obtaining the "gore", a narrow piece of land between the 28th township line (49th Ave) and the 4th meridian. Lloyd rode to Battleford, bought it, and donated it and his homestead to the town.

Rev. Lloyd left Lloydminster when his three years expired. He was Bishop of Saskatchewan from 1922 to 1931. He retired to B.C. and died there in 1940.

Photo courtesy of Doug Aston

The enormous quantity of baggage they had brought swamped the harbour's handling capability and forced the colonists to leave much of it behind to be forwarded on a fifth train. After a week of travel, through what soon seemed the never ending Canadian geography, the trains arrived in the village of Saskatoon on April 17, 1903. Since Saskatoon marked the end of the railway at that time, the colonists next had to arrange for horses, oxen, wagons, farm and household supplies, and travel 200 more miles, first to Battleford and then on to the land reserved for the "Colony".

Photo courtesy of the Glenbow Archives NA-303-72   *Photo courtesy of Doug Aston Collection*   *Photo courtesy of Grace United Church Archives*

1) Colonists had to live in tents until they could establish more permanent structures.

2) Sod shacks were a common sight in Lloydminster's early days.

3) Immigration Hall, built in 1904, became the most noticeable stucture in Lloydminster's prairie skyline.

Below: Rev. Lloyd dressed as Father Christmas for the colonists' first Christmas in 1903 and spread holiday cheer to children and adults.

Photo courtesy of Saskatchewan Archives Board

Life in the Colony

Barr's pamphlets suggested that a romantic adventure awaited those who emigrated to the "last best west". Very few were prepared for the rigours of real life on the untamed prairie. Most colonists had been lower middle class city dwellers who lacked any sort of farming experience. Only 28 percent of the heads of households had been farmers or in farming related occupations prior to leaving Britain. Accustomed to having sturdy roads, easy access to basic needs, and a more moderate climate, many challenges awaited the colonists in their chosen new world.

When they finally rolled into the "Headquarters Camp" in early May, after a strenuous two to three week trek across the untamed prairie, they saw only a tent community set up just north and north-west of the present Exhibition Grounds. Since the homesteads had only been reserved until April 15, the colonists immediately began to locate their choices, often made aboard ship as they crossed the Atlantic. Exploring the area was a challenge to people unfamiliar with the Dominion Land grid survey system.

In their first search for the survey posts, located every six miles along the 28th township line, they used a team and wagon. One man held the compass while Reverend Lloyd stood behind the driver to keep him rigidly on a straight line north, "slough or no slough". They tied a red cloth on the right hind wheel, while others kept tab of the revolutions. Having measured the outside of the wheel, they knew how many revolutions

Photo courtesy of Sylvia Baynton

went to the mile. At first they consistently missed to the west. Eventually someone explained the fact that in England the Magnetic Pole is 5 points west of the North Pole while here on the 110th meridian it is 12 points east of true north. As a result, they frequently ended up to the left of the survey holes. In addition, twenty years of prairie fires had destroyed the wooden survey stakes. Later, surveyors marked township corners with iron survey stakes, which became the inspiration for the current Border Markers.

Some colonists still resented what they believed were the false promises and shady schemes of Isaac Barr. On the other hand, Rev. Lloyd's leadership was applauded and he proved to be an organized and able administrator.

Records show that by October 1903, the thriving new Lloydminster had two large general stores, a post office, a drugstore, a saddlery and harness shop, a carpenters shop, three restaurants, and a livery stable plus 75 houses. By 1905, there were 100 houses, and 400 lots bought up. By then a Mounted Police Post, two butcher shops, a blacksmiths shop, a telegraph station, and of course, a log church, had been added. The "immigration hall" provided much needed temporary housing for the new arrivals. And settlers were still arriving, some in response to Barr's promotion or to join relatives who had preceded them.

Above: Pictured during the first winter (1903-1904), the Rendell Home was the first wood frame house built in Lloydminster. It served as family home for up to 15 relatives and friends, Police Station/Barracks, Nursing Station, Prisoner's Lock-up, Post Office and Social Centre.
William and Alice Rendell and children homesteaded the NE 1/4 of 36-49-1 W4, now the 25 square block area immediately south and west of the junction of Highways 16 and 17. The Rendell's positive attitude and success greatly encouraged the other early settlers. As of 2000, there are efforts being made to restore this home, the shell of which was moved to Weaver Park prior to destruction thanks to the work of Richard Larsen and R.J.R. Noyes.

Photo courtesy of Marjorie Brooks

Above: These colonists have just arrived and pose proudly for a photo to be dispatched to the folks in the "old country".

Photo courtesy of Provincial Archives of Alberta A 9382

Left: Lloydminster, winter 1907. Looking from south-east to north-west. The windmill, centre right, was near the present 49 Ave. and 50 St.

Archie Miller - Mr. Lloydminster

Born: Nov. 13, 1896, Lucan, Ontario
Died: Apr. 10, 1978, Lloydminster

Archie Miller was the best known Lloydminsterite in our first half century. He arrived in 1903 and for the next 75 years his smiling face and genial personality brightened Lloydminster's streets. He became a life member of practically every organization in the city.

"There was nothing here …" was the picture that greeted 6 year old Archie when he accompanied his father and uncles down from Edmonton on the North Saskatchewan River to set up a store in the new community. With the store built, they turned to constructing houses so their families could move here too. In the fall, Archie's father returned to Edmonton to pick up his family and provisions for the winter. Twenty-six teams pulling sleighs left Edmonton in late October to travel the already wintry trail. The trip took ten days.

Photo courtesy of Doug Aston Collection

Photo courtesy of Glenbow Archives NC-5-067

Photo courtesy of Doug Aston Collection

Friendly people find friendly communities and Archie was a prime example, even as a child. "I can remember in 1904, I went to school in the old log church and you have never seen a community and I don't care where you'd go, that you'd ever find a jollier bunch of people than these English people were."

Even though "there was nothing here", Archie found there was always something to do. "We made our own fun. Hockey, snowshoeing, cross-country skiing, they're nothing new to me."

Archie played these sports with a fierce zeal, later moving on to refereeing and then timekeeping. His determination and zest for life is no better illustrated than by his well known record of living in a tent for thirteen years "winter and summer". Archie's beaming smile made Lloydminster a better place.

Photo courtesy of Don Whiting

A re-union of Barr Colonists and pioneers in 1985. Standing (l-r): Pearl (Rankin) Payne, George Ives, Walter Page, Les Rendell, Olive Stevens, Mamie Rendell, Miriam Greupner. Seated left to right: Brian Payne, Kate (Kitty) Ives, Hattie Kitching, Edith (Forrester) Jones. The flag in the background was flown on the S. S. Lake Manitoba, obtained by Isaac Barr and flown here on the morning of May 6, 1903 to mark the official arrival of the party. It was preserved by the Barr family until presented to the City of Lloydminster by Isaac Barr's son William Barr, in 1969. It has been restored and hangs at the Barr Colony Heritage Cultural Centre.

Beyond the Colonists

The "Barr" Colonists were only the beginning of those who would choose to make Lloydminster their home in its first century of existence. Decade after decade, people kept coming to the little agricultural community which soon grew to be much more.

Even before the "colonists" were settled, others were arriving. Year after year they came, hoping to establish a livelihood and provide a safer, more stable life for themselves and their children. The new arrivals added to Lloydminster's prosperity by providing new opportunities for businesses to provide goods and services.

Louise Behm's father, William Whiting, was one of the early arrivals. He came from England in 1906 and took up his homestead six miles north of Lloydminster. Unlike many early settlers, William had worked on a farm and he brought with him some knowledge of agriculture.

Louise, the eldest of six children, was born in 1912. She attended Westdean School, four miles north and two miles west of the family home. In those days, there were no school buses, so children had to walk, ride or drive an open buggy called "a democrat" to school. In the winter months, straw would be placed in the bottom of a grain box. A heated stone would be placed in the box, and the passengers would sit in the straw as they travelled.

During the early years there were not many trees due to prairie fires, which would roar through unchecked. Breaking and maintaining the land was a labour-intensive job. Oxen pulled the ploughs and a field was ploughed one furrow at a time.

During the 1930's, Louise's grocery bill averaged $6.00 per month. She sold butter at 7¢ per pound or in exchange for groceries. Eggs cost 5¢

Photo courtesy of Glenbow Archives NA-4721-1

Colonists excitedly welcome a visiting bicyclist on his way to Immigration Hall, where he provided an afternoon of entertainment.

Photo courtesy of Glenbow Archives NA 303-78

Looking north on 49 Ave. from 49 St.; 1910

dozen. There was no health care, and medical bills came directly out of the family budget. Grain was hauled to the flourmill where it was ground into flour and put into 100 lb. sacks. Water had to be hauled winter and summer.

Louise married Tony Hamlin in 1934, and after living on a farm for three years, they moved into Lloydminster. Although Tony had been a painter and decorator the Depression forced him to supplement his income by mixing and pouring cement for cisterns. Cisterns were designed to store rain water that ran off roofs so that people would have soft water.

Photo courtesy of Glenbow Archives NA-898-3

Above in 1904, and left in 1910, Lloydminster has the appearance of a frontier town.

Below: Lloydminster, fall of 1905, showing the recently arrived railway

Photo courtesy of Glenbow Archives NA-1644-95

In 1939, Charlie Daniels came to Lloydminster to dig waterlines in the downtown area. Using a shovel, a five gallon pail, and a rope, he and other men dug ditches to accommodate the large pipe. Pay was 33¢ per hour. Like many of the workers, Charlie camped at the Exhibition grounds during his employment.

Daniels was one of many Metis around Lloydminster in its early years. The Metis, people of Aboriginal and European descent, were frequently the traders and freighters whom the colonists encountered.

Many purchased land and set up farms, while others, like Daniels, worked as labourers.

George Matheson came to Lloydminster in October 1941, from Provost, to manage the O.K. Economy store. Although he was only 23, he succeeded in business and opened his own store, Matheson's Groceteria, in 1949. During World War II, a challenge grocery store owners faced was handling rationed goods. Some customers went from store to store trying to buy up items. When rationing coupons came out, some of the pressure was relieved. The coupons were as valuable as cash. They were presented for items such as sugar, butter and jam. Once they had been accounted for at the bank, they were incinerated.

When George and his wife Kay moved to Lloydminster, they were told they would have running water and gas heating. However, running water was only available in the downtown section and along the main streets. Water had to be hauled from the pumphouse, located on the north side of 50 St., near the middle of the 5100 block. Dirty water had to be hauled out as well, a daily task which most Lloydminster citizens had to endure.

Housing was at a premium. Matheson served on the High School Board from 1946-48. He was in charge of finding accommodation for the teachers – a difficult task at the time. One principal even lived in a tent on the east end of town for a while. The population was growing rapidly, the schools were crowded, and not for the last time, finding a place to live in Lloydminster was a challenge.

George's ventures were not restricted to the grocery business. In 1958, afraid that he would be forced to move his store from the property he rented, he bought land and constructed several buildings which today house the Bank of Nova Scotia and Meridian Home Furnishings on 50th Ave. near 48th Street, and Paully's Restaurant and Border Paint on the corner of 50th Ave. and 49th Street.

The staff of Matheson's Groceteria in the 1950's. (l-r): Louis Dean, Maxine Willoughby, George Matheson (wearing his accustomed grocer's smock), Doreen Mallett, Cecil Scharf and Theresa McKevitt.

Photo courtesy of George and Kay Matheson

On August 3rd, 1961, Barb Collins and her family, from Houston, Texas, arrived at their new home in Lloydminster. Barbara's uncle Rev. Leo C. Owen came to be the minister at the local Church of Christ.

"Lloydminster was just a very small town in 1961," remembers Barb. "It seemed very quaint to us and I particularly remember that many homes had gardens in their yards, even the front yard! Everyone knew everyone and no one was too concerned about locking doors in either their homes or their vehicles. The residential areas did not extend further south than Highway 16 and along it were farmland and acreages. The main residential area was generally bounded on the west by 56th Avenue and east to 45th Avenue. Highway 17 was gravel."

Barb was an attraction to her high school class mates who vied to walk her home so they could hear more of her Texan accent. Now, with little of that accent remaining she says, "It has been great to see Lloydminster grow over the years from a small town to a bustling, thriving city. Our children and grandchildren were born in Lloydminster. We staunchly defend it to others and yet feel it is our right to voice our opinions on how things should be done. We have established a Canadian branch of the family that hopefully will continue for a long time. We are proud of our Texas heritage but are also proud of the place that's been our home for most of our lives - Lloydminster."

Rose Brassard witnessed first-hand, the growing ethnic diversity of Lloydminster. From 1979 – 1989, Rose conducted the LEARN (Literacy) program at Lakeland College. Growing numbers of immigrants made use of the program to improve their English language skills.

Brassard worked with people from Greece, Chile, China, Laos, Vietnam, Honduras, Czechoslovakia and the Philippines, all who had chosen to come to Lloydminster.

Some immigrants were sponsored by relatives, or by churches and still others came on their own. It was a challenge for many of these people to adjust to a new language and foreign culture.

Spiro Kokonas left Greece to come to Canada in 1959, initially settling in Saskatoon. Greece had experienced a civil war and as a result the country was in ruins. As a child, Spiro had heard Canada and America spoken of as "the land of opportunity". After living and working in Saskatoon for 11 years, Spiro and his brothers, Jim and Bill, were offered an

Year	Lloydminster, Alberta	Lloydminster, Sask.	Total Population
1906	130	389	519
1911	222	441	663
1916	294	494	788
1921	286	469	755
1931	539	977	1516
1941	572	1052	1624
1951	1706	2232	3938
1961	3052	2688	5740
1971	4738	3953	8691
1981	9029	6003	15,032
1991	10,042	7241	17,283
1996	11,305	7620	18,925

Above: Highway 17 stretching north. Alberta on the left, Saskatchewan to the right. A marvel to tourists but everyday life in Lloydminster.

Photo courtesy of Lloydminster and District Co-operative Ltd.

Hai Ma (above), who immigrated from Vietnam to Lloydminster in 1978, was a qualified mechanic and worked at several garages before opening Lloyd Hi- Quality Auto Repair in 1993.

Photo by Don Whiting; Inset courtesy of Glenbow Archives NA-4775-4

In the late '90's, the Parkview development, saw the growth of larger homes including the first home in Lloydminster to list at over $300,000 (left). Inset: A shack from 1903.

opportunity to run the Ranchero Restaurant in Lloydminster. The restaurant was located at the corner of 56th Ave. and 44th St. The family arrived in Lloydminster, a town of 8700, in 1970. There was nothing south of 36th St. and there were only three sets of traffic lights, all along 50th Ave. Spiro and his brothers ran the restaurant for seven years.

After Spiro's brother Jim died in 1976, the Kokonas family sold the Ranchero and opened a new larger restaurant, the 3K Family Restaurant, downtown on 50th Ave. just south of 50th St. In 1982 the economy dived, and they lost the business. With a private loan from Peter Gulak, Spiro and his wife, Tina, were able to open another smaller restaurant, The Lighthouse. After selling it in 1989, they opened Spiro's Pizza on the Saskatchewan side of Highway 17, south of 36 St.

Spiro and Tina are both from Southern Greece and were married in 1965. At first the flatness of the prairie was a shock to them but today the Kokonas take great pride in Lloydminster. "The planners did a good job of laying out the streets. They allowed wide streets long before automobiles were in general use," comments Spiro. For the first seven years Tina yearned for her homeland, but after returning to Greece for a visit in 1972 and seeing the changes there, she realized her attachment to Lloydminster. "Greece is my birthplace," she says, "but Lloydminster is my home."

Hai Ma arrived in Canada on April 23, 1980 at the age of 23 - the culmination of a two year journey of terror. Hai had trained and worked as a mechanic with the South Vietnamese Army until taken prisoner of war in 1975. In 1978, he escaped and began his journey.

Initially he and many others were taken by boat to Malaysia but the Malaysians refused them entry and towed them far out into the South China Sea. The refugees sailed to Thailand where they were once again turned back. Finally, after time on an uninhabited Indonesian island, they eventually found their way to a refugee camp where Hai stayed for three months. From there, Hai went to Singapore, Hong Kong, and finally to Canada where the Canadian government sponsored him to come to Lloydminster.

Ma could not speak English, but he did not let this hold him back. Soon he was working at Zellers but without English skills, Hai did not know how to cash his pay cheque. He simply put the paper in his pocket. Desperately hungry and weak, Hai fainted at work. One of his coworkers finally realized the misunderstanding and helped him to cash his cheque.

He had been a journeyman mechanic in Vietnam, so it was natural that he should migrate to the automotive industry. However, his training was not recognized, and Hai had to complete a four year apprenticeship. Within a short time, he was hired by the Nissan dealership. In 1993, Hai opened Lloyd Hi-Quality Auto Repair. In addition to his automotive work, Hai has been teaching Tae Kwon Do in Lloydminster for the past twenty-two years.

Dr. Gerald Charles came to Lloydminster in 1987 via a circuitous route – Baltimore, Yorkton and Regina. He had been practicing dentistry in Regina and was looking for a smaller community where he could set up a practice. At the time, dentists here were not accepting new patients and residents were often forced to go elsewhere to obtain dental treatment. Seeing the need for another dentist in the community, Dr. Charles moved to Lloydminster with his family and set up his practice.

Times were not great when Dr. Charles arrived. Lloydminster was in the midst of a recession, and many of his patients would opt to have a tooth pulled rather than pay for more costly procedures. Dr. Charles would see yet another benefit of the Heavy Oil Upgrader project. Pay and benefits such as dental plans improved and people were more willing to undergo restorative procedures.

As the economy changed, a new influx of people migrated to Lloydminster. Glen and Maggie Carroll moved here from Corner Brook, Newfoundland in April 1993. Their reasons reflect those of many others who have settled here: more employment opportunities and the presence of family members who had come West previously.

Since the recovery of the oil sector in 1999, there has been remarkable growth in the residential and business sectors of Lloydminster. Expansion to the west is most noticeable with the housing boom in the College Park and Parkview areas. The business sector received a new "Power Centre" of Wal-Mart, Staples, Canadian Tire and other retailers in 2000. Traffic issues are becoming increasingly important to Lloydminster's rapidly growing population of 22,000. As development progresses and businesses prosper, traffic congestion grows. For years, residents have complained about trains blocking the flow of traffic. Now with traffic volumes and business demands both increasing, traffic jams cause increased annoyance. Road widenings and a highway by-pass around the city loom on the horizon.

Throughout its growth over the last one hundred years, Lloydminsterites have worked hard and successfully to remain one cohesive community. There are some growing pains, as residents have to adapt to a faster-paced lifestyle despite having more conveniences and amenities. However, we still enjoy a lot of what is good about small town life. As the Barr Colonists did a century ago, families still arrive in Lloydminster seeking new opportunities, hoping to establish a new life for themselves and their children. We welcome those who come to grow with the City of Lloydminster as it now moves boldly into its second century - bordering on greatness.

Chapter Two

Agriculture

Research by Heather Gray and Penny Manners

For those who have experienced it, there is no mistaking or forgetting the smell of freshly ploughed prairie. The pungent aromas swirling up from the sweet crushed grass, the fresh black soil, and the split roots are a heady concoction. It is best experienced as a small child padding barefoot in the miraculous new furrow, leaving the complex task of keeping the share of the walking plough balanced and the team of horses straight and steady to one's father, while you concentrate on picking up the plumpest worms before a reeling Franklin's Gull swoops in. When you add to all this the dreams of the early settlers of establishing themselves as prosperous farmers in this new land of opportunity, and building a life for their families, then you can understand the persistent love affair with the land which has held so many in its grip over our first century.

Photo courtesy of Barr Colony Heritage Cultural Centre

Above: the entire family, and neighbours, gather to celebrate the turning of the first furrow, the hopeful beginning of a new life in a new land. Right: Newer but still labour intensive technology; the harvest practises common from the 1920's through the 1950's

Most Barr Colonists came to farm even though they had little or no agricultural background. They found here rich, fertile land and quickly attempted to put it into production growing their accustomed grains such as wheat, oats and barley; and raising the familiar livestock of cattle, horses, pigs, sheep and poultry.

There was plenty to learn and many a story about greenhorn Englishmen and their outlandish naiveté. For example, one settler laid potatoes on top of the ground and then carefully placed chunks of sod on top of them, another pioneer labelled the pieces of harness before taking them off the horses in order to be able to put them back on correctly. Before we get too smug though, we should remember we are still learning how to farm successfully in our dry, cool and unpredictable environment.

Robert Payne and family arrived in Lloydminster two months after the first Barr Colonists. Payne was a bricklayer with no agricultural experience. However, to secure title to a "homestead" one had to live on the land and make a portion of it productive. Robert started a mixed farm six miles northwest of Lloydminster, including a basic herd that could be used for dairy and beef production. As well, the family acquired horses, pigs, and chickens, and eventually some 500 sheep grazed on nearby undeeded land. As green as they were in the beginning, the Payne family established a farm which has successfully passed down through the generations for a century.

Above: A typical area view - this one near Lone Rock.

Below: the legendary Tighnduin Farm near Lashburn showed what a pioneer could do with a million dollars to spend.

In a new land, neighbours needed to help neighbours in order to succeed. While the majority of the colonists were inexperienced agriculturalists, there were those who brought with them a wealth of farm knowledge and experience. George Creech was one such man.

George Creech's first attempt at settlement in Canada was not successful. As a young man he arrived in Quebec and shortly realized that the language barrier made it too difficult for him to find work. He moved to Vermont but soon read about the Barr Colony heading west. He decided to follow them in the fall of 1903.

After arriving in Saskatoon, he walked to Battleford where he found employment for the winter. In the spring of 1904, Creech set out for Lloydminster with a team of horses, wagon, walking plough, disc and harrows. On the way he bought seed oats and a milk cow with a calf so young that it had to ride in the wagon.

Creech named his farm "Quantock" after a row of hills on the south shore of the Bristol Channel in England. On his farm he raised registered Shorthorn cattle, Clydesdale horses, sheep and swine. George Creech became involved in the community, serving on the council of the R.M. of Brittania, and the Lloydminster and District Agricultural Co-operative Association and the Lloydminster Exhibition Association.

Creech quickly became a valuable asset to Lloydminster farmers. He had grown up on a large mixed farm in Somerset, England and he brought with him a knowledge of farming passed down for generations. Creech's advice and help was much sought after.

Son Frank Creech, a veterinarian, continued to build the farm as the Quantock Cattle Co. He used quality grains and grasses to produce prize-winning herds. The family showed cattle in Lloydminster and Regina

H. C. Weaver

Horticulturist and Conservationist

Harvey Clayton Weaver had a basic philosophy from which Lloydminster still benefits. He is the man whose land became Weaver Park and whose farm home, and surrounding groves of trees, still survives as The Teahouse. It is often described as an oasis of green in an otherwise nondescript strip of highway commercial properties.

Weaver's philosophy was to "always leave a place a least as good as, if not better than, you found it".

Weaver was born in Ohio in 1887 and homesteaded near Swift Current in 1906. In 1924, he re-established his family on a farm south of Lone Rock and build a celebrated reputation as a registered seed grower. Weaver was featured in the April 23rd, 1936 issue of *The Country Guide*. In the article "He Started from Prairie Sod", R. D. Colquette wrote: "A weed would be positively lonesome on the Weaver place. I have seen clean farms, but this farm is as innocent of weeds as when it was in prairie sod."

Weaver also differed from his neighbours with regard to trees. He argued, "it isn't necessary to farm all the land in sight." He confessed he always hesitated before he cut down a tree. He thought they contributed a lot. "If they don't bring moisture, they certainly help to keep it. They are no trouble to raise, they save the soil, provide shelter, and they look pretty."

So it was that immediately after moving into Lloydminster in 1946, Harvey and Lydia Weaver began planting the groves of evergreens we still see today. He also experimented with growing fruit trees, ornamental shrubs, vegetables and of course the rest of his 160 acres was devoted to growing registered seed oats and crested wheat grass.

H. C. Weaver emphasized the importance of growing quality seed and believed that certain varieties were best suited to local soils. He still toiled to keep his fields free of weeds: "The inspector has yet to find the first wild oat in my fields" he claimed.

Mr. Weaver passed away in 1974. He was inducted into the Lloydminster Agricultural Hall of Fame in 1976. Touted as a "horticultural genius", Weaver was certainly ahead of his time. His love of the land, his conservationist approach, and his appreciation of beauty would all make fine examples for us to follow today. Harvey Weaver certainly left his part of Lloydminster better than he found it.

Photos courtesy of Barb Gulka.

Justamere Farms

Jonathan Fox II was born near Rochester, Minnesota, in 1873, to parents who had immigrated from Britain. During his youth, he learned many of the points of good farming from his father. In 1894, he married Jessie Lowrie.

By 1903, he had established Pleasant Grove Stock Farm in Olmstead County, where he raised Poland China hogs, Shropshire sheep, Shorthorn cattle, and Percheron horses. He also managed a farmers' co-operative that shipped beef cattle to Chicago. The Foxes raised nine children; the youngest of whom was Jonathan III, born in 1919.

Jonathan II came to Canada in 1918, first working for the ranching partnership of Kennedy & Davis at Blackfoot. In 1919 he established Justamere Stock Farm at its present location just east of Lloydminster. Here he developed a reputation as a skilful breeder of horses, cattle, sheep, swine and dogs. He was soon exhibiting his livestock and winning prizes all over Western Canada and at the Royal Agricultural Winter Fair in Toronto. In the early days he was probably best known for Justamere's prize-winning Percheron horses, the progeny of the Pleasant Grove stock, whose descendants are still being exhibited on the circuits today.

Jonathan III was learning the principles of good breeding before he started grade school. His father taught him to recognize the desirable and negative characteristics of an animal and would then quiz him as to which sire or dam could impart characteristics to improve those qualities. Jonathan III was an eager student whose curiosity went so far as examining closely the bones of animals who had recently met their doom.

Photo courtesy of Lloydminster Regional Archives

Above: a new generation emerges. Jonathan Fox II's grandsons; Bob (fourth from right) and Lyal (second from right) show their 4-H dairy calves c. 1955.

The management of Justamere's major lines of cattle and horses passed to Jonathan III in 1941, the same year he married Molly Sutherland.

Jonathan II still remained involved, specializing in raising purebred dogs and swine, until 1958. He was presented with awards and held the respect of Livestock breeders throughout Western Canada. Jonathan Fox II passed away on April 2, 1961.

One of the tenets of his philosophy was "Good enough is not enough." Putting this principle into practice led to continuing successes for Justamere's stock both in the show ring and marketplace. It is a principle that is still employed by his successors.

While Jonathan Fox III differed with his father on minor matters (raising Herefords instead of Shorthorns) he greatly extended the reputation of Justamere Farms. He had won awards for showing his father's Percherons as early as 1936 and now he went on to breed and show the Grand Champion Percheron Stallion at the Royal Winter Fair in 1964, 1966 and 1967. His interest in Holstein cattle produced another national champion but he became known around the world for his work with Polled Herefords.

Ahead of his time, as usual, he was convinced that the practice of de-horning was a serious blow to a rancher's productivity. What better way to increase returns than developing a breed known for its good beef characteristics but without horns. Fox's cattle won championships at shows from Toronto to Calgary, from Georgia to Texas. In 1969 alone, he won three of the four grand championships for Herefords in Houston.

In 1968, the Edmonton Exhibition named Jonathan Fox III the Livestock Man of the Year. In 1969, it was induction into the Livestock Hall of Fame in Billings, Montana; in 1970, Saskatchewan Salesman of the Year; in 1971, President of the Canadian Cattleman's Association; in 1973, the Canadian Agricultural Hall of Fame, (only the second living person to be so honoured) and so the list continues to a total of six different halls of fame in Canada and the United States. He was inducted into the Lloydminster Exhibition Hall of Fame in 1985.

One of Jonathan's fondest achievements is being named in 1983 by the U.S. publication, *The Record Stockman*, as Canadian Man of the Year. The magazine stated Fox was known and respected throughout North America for his "look ahead vision". Here they identified one of the main qualities responsible for Fox's success not only as a breeder but as a business manager - the skill to anticipate where the market is going. As a breeder he once said, "it's not enough to know what current demand is, you have to anticipate the demand five years down the road."

Not to be overlooked are Fox's management skills considering that for an extended period he was CEO of an organization that operated several farms and ranches totalling approximately 10,000 acres and spread over three provinces, had an active import-export business (with a branch office in Britain) which exported cattle to Japan, Australia, Central and South America, South Africa, and almost all parts of Europe, and sold breeding stock into 45 of the U.S. states. At the same time he bred and showed to championship levels draft horses, beef cattle, dairy cattle, sheep, swine and dogs.

Fox's reputation as a breeder and showman soon led to livestock judging (as many as 80 shows per year). He raised eyebrows by judging from horseback. His rationale

Photos courtesy of Lloydminster Regional Archives and (inset) Don Whiting

Lyal (centre) and Jonathan (left) show champion Polled Hereford bulls at Toronto in 1968. (Inset) Jonathan Fox III continues as an active ambassador of the places and livestock he loves.

was that cattlemen usually survey their herds this way and he enjoyed it. "I'm never happier than when riding a good saddle horse among a bunch of good beef cattle".

Son Lyal Fox took over the operational management of Justamere Farms by the 1980's and Jonathan and Molly moved to a small ranch near Kamloops. Allegedly semi-retired, they actively bred and raised championship Morgan horses while Jonathan remained an active ambassador of Justamere Farms and of Lloydminster and Canada.

In his later years, Jonathan Fox gives increasing credit to his father for teaching him the essential values that led to his success. "I give credit to my Dad for teaching me to look after the person on the other side of your ranch line," he says. "If you do that, the world will come to your door." Another of his father's adages he often quotes is; "Always step up to your problems. Never take the line of least resistance because that makes for crooked rivers and crooked men."

In recent years, under the direction of Lyal Fox Sr. and his wife Virginia, Justamere has expanded to provide opportunities for the next two generations of family members. In addition to the purebred operation in Polled Herefords and Angus, they now operate a commercial cattle enterprise in Manitoba. In 1995, a livestock assembly station was set-up at the Lloydminster location that taps into the family's noted expertise and enthusiasm for marketing practical and sound livestock.

From time to time there occur exceptional examples of leadership and high degrees of excellence. Justamere Farms stands unchallenged in these regards making Lloydminster's agricultural community internationally known.

for 25 years. They were named Premier Breeder of the Year for twelve years in a row. The Creech family also showed cattle at the Denver Stock Show for 23 years in a row. Frank was inducted to the Honour Roll of the Canadian Hereford Association, the Saskatchewan Livestock Association and the Lloydminster Exhibition Association.

Frank's sons continue in the cattle industry. Eldest son Barney operates a purebred Angus and Charolais ranch as well as owning the local Wendy's Restaurant. In 1969, second son, Mac, became one of the first breeders of Red Angus in Canada while continuing to raise Herefords. Mac and younger brother Bill sell purebred bulls across the country. They all continue the Creech tradition of developing beef breeds, thus making a significant contribution to food production in Canada.

Above: Reserve Grand Champion Hereford Bull at the 1963 Lloydminster Exhibition Association Bull Show. Bull shows and sales have always been major events in Lloydminster. At one time, local schools closed for the day of the Bull Sale.

Below: (Inset l-r) March 1955; Rawson Lister, his wife, Margaret, and mother, Mrs. B. Lister accept, for the third year running, a trophy for the highest producing Jersey herd in Saskatchewan. From their dairy four miles south on Highway 17, the Lister's delivered milk into Lloydminster virtually every day from 1930 to 1977. Below right: some contented cows.
Photos courtesy of the Lister family.

Lloydminster Exhibition

Many settlers recognized their need to learn and actively sought information, compared notes with neighbours, and celebrated their successes. It was this spirit that led to the first agricultural exhibition, held in October 1904. Beaming "Colonists" showed off their achievements in garden vegetables, grains and a few classes of livestock.

This desire to succeed and improve has remained over the years and has led to well attended short courses and boys and girls farm camps. The Lloydminster Exhibition Association also played a central role in this effort, providing a showcase for local producers and often a stepping stone to provincial, national and even international success.

Lloydminster's being split by the new provincial boundary in 1905

created complications. The Lloydminster Saskatchewan Agricultural Society was chartered in 1906, and the Lloydminster Alberta Agricultural Society in 1908. The two societies operated separately for years, each holding a fair on the same Exhibition grounds but on separate dates.

During World War I, the two societies were finally amalgamated into one Lloydminster Agricultural Society by special orders-in-council passed by both governments. Each province was to pay half the grant monies paid to other societies of the same status, an arrangement which existed until 1978 when Lloydminster received its "A" status.

"A Way of Life"
for Lloydminster Veterinarians

Dr. Glenn Weir graduated from Veterinary College in Guelph, Ontario, in 1949. He returned to his hometown of Aberdeen, Saskatchewan, and started his own practice. Unfortunately, in 1950, he contracted Ungulant Fever, an illness spread to humans from cows. After recovering, Dr. Weir worked in animal pathology in Edmonton before coming to Lloydminster in 1952.

Dr. Weir and Dr. Frank Creech were the first university-trained veterinarians in Lloydminster. Dr. Creech was also the first federal veterinarian in the area. Until this time, local farmers acquired veterinary services from local "horse doctors". Horse doctors were usually people who had a love of animals and had learned to treat them. Dr. Weir had great respect for these people who were often paid in kind, with a few dollars, a chicken or not at all.

One major focus of Veterinary Medicine is to prevent the transfer of diseases from animals to humans. Dr. Weir assisted in a federal program to test all cattle for tuberculosis and brucellosis.

Above: The Weir Veterinary Clinic. Inset: A newborn calf struggles for life. The veterinarian's role is crucial in assisting farmers and ranchers to have productive herds as well as insuring society is protected from animal borne diseases.

Dr. Weir recalls there were many miles to cover to test all the animals. His area was Lloydminster and as far north as there were cattle. In winter, Dr. Weir had two teams of horses pulling a cutter. He would take one team out as far as fifteen miles in the morning and return at noon. He would take a second team out as far as ten miles in the afternoon and return around suppertime. In 1955, he bought an airplane to fly into the northern areas.

Dr. Weir opened the Weir Veterinary Clinic in 1961 and it has undergone many additions since then. In 1967, Dr. Ellis joined the practice. Dr. Weir's son, Doug, graduated from Veterinary Medicine in 1982 and also came on board. Dr. Doug Weir and Dr. Ellis took ownership in 1986. Although Glenn Weir entered semi-retirement in 1997, he is still seen around the office on a daily basis.

For the Weirs, Veterinary Medicine is a family practice. Glenn's wife Kelly managed the office from 1952 to 1986. In addition, nine members of the Weir family are veterinarians. A tenth, Weir's grandson, recently entered Veterinary College.

Dr. Weir has travelled to many countries, including South Africa, England, Scotland, Australia, New Zealand and Holland, to visit institutions of Veterinary Medicine, and give lectures at Universities in these countries as well.

Advances in technology have had a great impact on veterinary medicine. The Animal Hospital, owned by Dr. Richard Starke, Dr. Alison Chiswell, Dr. Daryl Hanely, Dr. Sonia Kollassa, and Dr. Corin Berg, is a mixed animal practice, tending to 60% small animals and 40% large animals. Today, more and more families have companion pets such as dogs, cats, or horses used for recreation.

A state of the art clinic, the Animal Hospital, uses computers and cameras with microchips to take "e-rays" which can be e-mailed to the Veterinary College in Saskatoon for expert opinions, if necessary. They also have their own lab where the staff completes cultures from samples. The clinic can provide test results within minutes.

As in human medicine, there is a growing trend toward holistic medicine in veterinary practices. This includes feeding animals the best quality food and supplements. Massage therapy is also used, particularly on horses, and behavioural therapy is used to treat pets.

For Dr. Glenn Weir and the other Lloydminster veterinarians, Veterinary Medicine has been more than a profession; it has been a way of life that offers great fulfilment and rewards. Although the profession has changed over the years, the doctors' concern for their patients and for their community has remained a constant.

Photo courtesy of Don Whiting

The grain elevator was a prairie institution and one of the most recognizable symbols of the West. Lloydminster once had seven, plus a flour mill, but over the years economics has dictated larger facilities and so the old wooden structures are rapidly disappearing to be replaced by concrete terminals such as the Lloydminster Joint Venture Elevator pictured at bottom.

Photo by Don Whiting

Photo by Don Whiting

Photo by Don Whiting

During the early 1920's the Society suffered financial losses and three Directors had to guarantee its bank loans. In order to reduce this liability of the Directors, the Lloydminster Agricultural Exhibition Association Ltd. was formed under the Company's Act of Saskatchewan.

As farmers added to their knowledge, some won national and international prizes. Remembering that many local farmers had once struggled to learn the basics and now saw their peers winning prestigious awards helps us understand how these wins became the stuff of local legend. J. C. Hill and sons, won the Colorado Cup for best sample of oats in 1911, 1912 and 1913. An unrelated family of Hills, Dr. J. T. Hill who farmed with the help of his brothers Hugh and Jim, won international awards for wheat and field peas in the 1920's. Local school superintendent, A. R. Brown, developed a national reputation in horticulture and for many years hosted a popular CBC radio program, "The Prairie Gardener".

What made learning to farm successfully even more challenging was that our early settlement occurred at the beginning of revolutionary changes in agricultural technology. After centuries of hand labour, and little more than fifty years of horse drawn equipment, agriculture was about to become fully mechanized. From the beginning our fields saw the continuing arrival of new technology: first steam powered but soon gasoline and diesel powered tractors capable of pulling bigger field implements and driving them with power take-offs and hydraulics.

One result of this technological change was that the prediction by experts that the West would be covered with quarter-section family farms and support a rural population of 6 to 8 million people was obsolete before it began. With generally low commodity prices, farmers sought to support their entrepreneurial dreams by increased production. Mechanization allowed fewer people to work larger farms. So the trend began toward larger farm size, fewer agricultural labourers, and more emphasis on technologically enhanced production as a means of boosting farm incomes.

Along the way, farmers in our area, as well as across the West, grappled with such issues as the Crow Rate, the formation of farmers' organizations such as the wheat pools and co-operatives, and more recently the controversy over the role of the Canadian Wheat Board (CWB). These issues often revealed a sharp difference between farmers in Saskatchewan and Alberta, despite the fact that some farmed, literally, across the road from each other. Supporters of the Crow and the CWB argue that they represent necessary and desirable government support for Western agriculture. The opponents argue that government programs distort the market and thus stand in the way of necessary and desirable diversification and the development of value added secondary and tertiary industries. They point out, for example, that the Crow Rate helped make it more economical to produce breakfast cereals in Peterborough and Niagara Falls, Ontario than in Saskatoon or Red Deer, next door to the source grain fields.

Lloydminster farmer Rudy Jurke fought to save the Crow. The Jurke family came to Lloydminster in 1927. Jurke worked with the Saskatchewan Wheat Pool and the National Farmers Union to promote policies to help agriculture and its people. Rudy is also president of the Lloydminster and District Co-operative Ltd. and strongly believes in co-operatives as one way of preventing the large multi-national companies from taking over the market.

While our first century saw ongoing technological development and a deeper understanding of production issues, the question that remains unresolved is the issue of low commodity prices. Farmers are selling grains and livestock at prices substantially the same as those that existed 100 years ago yet the cost of many other products, including those farmers purchase, has increased tenfold.

After exhaustive efforts to increase production by more and more expensive inputs, a few farmers are turning back to organic farming; that is, farming without chemical fertilizers, herbicides and pesticides. One such farmer, Joe Holden, was recently quoted as saying, "It's a major change in that we are working with nature, rather than controlling it. That is the enjoyable part, because it's finding where I fit into [nature] rather than how do I control it."

Photo courtesy of Lloydminster Regional Archives

Above: Blonde Wonder (20K-464102) Grand Champion Yorkshire Boar Edmonton Show and Sale (late 1950's) [Note: his Sire and Dam and Grand Sire and Grand Dam were all show champions.] Shown by Ken Hougham who exhibited livestock at the Lloydminster Exhibition for 50 years beginning in 1928. Mr. Hougham was a member of Alberta, Saskatchewan and Canadian swine breeders associations. A Director of the Exhibition Association for 19 years, he is a member of their Hall of Fame.

Photo by Don Whiting

Left: A field of canola ripens in the August sun. As many as 10,000 farmers deliver canola to the ADM crushing plant in Lloydminster. Both canola oil and canola meal have emerged as important products for both domestic and export sale.

Another controversy is rapidly emerging around the use of genetically modified seeds. For the time being though, most farmers are turning to the marketing side of the equation. Hence the remarkable efforts in the last quarter century toward diversification. Where once wheat was the dominant cash crop, and a modicum of oats and barley were grown, canola has emerged as the major cash crop. Oldtimers might be

The Lloydminster area has become a leading player in the development of diversified livestock with several active breeders and producers and annual shows and sales.
Below left: After an absence of 125 years, buffalo again graze the plains near Lloydminster.
Below: Dr. Doug Weir (right) and assistant remove elk horns which are processed locally or exported to be used in traditional oriental medicines.

Photo by Don Whiting

Photo courtesy of Dr. Glenn Weir

Photo by Don Whiting

Above: Cattle graze contentedly with the Lloydminster Joint Venture Elevator and the Husky Lloydminster Upgrader in the background - the three pillars of Lloydminster's primary economic sector.

Below: When it comes to farming, it helps to have a sense of humour.

Photo by Don Whiting.

amazed at the fields of peas, lentils, flax and triticale.

On the livestock side, there was a long period of dominance by British breeds such as Hereford and Angus in beef cattle. Then there was an era of continental European lines such as Charolais and Limousin. Now on the leading edge are such exotics as elk and the old king of the plains - the buffalo.

Matthias Alsager developed one of the earliest Hereford cattle herds in Lloydminster. He arrived from Illinois in 1903, and quickly became active in the community as the Reeve of the Streamstown Municipality. He was later elected to the board of the Lloydminster and District Cooperative Association. A. A. Mitchell was another cattle breeder who did much to establish sound genetic lines in the Hereford industry. Ken Hougham in swine and Robert Golightly in sheep, along with their families, established national reputations as breeders over a 50 year period from the 1920's to the 1970's. There are many others who could be mentioned if space permitted.

While this area has excellent pasture and range land, the 1960's saw the introduction of feed lots as an alternative way of finishing animals before they are sold. Previously the animals were kept on the farm until they were sent to market, sometimes by rail to packing plants as far away as Eastern Canada. During the Depression in the 1930's, the cost of sending an animal to market by rail was sometimes as much as the market value of the animal.

The 1970's saw the development of two major custom feed lots in the Lloydminster Area. Vee-Tee Feeders, to the north-west, is owned and operated by Richard and David Davies and their families. Hi-Gain Custom Feed Lot situated to the west, established by Dennis Wobeser and Keith Pawsey once fed up to 7,500 cattle but is now a cow/calf and backgrounder operation run by the Wobeser family.

Photo by Don Whiting

Much of the virgin land in our area was broken by the labour of horses, once the primary source of power, pulling farm machinery as well as wagons and buggies. There were some major producers of horses in the Lloydminster area. Justamere Farms raised Clydesdale and Percheron draft horses (see page 18). Another well known local horseman was Tom Halstead who took over his parents' farm south of Blackfoot in the 1950's. At one time, he and his father had over 100 purebred Percheron horses which sold all over Canada and the United States.

Mr. Halstead, a Director of the Lloydminster Exhibition Association for 29 years, encouraged the draft horse and saddle horse competitions which were long a highlight of the Exhibition, attracting horsemen and women (such as Audrey Henry) from throughout Western Canada and well known judges (such as Grant MacEwan). Tom Halstead was a good judge of horses as well and spent many weekends judging horse shows. He was considered one of the best judges in the area. He was fond of saying "I like any kind of horse as long as it is a good one." Tom also promoted rodeos and horse races. He encouraged the racing of other animals so raced pigs, goats, and ducks all over Alberta for 5 - 6 years. He wanted to race one more year because he was training a skunk to race, but it never came to pass.

As well as horse shows, Tom Halstead helped bring the Rare and Exotic Show and the Fur and Feather Show to Lloydminster. Tom received many awards for his accomplishments. In 1963, the Rotary Club gave him a silver belt-buckle for helping to promote an all-girl rodeo. He was selected the Kinsmen sportsman of the year and inducted into the Lloydminster Agricultural Hall of Fame. The Race track at the Lloydminster Exhibition Grounds is named Halstead Downs to recognize the work and dedication that Tom Halstead invested in developing our agricultural heritage.

At present horses are seldom used as a work animals but their role as a companion or recreational animal keeps horses a part of our rural landscape. A recent example of a promoter of horses is Jean Wobeser who came to Lloydminster in 1961. Jean has been very involved in the local community, and a Director of the Lloydminster Exhibition Association for 30 years. Jean holds the distinction of being the Association's only female President, from 1995 - 1997.

From uncertain beginnings, our agriculture has flourished. The children who saw the first furrows turned have since passed away but the industry they saw begin is a major factor in our community's well being today. Agriculture in the Lloydminster District has been a major contributor to our local economy and to the food resources of Canada and beyond.

Photo by Don Whiting

Chapter Three

Religion

Research and original draft by
Ian Goodwillie

Photo by Don Whiting.

Not only were the Colonists of a generation which celebrated the British Empire, they were also of an era which proclaimed Christian virtues as the pinnacle of human achievement. They strove to meet such standards as: sacrifice for others, decency in personal and community life, and doing one's duty to God, King and fellowman. While some fell far short, there was widespread agreement, even by those, that these were the values to be nurtured and cherished.

So it was not surprising that the Colonists chose to honour their religious heritage when choosing a name for their new town. "Lloyd" was to recognize Reverend George E. Lloyd who led the community in its earliest days. Rev. Lloyd insisted on appending the word "Minster", meaning "Mother Church" to reflect the central role he saw for the Church. As it turned out, Rev. Lloyd's vision that the new church and town would act as a regional centre for the surrounding districts was remarkably accurate.

While there have been individuals and families of Jewish, Muslim and other backgrounds over our first century, Christian churches have been almost the sole institutional expression of religion in our community. However, within that tradition, the number and variety of religious communities has grown remarkably. British Protestant denominations such as: Church of England, Methodist, Baptist and Presbyterian came with the Colonists but soon other denominations were appearing. In recent years, evangelical, independent churches have emerged to provide their forms of worship and ministry in the community.

Photo courtesy of Lloydminster Regional Archives.

Predictably, the Anglican Church was the first church in Lloydminster. Both Barr and Lloyd were Anglican clerics and the majority of the 1,700 or so Colonists who settled in the area were members of the Anglican Church. A service of thanksgiving was held in Headquarters Tent soon after the Colonists arrived, in early May 1903. Next, services were held in Rev. Lloyd's home until the summer of 1904 when it was decided to build a log church. Then, with the help of native people from Onion Lake, logs were transported, assembled and mudded. A foundation log inscribed with the phrase "St. John's Minster, laid July 10, 1904" was placed at the centre of the building and the first services in the new church were conducted by Rev. Lloyd. In 1906, Reverend Carruthers succeeded Rev. Lloyd as rector.

Photo courtesy of Sylvia Baynton

As early as 1907, it was realized that the congregation had outgrown their place of worship. In 1910, a ceremony to lay the cornerstone for the new church was held. Rev. Lloyd, now Principal of Emmanuel College, was on hand for the occasion. Inside the cornerstone was an hermetically sealed bottle containing a photo of the old Minster, coins of the realm, canons and constitutions of the parish and diocese, a copy of the Lloydminster Times, and the latest circular of the Board of Trade. The new St. John's Minster was dedicated on December 4, 1910.

Above: Rev. George Lloyd officiates at the first service at Stoney Creek - June 1904 - held on Freddy King's Farm. St. Peter's, Stoney Creek became one of several small rural churches operating under the auspices of St. John's Minster.

Below: a large crowd gathers to marvel at the partially constructed St. John's Anglican Church. James Gee (on platform, far left - rear) and Sons were the contractors. The school later known as "the old high school" is in the distance, top left.

LAYING CORNER STONE OF NEW ST JOHN'S CHURCH, LLOYDMINSTER, CANADA.

Photos courtesy of Peggy Peckover and Sandy Hill

The ceremonial laying of the cornerstone of St. John's Minster on August 25, 1910. Clergy present include (l-r): Rev. J. D. Mullins, Secretary, CCCS; Rev. Principal G. E. Lloyd, and Rev. C. Carruthers, Rector of St. John's.

Below: A hearty rendition of the hymn, Rock of Ages, *was sung at the official laying of the cornerstone for St. John's Minster. It was a favourite hymn at funerals during our first century..*

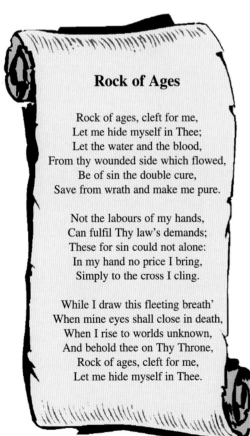

Rock of Ages

Rock of ages, cleft for me,
Let me hide myself in Thee;
Let the water and the blood,
From thy wounded side which flowed,
Be of sin the double cure,
Save from wrath and make me pure.

Not the labours of my hands,
Can fulfil Thy law's demands;
These for sin could not alone:
In my hand no price I bring,
Simply to the cross I cling.

While I draw this fleeting breath'
When mine eyes shall close in death,
When I rise to worlds unknown,
And behold thee on Thy Throne,
Rock of ages, cleft for me,
Let me hide myself in Thee.

As the years continued, many special services were held in St. John's. On May 29, 1919, the Royal and Battalion colours of the First Canadian Mounted Rifles were deposited. On June 26, 1921, a new bell was dedicated and a memorial tablet unveiled listing the names of those from Lloydminster who had died in the Great War.

One of the largest funerals held in St. John's was for Nurse Mabel Drewe who died on April 25, 1914. Residents honoured this pioneer who had provided her own home for a hospital. Her death was felt especially by those at St. John's as she had been a devoted member of the congregation and a long time member of the choir. Later that year, money was raised to purchase the Eagle Lectern Memorial dedicated to Nurse Drewe. It was meant to recognize the devoted service she had given to the Lloydminster community.

At the Diamond Jubilee of the Colonist's arrival, in 1963, a project was announced by the City to restore the Old Minster, recognizing that it was one of the most important pieces of Lloydminster's history. It is the oldest surviving building in Lloydminster. After its retirement in 1919 as a Church, the building was used for a variety of purposes including school house, general store, second-hand store and bottle exchange. Through these years, it had fallen into a state of great disrepair. After the restoration and relocation to Weaver Park was completed, Bishop Steer came to Lloydminster on June 2, 1968, to rededicate the Old Minster to the service of God and the community. It was officially renamed "The Old Minster Church" and it was decided that an annual service should be held at the church to emphasize it was still a place of worship.

With a new life, The Old Minster Church continued to make history. In 1978, in an event which would have warmed the hearts of all the Colonists, Her Majesty Queen Elizabeth II, Prince Phillip and Prince Edward toured the church and signed the visitor's book. In 1979, a special service marked the 75th Anniversary of the first service there. A Bible was dedicated for lectern use in commemoration of the event.

St. John's Minister continues its active role in the community. In 1975, a hall was added that has hosted many community functions such as fall suppers, dramatic presentations and blood donor clinics. Various community organizations, such as Alcoholics Anonymous, hold their meetings at the church. Recently, The Gate youth centre moved into the second floor and the Sunday School relocated to the basement. St. John's plans to host a Provincial Synod of the Anglican Church in 2003 as both St. John's Minster and Lloyd "minster" mark their centennial.

Although the Anglican Church was a strong force in the community from the outset, by 1906, four other churches had begun to grow in numbers and build homes. The first of these began on July 3, 1904, when ten members assembled under Rev. W. P. Freeman, an interim student pastor, for the first service of what became the First Baptist Church.

Photo courtesy of Peggy Peckover and Sandy Hill

By 1915, the Baptist Church was experiencing difficulties due to membership fluctuations and the outbreak of the Great War. The church was forced to close and for twelve years the building was used as a school and the manse became a private home. Finally on August 7, 1927, the doors of First Baptist were reopened under Rev. Robert with the support of twenty members and the Baptist Union of Western Canada.

An example of their outreach efforts is provided in a Lloydminster Times article of 1940 which describes "Gospel teams" going "to all points in the country districts where an open door can be found and a meeting place arranged" in order to revive "the old-fashioned Gospel preaching" and feature the "singing of the old Gospel hymns in which all can join."

Plans emerged in 1953 for a new First Baptist Church. It was built in stages. The basement was completed in 1954 and services were held there until the church was completed in 1959. Rev. L. E. Jones led the building of the new church. In addition, he initiated the Baptist Bible Hour radio broadcast which lasted until 1973 and was one of the driving forces in establishing Pleasantview Bible Camp.

Rev. Vern Priebe came in 1970 and, in addition to a variety of local efforts, he established a daughter ministry in Vermilion. Pastor Harvey Peters continued the trend by creating another daughter ministry in Maidstone during his 1977 to 1982 term.

Many devout Presbyterians were part of the earliest stages of the colony. Mr. E. Morgan held an organizational meeting in the Immigration Hall on August 29, 1904, to discuss the intricacies of setting up a new church. Details, such as trustees and space, were hammered out and it was decided that Mr. Morgan would conduct the services until an ordained minister could be found. That minister was the Reverend A. R. McLennan who was appointed in March of 1905 and stayed for two years.

Services were held in the Immigration Hall until the authorities notified the congregation they had to move as all the space was needed. With a church building now a necessity, in October of 1905, lots were purchased and the work of raising funds and drawing plans began. The church was completed and dedicated by the Presbytery of Saskatoon on February 6, 1906 and incorporated as Knox Presbyterian Church on November 6, 1911.

The church lost self-supporting status in 1925 due in part to financial

Photo courtesy of Jack McGuffie

The first Baptist Church in Lloydminster, and accompanying manse, occupied the south-east corner of the intersection of 48 Ave. and 50 St.

Below: Generations of children have enjoyed Church summer camps such as Silverbirch Bible Camp at Loon Lake, shown here.

Photo courtesy of Lloydminster Gospel Fellowship

Religion

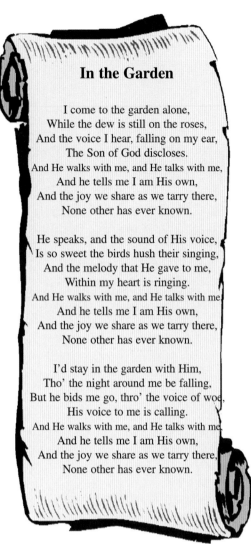

In the Garden

I come to the garden alone,
While the dew is still on the roses,
And the voice I hear, falling on my ear,
The Son of God discloses.
And He walks with me, and He talks with me,
And he tells me I am His own,
And the joy we share as we tarry there,
None other has ever known.

He speaks, and the sound of His voice,
Is so sweet the birds hush their singing,
And the melody that He gave to me,
Within my heart is ringing.
And He walks with me, and He talks with me,
And he tells me I am His own,
And the joy we share as we tarry there,
None other has ever known.

I'd stay in the garden with Him,
Tho' the night around me be falling,
But he bids me go, thro' the voice of woe,
His voice to me is calling.
And He walks with me, and He talks with me,
And he tells me I am His own,
And the joy we share as we tarry there,
None other has ever known.

problems resulting from the Church Union movement in Canada. In 1925, all Unitarians, most Methodists and some Presbyterians joined to create the new United Church of Canada. The merger was defeated at a local Presbyterian church meeting on January 25, 1925 but many of the congregation left anyway to join the United Church. The Presbyterian congregation here did not become self-supporting again until 1958.

During the Great Depression, Rev. Andrew Walker came to Lloydminster. His circumstances were similar to many in that era. His stipend was often late and almost always reduced. It was common for him to be paid in produce, which he often gave to someone he felt was more in need than himself. He continued his work here until his death in 1947. His contribution would be saluted by the addition of the Andrew Walker Memorial Wing, formally dedicated on September 9, 1959.

At the 60th Anniversary of the congregation in 1964, Rev. J. E. Bigelow brought forward the idea of a three stage building program culminating in the completion of a sanctuary. After many trials and tribulations over cost and construction issues, the first service in the new sanctuary was held in June 1968. The first funeral in the church was for choir director and assistant organist Blanche Squires in 1971. During that service, the organ quit working during one of the hymns. Whether a coincidence or a sign, this prompted the decision that day to purchase a new organ and dedicate it as the Blanche Squires Memorial Organ.

As of 2001, the Pastor of Knox Presbyterian, Dave Leggatt is involved in many aspects of the community. One of the volunteer chaplains at the hospital, he is also a spiritual advisor at the Thorpe Centre. He continues the involvement of the church in the community through volunteer programs and various fund-raising initiatives.

Lloydminster's Roman Catholic history began in 1905 when Father Auguste Bemier began visiting Lloydminster by train. The first church was not built until 1910 after Father Henry Goutier was appointed parish priest in Vermilion in 1909. The first resident priest here was Father Thomas Dobson who arrived in 1924. He remained until 1948 when he was called to St. Joseph's Seminary in Edmonton to become a professor of English.

Below: St. Anthony's Roman Catholic Church, rear view, late 1950's.

Photo by Don Whiting

On July 1, 1948, he was succeeded by Father Bernard Gorman. It was seen immediately that a new church building was required and it was soon completed on the corner of 52 Ave. and 44 St. The congregation moved into it in August 1949, with a few modifications to be completed later. The Catholic Women's League held a variety of fund-raisers including suppers, teas and bazaars to raise money for the new church. The entire St. Anthony's Parish supported in any way they could, making it a true parish effort.

In 1961, the Roman Catholics of Lloydminster established a Separate School Board and St. Thomas School became the first Roman Catholic School to open in the border city, affirming the role of Roman Catholics in the community. Eventually, a new church was needed for the parish to continue its work. On April 12, 1987, Palm Sunday, the new church at 56 Ave. and 27 St. saw the celebration of its first mass.

Photo courtesy of Grace United Church Archives

Above: Grace United Church, late 1950's

In 2001 Grace United Church celebrated its 95th Anniversary in Lloydminster. Originally, Methodists met in the Immigration Hall until the Wesleyn Church was built in 1906. Various areas have been a part of the Lloydminster parish during its existence, including at different times Southminster, Marshall and Hillmond. The Wesleyn Church became Grace Methodist Church in 1920 and then changed again in 1925 when a number of Presbyterians moved from Knox to join the Methodists in creating Grace United.

The first church to be built after the amalgamation was in 1950. It continues to serve as the upper and lower halls. The present sanctuary was finished and dedicated on October 21, 1961. Over the years, many renovations have been made. A new kitchen and additional offices alleviated some congestion in such popular areas as the Sunday School which was often held in private homes and sometimes in shifts. The additional space also gave room for such groups as the Bible Study and U. C. W.

Another important physical presence of Grace United has been the booth operated at the Exhibition, which has always been an excellent place to get home style food while attending the Fair. The newest booth was built in 1962 and operated by the U.C.W. until 1988 when it was turned over to the Exhibition Board due to an earlier agreement. It was sold back to the church in 1990 for $1.00. A committee formed from the congregation manages the continued operation of the booth.

Music is an important part of the history of Grace United as it has been for other churches in Lloydminster. Senior and junior choirs, and instrumental components have played an important role in services. This has recently culminated in events such as the Gospel Service.

The first of the non-traditional churches to arrive was the Salvation Army which officially began in Lloydminster on April 17, 1920. The Salvation Army brought a unique focus grounded in community service, especially to the less fortunate. They offered to change peoples lives and called on their clergy to observe a military-style discipline. The term "army" was not just a figure of speech. They often held open-air services in the street with the Salvation Army band present. Their very public presence and obvious good works soon earned them respect.

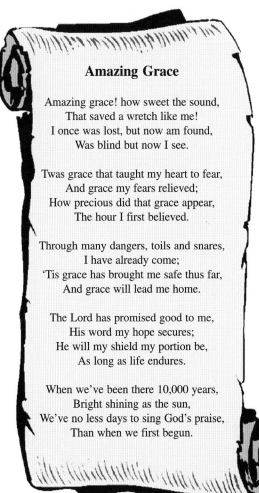

Amazing Grace

Amazing grace! how sweet the sound,
That saved a wretch like me!
I once was lost, but now am found,
Was blind but now I see.

Twas grace that taught my heart to fear,
And grace my fears relieved;
How precious did that grace appear,
The hour I first believed.

Through many dangers, toils and snares,
I have already come;
'Tis grace has brought me safe thus far,
And grace will lead me home.

The Lord has promised good to me,
His word my hope secures;
He will my shield my portion be,
As long as life endures.

When we've been there 10,000 years,
Bright shining as the sun,
We've no less days to sing God's praise,
Than when we first begun.

Brigadier Faie Everson

Born July 5, 1905, Faie Everson always sought to serve God in her life. She attended youth councils where she prayed the Lord would give her direction. In 1926 she moved to Winnipeg to train at Grace Hospital and graduated in 1927, returning to Lloydminster to work. Following Lloydminster's great fire in August 1929, Faie noticed how much the local Salvation Army was doing to assist the community recover. In 1930, she returned to Winnipeg, this time to enter the Salvation Army's Offic-

Brigadier Everson celebrates her 90th birthday in Lloydminster with family and friends.

er's Training College.

On June 26, 1931, Faie Everson was commissioned as a Salvation Officer, eventually reaching the status of Brigadier. Her long and outstanding service to the Corps earned her great praise. On February 19, 1978, the Brigadier received the Queen's Silver Jubilee Medal in recognition of her many years of caring and community service. She was honoured again in 1985 for 58 years of service, an outstanding commitment in any field.

Below: Lieutenant Margaret Stratton, one of the founders of the Salvation Army in Lloydminster - 1920's.

The first First Officer of the Lloydminster Corps was Captain Eveyln Gain assisted by Pro-Lieutenant Margaret Stratton. They opened the first Salvation Hall in May 1920 in a former grocery store. The building burned in the great 1929 fire. Captain Florrie Walker, who was in charge at the time, was away leaving Stratton and Faie Everson to save what they could, including the flag and the drum.

It was a devastating loss for the Corps. It was over thirty years until the New Salvation Army Citadel was opened and dedicated by Brigadier A. P. Simester on June 10, 1961. For a period, the Corps worked out of Vermilion for lack of suitable space in Lloydminster. In 1976, the Vermilion Corps was closed and amalgamated with the Lloydminster Corps. On May 2, 1992, the Corps moved into a new building on the south side.

The good works of the Salvation Army have garnered the church the respect of the community. The most obvious example is the Thrift Store, which also houses the food bank. The League of Mercy visits those who need good cheer in hospitals, nursing homes, and private homes. The presence of the Salvation Army is especially felt at Christmas when members and supporters can be seen in the stores and on the streets of Lloydminster ringing bells and collecting donations.

Other non-traditional groups which had some presence before World War II included the actively proselytizing Jehovah's Witnesses and the Church of Jesus Christ of Latter Day Saints.

Pentecostal services were introduced as early as 1927 with celebrations held in private homes until a small gospel tent was erected in a field (now 47th St. and 54th Ave). Samuel Peregrym moved to Lloydminster with his family in the late 1940's and began conducting Ukrainian Pentecostal meetings. Fred Shorland, an apostolic brother, and his wife, moved here just after the Peregryms and joined their meetings. Dual language services developed and the congregation grew. It was decided a church building was needed. Finally, on the third Sunday in March, 1954, the Pentecostal Tabernacle of Lloydminster was opened, ending the days of services in homes and tents.

In the mid-1950's Rev. Peter Kerychuk became the minister and performed the services in both Ukrainian and English. The church continued to reorganize, eventually being named "Living Faith Pentecostal Tabernacle Lloydminster". The new building on 31st St. was dedicated on April 7, 1974.

The Ukrainian Catholic Church had a presence in Lloydminster as early as 1933 with liturgies held in private homes in and around Lloydminster. For a time, services were held in St. Anthony's Roman Catholic Church. The Descent of the Holy Spirit Byzantine Ukrainian Catholic Parish was officially incorporated on March 30, 1952. Shortly after, a new church was built which stood where the parking lot of the current church is today. The current structure was completed and the first liturgy performed there on April 8, 1984, with the old church being moved to Clandonald. The domes from the top of the old church, constructed by Mr. Walter Stoyko, were retained for the new one and are still in place today.

Reverend Herbert R. Brase was sent to Lloydminster by the Mission Board of the Lutheran Church Missouri Synod in the depths of the Great Depression - fall 1936 - to establish a Lutheran congregation. He held his first service in the rented basement of the First Baptist church. The congregation organized the First Lutheran Church of Lloydminster on December 10, 1939.

When it was decided in 1944 to build a Lutheran church, it was financially necessary to do it in stages. In 1945, the basement was completed and dedicated and the rest of the church on December 19, 1949. This was a great moment of joy followed by a great moment of sadness as only a few months later Pastor Brase left the congregation.

However, Pastor Brase returned in 1964 as a special guest for the 25th Anniversary celebrations of First Lutheran Church. His contribution was further recognized in November 1974 by naming the new wing the "Brase Memorial Hall." Almost nine years after this joyful occasion, the unthinkable happened. On Christmas Eve 1983, the church and Brase Hall were completely destroyed in a fire, later determined to be arson. Christmas services had to be held in the Anglican Church Hall. The congregation rebounded and dedicated the new First Lutheran Church on September 16, 1984.

Photo courtesy of the Salvation Army

Above: 1950's, children prepare to embark on a day of outdoor fun and fellowship thanks to the Salvation Army's "Hallelujah Chariot".

Below: The Descent of the Holy Spirit Ukrainian Catholic Parish used this structure from 1952 to 1984.

Photo courtesy of Descent of Holy Spirit Church

Above: The March for Jesus - 1997. An inter-denominational event attracting participation from many of Lloydminster's 25 plus Christian churches.

In 1960 a small group of faithful Ukrainian Orthodox followers decided to form a church. The earliest services were led by Reverend M. Kryschuck. In April, Ben Gulak was elected the first president of the church council. The All Saints Ukrainian Orthodox Church of Lloydminster was incorporated February 8, 1962.

Their first church was not completed and the first mass held until September 1964. The official dedication was in June 1970, when the cost of land and construction had been paid off. The church continues with a priest who drives from Vegreville approximately fourteen times a year. The liturgy is now conducted in English. The year 1998 was important for the entire Ukrainian Orthodox Church as it marked the 1,000th anniversary of Christianity in Ukraine

The Church of God was incorporated in 1962 with Gabe Adams as the first pastor. Their first location was the Boy Scout Hall, near the present City Hall. Later, the congregation purchased the former Baptist Church. Their first service there was held on July 22, 1980, with the dedication service a few months later on Thanksgiving weekend.

Conveying God's Word - Dramatically

Christmas pageants have been presented by local churches since the very first Christmas was celebrated here in 1903. Over recent years, Southridge Community Church has established an outstanding reputation for the quality and impact of its dramatic productions. For example, in 1999 the play, *Trip to Bountiful*, depicted the attitudes to aging and the hopes and fears of the aged. The talented cast left the packed audiences moved to tears.

Below: Denise Block (left) as Mary and Sarah Morgan as Elizabeth discuss the miracles of conception and birth and speculate about God's plan for their children in **Two From Galilee**. *Above right: Reg Block and Linda Shakotko appeared as Mary's parents in the same production.*

Worship Pastor, Brad Berkan has provided the skilled direction for many of these professionally staged productions. He draws on a talented congregation who devote many hours to rehersals. When asked why the Church puts such effort into drama, Pastor Mike Morgan responds; " Our God is a creative God. He expresses His love and His message to us in many ways, including throught the arts. Some people who attend our productions may not attend church and the arts provide us with a way of conveying God's message of love for all."

With their success in drama, Southridge plans a musical theatre youth camp which may develop into a veritable Christian School of the Arts.

The Seventh Day Adventists first opened their doors in 1975 under Pastor Las Saylor at their present location on 31st St. Now led by Pastor Darrell Beaudoin, they follow strict Biblical teachings such as observing the Sabbath on the seventh day of the week - Saturday. They are also involved in humanitarian work such as the Anglican Church's soup kitchen.

Southridge Community Church began in the Stockade Building, on September 11, 1976 under the leadership of Al and Lois Torhjem. As the congregation grew, they moved to the Civic Centre and finally to their own new building on the corner of 57th Ave. and 41st St. The first worship service there was on May 6, 1979, with the dedication on October 19, 1980.

An evangelical church, they stress worship and discipleship as a means of celebration and education. In addition to weekly ministries and other services, they also offer a summer camp for children and families. Southridge Camp began in 1978 and is held at Ministikwan Lake. Continually expanded to create an even better experience for the campers, it celebrated its 20th year of operation in 1998. Southridge Community Church itself celebrated its 25th anniversary in the summer of 2001.

The Word Outreach Centre began in Loon Lake in 1979. Then Pastor David Bounds started a ministry to Lloydminster, moving here permanently in 1990. The Word Outreach Centre is a Pentecostal church which includes speaking in tongues. Music factors very highly in their services as do dramatic presentations.

In January 1988, what became the Lloydminster Gospel Fellowship (LGF), began with meetings in private homes. Once their numbers grew to a sufficient size, they rented the former Senior Citizens Centre at 4723 - 49th St. Rapid changes for the L.G.F. continued in July of 1988 when they leased the former Jubilee Nursing Home. In August 1988, Pastor Dave Postal became the group's first pastor. Renovations and improvements have continued under the current pastor, Kevin Olive.

Another recent evangelical denomination is the Alliance Church of Canada. Initially, Southridge Community Church was affiliated with the Alliance but it became a non-denominational community church in 1990. Robin Hurlburt became the pastor of those who wished to continue with the Alliance

Many people have contact with the Church only on special occasions such as weddings or funerals. The church provides solemnity and meaning to all these occasions. While we are often caught up in our daily mundane lives, these special occasions remind us of the great mysteries of life and death, and of the spiritual dimensions which can console and inspire us, just as they have so many generations who have gone before. For Christians, the miracles inherent in this life foreshadow the miracles awaiting in the next.

Religion

Photo courtesy of Marlene Cherry

Above: Most churches assist with community activities. The First Baptist Church has hosted the Lloydminster Musical Festival for many years.

Below: Teen councillor Aron Klassen assists a group of Sparks to prepare for a flag ceremony on Awana Sunday, 2000. Awana is an international youth program in Christian fundamentals. The girls' badges indicate knowledge of Bible stories.

Church. The congregation was next led by Ross Plews, until 1998, when Don Williams took over. The Alliance was an unlikely beneficiary of the Alberta government's privatization of the liquor trade. The congregation purchased the former Alberta Liquor Control Board building on 51st Street and, changing its spiritual character, transformed it into their home church.

The first meeting of the New Life Community Church took place on September 29, 1991, under Pastor Marty Wagantall and is currently led by Pastor Dwight Brown. They held services in a Lakeland College lecture theatre until they bought the former Knights of Columbus building in 1996. Dick Vokins, moderator of the board, describes New Life as a church for the unchurched. It is a very non-traditional as they believe that traditional approaches separate people from a relationship with God. The music is upbeat, there are no hymns, and no collection.

Each church carries out its form of pastoral care in our community. The earliest churches relied purely on their ministers, pastors or priests for pastoral care and all other matters involving their spiritual needs. But times changed and congregations grew and so did the demands on the pastors. One solution was an increase in staff. Some churches hired an assistant pastor. First Lutheran chose this path. Another solution is to involve lay members more in the functions of the church. Such individuals can be, but are not necessarily, pastors. They are individuals willing to volunteer their time to the ministry of the church.

First Baptist has a Senior Pastor, a Youth pastor and a Ministry Coordinator. Southridge also created a variety of positions, one specifically dedicated to the pastoral care of the congregation and occupied for several years by Robert Myers. Knox Presbyterian took this concept to the next level. In 1955, the congregation was organized into districts. These districts were managed by elders who would oversee the spiritual welfare of the congregation. Another option is the one chosen by the Church of God. They have divided their congregation into cell groups where personal studies and ministering is performed. The leaders of these groups are in turn ministered to by the pastor.

As we have seen by reviewing the churches begun in Lloydminster in the past quarter century, the trend seems to be toward non-traditional, evangelical churches. Many members of these congregations emphasize a personal relationship with God and believe the traditions and practices of the older churches are no longer relevant to that. Many believe that this is especially true for younger people. For whatever reasons, it does appear that traditional congregations are growing older and declining in numbers.

Photo courtesy of Southridge Community Church

Rev. Don Byrt leads the 2000 edition of the annual service at the Old Minster, now located on the grounds of the Barr Colony Heritage Cultural Centre.

Photo by Don Whiting

Organist Pat Skinner prepares to play the antique organ at the Old Minster Church.

Photo by Don Whiting

At the same time, evangelical churches are more youthful and are often growing in numbers.

"Old Line" churches have also made changes to attempt to attract new members. Some believe the message of the Church needs to be changed to fit what are assumed to be the changing needs of the people. On the other hand, if religion, in all places and at all times, is about the quest for meaning and value in life, then perhaps we should note that the successful "new" churches often espouse a "back to the basics" approach. Their emphasis on personal spiritual experience is part of the continuing renewal that has characterized Christian history.

As other world religions become more prevalent in our community, and as interest grows in other forms of spiritual questing, from aboriginal to oriental, we can be sure that religion will continue to play an important role in the Lloydminster community.

In the year 2000, 96 years after Lloydminsterites first worshipped within its walls, the annual summer service at the Old Minster attracts a congregation of regulars and tourists to praise and give thanks to God.

Photo by Don Whiting

Religion

Chapter Four

Local Government

Research by Jean Henry and Alan Griffith

Above: Bishop G. E. Lloyd stands in the doorway to address a crowd of proud Lloydminsterites at the official opening of the new Town Hall for Lloydminster, Saskatchewan in 1927. Such an imposing structure within site of where the first settlers had camped less than 25 years earlier seemed a remarkable achievement.

Below: Mayor Harold Huxley (centre in light coat) poses along with other members of Town Council and Bishop Lloyd on the same occasion.

Photo courtesy of Don Whiting Collection.

Photo courtesy of Doug Aston Collection

B order City - the name appears in our City's motto - "Canada's Only Border City" - and in the names of many local businesses, organizations and teams. Our border reality intrigues tourists who often take pictures of themselves with one foot in Alberta and the other in Saskatchewan. Locals come to take it for granted, traveling from homes in one province to restaurants in another on the basis of choice of food rather than provinces. In fact though, we have had to work hard for almost our entire history to build and maintain one community despite our bi-provincial reality. Despite our success in doing this, even veteran Lloydminsterites do not fully appreciate that Lloydminster's status as ONE municipality having territory and population in TWO provinces makes it truly unique, in Canada and perhaps even in the world.

Perhaps no aspect of our community must confront the problems and opportunities of bi-provincialism on a day by day basis more than our local government. Over the years, village, town and city councils, and staff, have contended with two provincial bureaucracies, each with different regulations and policies on public works, taxation, health care and education. Yet there are opportunities. The uniqueness of the Lloydminster Charter allows the City to pick and choose areas of legislation from either province, thus sometimes getting the best of both worlds. The mayor and council, along with the citizens, have learned to operate a local government which is truly unique.

The Border Split and the Amalgamation

On November 30, 1903, Lloydminster, Northwest Territories, was officially recognized as a village. The first overseer was Dr. W. W. Amos who succeeded the colony's chosen leader Rev. George Exton Lloyd and his "Council of Twelve" who had managed the town-site until then. The aim was to organize an efficient village government for the years to come.

However, Dr. Amos, Rev. Lloyd, and the other residents did not expect that less than two years later their community would be split down the middle by an arbitrary line marking the border of the two new provinces of Saskatchewan and Alberta. There had been several proposals for borders for the new provinces. Some wanted to simply turn the previous territories into provinces which would have resulted in five prairie provinces. Most wanted one new province along with the existing Manitoba but the federal government was fearful of the influence of such a potentially large province. Some wanted a northern and southern province. Right to the last minute the decision could have placed the boundary 60 miles to the east. However the final selection of the Fourth Meridian as the provincial boundary confirmed the feared rumours. Village officials pleaded with the federal government to at least run the border around the already surveyed townsite so that it would be contained within one province but, of course, that did not happen.

Above: When first constructed, the Town Hall contained two bays for the use of the fire department. When a separate fire hall was constructed to the north of the Town Hall, the former fire truck bays were converted into office space. The structure served as Lloydminster's City Hall until 2000.

So, Lloydminster became a town in Saskatchewan and a separate village in Alberta, each with its own municipal government, waterworks, and school district. From the beginning, many citizens recognized the needless expense and bureaucracy of such a situation. The town and the village would be much stronger if they were united as they had been in the first place.

It has been long believed that the fire of 1929, which destroyed the downtown core of Lloydminster, was the major impetus for amalgamation. While it definitely played a role, people had discussed the issue of amalgamation as early as 1905.

In May 1907, councillor J. T. Hill of the town and Reeve R. W. Miller of the village visited Edmonton and Regina to gain support from the provincial governments for amalgamation. The idea was to include the amalgamated town under one province's jurisdiction. At the time, it appeared that Saskatchewan would become Lloydminster's governing province.

The town and village councils agreed to hold a vote on July 15, 1907, to gain the residents' approval of the amalgamation proposal. However, the vote was cancelled at the last minute. A group of residents objected to the amalgamated town being governed by Saskatchewan, and a petition, containing twenty-one signatures, was to be presented to the federal government. In light of the petition, the town and village councils decided to put their amalgamation proposal on hold. Others, such as J. G. Willard, *Lloydminster Times* editor, wondered whether the petition would have had any effect: "It seems to us a great pity that it should be in the power of such a small minority to stop the vote and thus prevent what would possibly have been the greatest benefit that could accrue to our town."

A plan of the townsite of Lloydminster from 1904

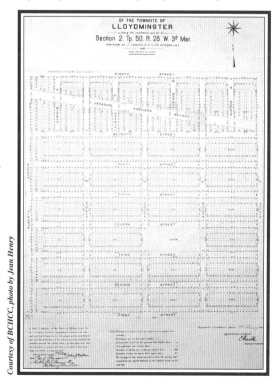

Photo courtesy of Don Whiting Collection.

Above: The Lloydminster Public School resulted from a combined effort of the two local school districts working together despite the fact that they had been forced apart by provincial regulations. Their determination brought a much needed educational facility to reality in 1925 with the opening of the new school. Their work provided an example of the benefits of residents of both provinces working together to build one better community. Later renamed, Meridian School, in recognition of its fronting on the border, the building was demolished in 2000 to make room for the new City Hall.

Below: A photo of the Board of Trade Executive in 1954. Throughout its history, the Board of Trade had a strong influence on Town Council, forming an Amalgamation Committee in the 1920's and later pushing council to install a waterworks system for the good of the town. In 1955, they became known as the Lloydminster Chamber of Commerce.
Back row (l-r): R.J.R. Noyes, ?, Ken Fisher, Marshall Tindall, and Ray Nelson. Front row (l-r): Harold Fossey, George Wiens, Joe McLean, Art Shortell, Bill Cardiff

The major issue then became which province was preferred to govern the whole community. The issue divided people for years, and provincial loyalties ran high. School boys divided into "our province only" gangs. Pranks such as towing the early wood frame Post Office across the border became local legends. It was not until the mid-1920's that the two local governments began once again to discuss the issue in earnest. In March 1927, Mayor Hall of the town and Reeve Cooke of the village visited Edmonton to discuss the possibility of amalgamation with members of the Alberta Legislature. The mayor and reeve suggested that the Border Areas Act of 1924 could be amended to deal with a combined community.

Both the Lloydminster Ratepayers and the Board of Trade also began to push for amalgamation. In February 1928, Board of Trade president J. D. Hamilton sent a letter to the premiers of both provinces asking them to meet with a Lloydminster amalgamation committee to discuss the issue. "The council is of full sympathy and accord with the proposed amalgamation of the town and village and would take any steps necessary to bring about a workable plan to present to the ratepayers of the town of Lloydminster," the letter stated.

The councils trudged through five drafts of the Lloydminster Municipal Amalgamation Act 1930, before it met with approval by the Saskatchewan and Alberta governments. The Act was general, including all that was legally necessary without dictating specific matters that would concern the community. Commissions were appointed by both provinces to handle transitions such as schools, debts, lands, bylaws, and tax rates until a new town council could be elected. There were two versions of the Act: one for Saskatchewan legislation, and the other for Alberta legislation. The residents of the town and village also had to approve the proposal in a referendum.

The vote was to be conducted on February 3, 1930 and notices of polls were published in the *Lloydminster Times*. Voters were asked the question, "Are you in favour of the Amalgamation of the Town of Lloydminster and the Village of Lloydminster on the basis as advertised?" Polling took place at the Town Hall and Alberta Hall, and the overwhelming majority of Lloydminster residents voted in favour. In the town, the exact tally was 431 "Yes" to 4 "No", and in the village 152 "Yes" to 3 "No". With the approval of the people of Lloydminster, the Act was passed by the Alberta government on May 20, 1930 and the Saskatchewan government on May 21, 1930.

Photo courtesy Lloydminster Regional Archives

The Lloydminster Wedding

At the amalgamation of 1930, a ceremony was held complete with a performance of wedding vows to mark the "marriage" of the town and village as acted out by several local school children. The ceremony was as follows:

Minister:

"Dearly Beloved, we are gathered here to join this Town and this Village in serious Amalgamation. First, it was ordained at the commencement of the New City of the West. Secondly, it was ordained for a remedy against haughty remarks and facetious digs from either side. Thirdly, it was ordained for the mutual welfare of the citizens of Town and Village, that each may have the benefits of the town pump and the

Above: Children who enacted the "marriage" of the town and village have been identified as Ted Howell, groom (third from left) and Kathleen Yates, bride (fourth from left).

fire siren. Therefore, if any man can show any just cause why they may not be joined together, let him ring the fire bell now or forever hold his horses. Wilt thou have this village to be thy wedded wife; to give her Mayor Huxley; to co-operate in hustling along the water works; to install cement sidewalks in all directions and sit in chairs of unity in the Town Hall?

Lloyd, SK: I will.

Minister: Wilt thou have this Town, to be thy big noise; to assume his debts, use his post office and work with him to obtain waterworks?

Min, AB: I will.

Minister: Who giveth this village to be united to this town?

Lloyd, SK: I, Lloyd Saskatchewan, take thee, Min Alberta for better, for worse, for good crops, for poor crops, in big fires and small fires, till the crack of doom, and here I'm thine.

Min, AB: I, Min Alberta, take thee Lloyd Saskatchewan, for better, for worse, for good waterworks, for any waterworks, for big rains and small rains, till the day after the last, and here I'm thine.

Minister: With this ring I thee wed, with Mayor Huxley at the head, Nicholas, Crossley, Miner, Cooke, Miller and Wallis to fill the book. All ye that are united, sing. Let us all sing."

"So, an important and happy event drew to a close, and Lloydminster was on its way to prosperous years ahead."

Linda Goad, *The Lloydminster Times, 1930*

Lloyd and Min Celebrate 70th Wedding Anniversary

May 30, 2000

It is hard to believe that seventy years have passed since our dear friends, Lloyd Saskatchewan and Min Alberta, first joined together in the union of marriage. A come and go tea was held last Saturday at the Legacy Centre in honour of their wedding anniversary. Friends and relatives poured in to offer their congratulations.

Lloyd and Min recalled how there had been enormous pressure on them to marry back in 1930. "Everyone was trying to fix us up," Lloyd smiled. "The fire departments, waterworks, you name it."

There is no denying that the couple had some hard times. Soon after they married, they both experienced great depression and then it seemed like out and out war. Finally, they adopted a Husky and this began to pour oil on their troubles.

In the beginning, Lloyd, undeniably the leader, lovingly provided for his wife. As the years went by, however, Min came into her own. "It was an exciting time," she says. "I felt a newfound sense of control in my life." She began to assert her family name - Alberta. It was difficult for Lloyd to accept his wife's success. "At first I felt threatened. Min didn't need me any more" Lloyd said. He seemed to be standing still while he watched his wife continue to grow. "Our marriage needed to operate on an equal playing field," insisted Lloyd.

There were many who thought Lloyd and Min's marriage would never last. The two came from fundamentally different belief systems. Lloyd's socialist rhetoric often fell on deaf ears as Min became more and more committed to the free enterprise system. Still, Min stuck with him.

As the times changed, a new booster came to support their relationship. After many invitations, eventually family friend Mr. Up Grader came to town. "Mr. Grader really helped to blend Min and Lloyd's relationship," a confidante reports. He also helped Lloyd to regain his confidence. Since Mr. Grader's arrival though, Min has continued to achieve prosperity while Lloyd struggles to keep up to her.

Lloyd and Min are truly a unique husband and wife, and all who come to know them marvel at their continuing deep attachment to each other. It may take more than a lifetime for Lloyd and Min to sort out all their differences, but one thing is for sure: a more committed couple, you will not find.

(Gifts can still be delivered to City Hall.)

Amalgamation served to unite the community and combine the resources of the former town and village. With the unification in place, there were great hopes that a more efficient and less costly local government would emerge with an agenda to develop the new town and establish a water system. However, Lloydminster's bi-provincial difficulties did not cease with the Amalgamation Act of 1930. Lloydminster's leaders would still have to continually explain to the federal government and the two provincial governments that Lloydminster was a single unit.

Photo courtesy of Jack McGuffie

Above: Drayman Bob Chapman delivered a variety of goods around Lloydminster, including water in barrels such as those on the left.

Below: Lloydminster's water tower stood tall for many years until it was declared obsolete in 1980.

Photo courtesy of the Provincial Archives of Alberta PA-4473

The Issue of Water

From Lloydminster's very earliest days, residents were urging the mayor and council to establish a waterworks system. Water was an obvious necessity of life, and wells had been dug, but they quickly ran dry. There was also the inconvenience of having to haul water in pails or barrels from the town well to one's home or business. As well, fire was a great concern. It was difficult to fight a blaze without adequate water. While the town and village continued to dig wells to service their growing populations, it would be many years before a water system was put in place. The Lloydminster Ratepayers pushed the Council on the issue. They recommended a deep well be sunk to ensure an adequate water supply and that the wheels be put in motion for the installation of a water system. Despite the ratepayers' insistence, Town Council had reservations. There was the problem of winter freezing and concern by some that Lloydminster's hard water would corrode the pipes over time. On the point of fire protection, one alderman, Dr. J. T. Hill, stated that many of the town's buildings were not worth saving at such an expense. However, the town and village council agreed jointly in 1914 to sink a deep well and citizens hoped it was the first step towards the installation of a municipal water system. However, by 1917, that very well began to fail, and Council had to act quickly to have another well sunk. The issue was still prominent in the 1930's. The February 12, 1931 issue of the *Lloydminster Times* contained an editorial entitled "What about Water?": "Will Lloydminster ever have a water system? For years the citizens of this promising town have been asking for this very necessary convenience, but the fulfillment of the hopes seem as far off as ever." The councils had promised that when amalgamation was complete, discussions concerning waterworks would be on their agenda. The editor noted, though, "it is evident that no one considered themselves responsible for summoning the meeting and the result is the citizens are still talking about water."

While the people seemed desperate for a water system, many wondered what the cost would be to them. The fear was that the cost of home installation would be well above the means of an average homeowner. With the Great Depression now in full stride, people were even more cautious.

The Council attempted to use the Depression as a means to secure Saskatchewan government funds to establish a waterworks system as a relief measure. A delegation went to Regina for interviews but they met with little sympathy. They were told that Lloydminster did not merit assistance as good crops were expected in the area since drought had not hit the region as it had in southern Saskatchewan.

By the late 1930's, the issue was revived. Council pushed through the necessary approvals and a proposal was forwarded to the Saskatchewan authorities of the Municipal Improvements Assistance Act. The provincial authorities agreed to back the town's debentures, and the proposal was passed on to the federal authorities. The federal officials discovered that part of the expenditure was to be made on the Alberta side of the border and they would require the Alberta Government's sanction before they could authorize the town to go ahead with the necessary arrangements for the financing.

In early August 1939, Mayor Miner and Councillors Cooke and Shaw made an emergency trip to Edmonton to present their plan to Judge A. A. Carpenter, chairman of the Public Utilities Board of Alberta. However, Carpenter stated that the Alberta Government had no authority because the Amalgamation Act took away Alberta's jurisdiction over Lloydminster in such matters. Internal Affairs had been passed over to Saskatchewan. "Alberta has no right to dictate to the town and therefore has no right or authority to either endorse or repudiate any expenditure in relation to the town," he commented.

The councillors headed back to Lloydminster, and shortly continued on to Regina to relay Carpenter's position. The Saskatchewan government conferred with the Federal officials who disagreed with the Alberta Government. After a long summer of legal entanglements and many exhausting visits to the two provincial capitols, the issue was resolved and the Alberta government agreed to counter-sign the water scheme debentures.

Even after the announcement had been made, in an October issue of the *Lloydminster Times*, that the water system was now assured, the public was sceptical. It turned out that they had reason to be. Early test holes indicated an excessive amount of iron in the water and further test holes had to be sunk at an unexpected expense to the town. Some councillors believed that it was futile to waste further town money to dig test holes which would likely continue to contain excessive iron. After some debate though, they agreed to follow the water representative's advice and drill again. An adequate supply, billed as healthy enough for human consumption, was finally found and the project was underway.

Photo courtesy of George and Sylvia Baynton

George F. Baynton (left of centre), owner of the Lloydminster Times, is shown here presenting Town Council with several copies of the Jubilee Edition of the newspaper in 1953. Mr. Baynton used the Times to argue tirelessly for civic improvements such as the installation of a waterworks system. (l-r): Ernie Morlidge (reporter) Frank Turvey, Ted Mitchell, George Baynton, Russ Robertson, Vern Miner (Mayor), W. D. Green, Tom Steele (Town Engineer), Gordon Hudson and Bill Cardiff (Town Clerk)

First Council of the City of Lloydminster, January 1958. Back row (l-r): Tom Steele (City Engineer), Ted Mitchell, Russ Robertson, Nick Ewanowich, Gordon Hudson, Bill Zier. Seated (l-r): Bill Cardiff (City Clerk), V. U. Miner (Mayor) and Frank Turvey.

Photo courtesy Lloydminster Regional Archives

Many dedicated citizens have answered the call of local government, making Lloydminster what it is today. Before 1930, there were two separate entities, the town with its mayor and the village with its reeve. Pictured on these pages are all of the mayors since amalgamation. All photos courtesy of the City of Lloydminster except Ilston Plant, by Don Whiting, and Ken Baker, by Charles Lamb Photography.

J.D. Munro (Village) 1921-1926

Dr. G.L. Cooke (Village) 1926-1930

Amalgamation of the town and village 1930

Dr. G.L. Cooke 1932-1935

Dr. G.L. Cooke 1939-1947

V.U. M 1950-1

W.L. Cameron (Town) 1923-1925

Harold Huxley (Town) 1925-1930

Harold Huxley 1930-1931

V.U. Miner 1935-1939

R.L. Shaw 1947-1950

W. Willis (Village) 1920-1921

J. Lindsay (Village) 1919-1920

G.M. Cook (Village) 1917-1919

H.B. Hall (Town) 1915-1917

Dr. J.T. Hill (Town) 1920-1923

Harold Huxley (Town) 1917-1920

Dr. W.W. Amos (Overseer) 1903-1906

H.B. Hall (Overseer) 1906-1907

Town and Village are created 1907

H.B. Hall (Town) 1907-1909

J.P. Lyle (Town) 1909-1910

James Gee (Town) 1910-1911

J.P. Lyle (Town) 1911-1912

Dr. J.T. Hill (Town) 1912-1913

D.S. Tuckwell (Town) 1913-1915

R.W. Miller (Village) 1907-?

Page opposite, top (l-r): Harold Huxley, Dr. G. L. Cooke, V. U. Miner;
Below, top (l-r): R. L. Shaw, E. G. Hudson, Leo Cavanagh
Page opposite, bottom (l-r): Russell A. Robertson, Kay G. Matheson, William Kondro
Below, bottom (l-r): Patricia Gulak, Ilston Plant, Ken Baker

The town becomes a city: Jan. 1, 1958

V.U. Miner 1958-1962

E.G. Hudson 1962-1968

Leo Cavanagh 1968-1970

E.G. Hudson 1970-1972

R. Robertson 1972-1978

K. Matheson 1978-1981

W. Kondro 1981-1987

Pat Gulak 1987-1994

Ilston Plant 1994-2000

Ken Baker 2000-?

Mayor Facts

H.B. Hall was the first mayor of the town of Lloydminster, serving terms from 1907-1909 and 1916-1917. Hall came to Lloydminster with the Barr Colonists with the intention to farm, but instead he decided to open a business in town. The general store Hall, Scott, and Company opened under the partnership of Hall, local doctor W.W. Amos, and George Scott of Northern Hardware Company in Edmonton. H. B. Hall always had the town's best interest in mind; in the early days of the colony, Hall, along with Bishop Lloyd and a Mr. Ellis, secured a section of land on the Saskatchewan side. They later abandoned their claim to it and turned it over for the benefit of the town, sacrificing their opportunity to secure some of the best homestead land in the area. Hall's son, Steve, was a local war hero, who served in World War I.

Harold Huxley was born in Wem, Shropshire, England in 1881. Harold and his two brothers, Leonard and Frank, came to Canada with the Barr Colonists in 1903. He was town councillor for many years before the amalgamation and served as mayor from 1918-1920 and 1926-1929. Instrumental in the amalgamation process, Huxley continued as mayor of the newly united town from 1930 to 1931. Huxley was greatly respected for his tireless efforts during the influenza epidemic of 1918-1919, which took the lives of his two brothers. The mayor was involved in almost every community organization, including the Masonic, Oddfellow and Orange fraternities, and he was a charter member of the Elks Lodge and the Rotary Club. A founding member of the Exhibition Association, Huxley served as secretary/treasurer from 1907 – 1932 and was inducted into the Lloydminster Agricultural Hall of Fame on July 12, 1985. Harold Huxley died suddenly in 1933.

E. Gordon Hudson was born and raised in Lloydminster. In 1927 he started a theatre business and operated it until 1963. Gordon joined the town of Lloydminster fire department in 1935 and three years later, he was appointed Deputy Chief, a rank which he held until his retirement in December, 1988. In 1950, Gordon was elected to Council and served as an alderman until 1959. He was elected Mayor from 1963-1968 and, following a short break, he was re-elected from 1971 to 1972. Gordon also served as Justice of the Peace for twenty-two years. In recognition of his 54 years of service, the fire station was renamed the E.G. Hudson Fire Station No. 1.

Leo Cavanagh first called Lloydminster "home" in May of 1947, when he began working with Husky on the construction of the first Husky asphalt refinery. By mid 1954, he was named refinery manager. His community and civic interests resulted in him capturing a seat on Lloydminster City Council as alderman from 1963 to 1966. In 1969 he became mayor of the City, a position he held until 1970.

In 1941, teacher **Kathleen (Kay) Matheson** and her husband George moved to Lloydminster. While raising their daughter and son, Kathleen remained active in community affairs. In the 1940's and 1950's, Kathleen held office in the Catholic Women's League, the Home and School Association, and the Kinette Club. In 1959, she was elected to the first Catholic School Board and served for eleven years, four as chairperson, becoming the first Lloydminster woman to hold public office. Kathleen later served as president of the Allied Arts Council. In 1988 she received a special volunteer award from the Saskatchewan government for her service in promoting culture.

Matheson became a city alderman in 1971 and continued until she was elected mayor in 1979, becoming the first woman to hold the prestigious title. During the following three years in office, some of the major items on her agenda were the water and sewer project, the 75th anniversary celebration of Alberta and Saskatchewan as provinces in 1980, the Alberta Winter Games in 1982, and the continued promotion for an oil upgrader in Lloydminster.

Above: Mayor Bill Kondro welcomes cross Canada runner, Steve Fonyo, to Lloydminster.

Photo courtesy Lloydminster Regional Archives

The town promptly received more than forty tenders for the contract to install the water system, and in April 1940, the newspaper headline read "Water Installation Now Sure". By May, work had commenced, and there was an influx of workers into Lloydminster to dig the deep trenches required for the laying of the pipes. After many years of financial concerns, issues of water quality, and bi-provincial legal entanglements Lloydminsterites could finally have water in their homes.

Well, not exactly. The cost of the necessary plumbing was too high for the average homeowner and many chose the more economical option, which was to lay pipe about 10 or 15 feet over the property line and then purchase a rubber hose for garden purposes. After years of hauling water from the town well to their homes, walking a few steps into the backyard for a pail of water was a luxury.

With a the installation of a waterworks system completed, a new movement emerged. In a May 28, 1942 editorial in the *Times*, George Baynton wrote the following: "It is really a pleasure to walk around town and see everyone spraying their flowers, lawns and gardens and it should stimulate that interest in natural beauty which has been characteristic of this town." People began to focus on making their environment more beautiful. The council sponsored competitions for the most beautiful block in Lloydminster, and people were encouraged to plant trees and make the town more pleasing to the eyes.

By the late 1940's, the attraction of a water system and natural gas drew many newcomers to the town. Lloydminster was booming and the increased number of water users was taxing the town well to the limit. Until a new well was drilled, Lloydminsterites had to curtail their water usage. Council divided the City into circuits and water would only be available to certain areas on designated days. People were urged to conserve and not use the water for their gardens.

In the late 1950's and early 1960's further wells were sunk in the Sandy Beach area, and the water was piped into Lloydminster. Another boom in the late '70's once again strained the water and sewer system. Council faced many complaints about regular water breaks, and Mayor Russ Robertson informed the concerned citizens that the cast iron water mains were corroding and deteriorating and they needed to be replaced. The threat of a water shortage loomed over council's head, and it was decided to pursue funding to pipe water from the North Saskatchewan River. At the same time, it was recognized that the sewer system was seriously antiquated, and it would be in the best interest of the city to deal with that issue as well.

It would cost 16 million dollars to put the system in place, and city engineers pushed Council to invest the money to allow for the long term growth of the City. Provincial and federal money was acquired for the project, and the City used profits from its increased water rates to pay back the debentures.

The Border Markers

Even after amalgamation, the border continued to be a constant fact of life. Over the years, it has been marked in many ways. Initially, a wooden post at the former C.N. Railway station marked the dividing line. Later, a pair of yellow culverts could be seen at the junction of Highway 16 and 17. Some came to believe the community should do more to highlight one of its most unique attributes.

In 1990, the Lloydminster Tourism and Convention Authority formed a Border Marker Committee and hired a consulting firm to prepare a design. The final proposal was to erect five one hundred foot towers at the junction of 44th Street and 50th Avenue which would emulate the markers used by Dominion land surveyors to stake the original boundary.

Little was heard from the public at first. However, as the final approvals neared, many began to question the high cost. City Council was split, approving the construction only after the project was downsized to

Lloydminster Becomes the Tenth City in both Saskatchewan and Alberta
Lloydminster's rapid growth made it eligible for city status in 1957 when the population hit 5000. Council applied to both provinces for revisions to the Charter and Lloydminster officially became Canada's only bi-provincial city on January 1, 1958.

Below: Sharp eyed train passengers might catch sight of Lloydminster's first border marker, supplied by CN Rail. Locals didn't pay much attention to it and it eventually succumbed to abuse.

Photo by Don Whiting

City Council decided in a 4-3 vote in 1993 to erect the controversial Border Markers, even without Alberta lottery funding.

Photo by Don Whiting

four poles instead of the original five. Lottery funding provided by the Tourism Industry Association of Alberta was to cover $260,000 of the $300,000 plus project

Construction began in August of 1993 but the controversy increased. Much was made of an allegedly secret letter to Mayor Pat Gulak from the Tourism Alberta, dated May 18, 1993, stating that the project needed to be re-evaluated due to "the overwhelming public outcry." However, the Mayor said she had received a letter dated July 13th stating that the project had been re-considered and was approved to proceed. Two weeks after construction began, M.L.A. Steve West, Minister of Municipal Affairs, advised that Alberta Lottery Funding was to be withdrawn. Contractor Dawson-Wallace was ordered to cease construction, leaving the city with four large $60,000 holes in the ground and no government funding to complete the project.

The debate continued: Fill the holes and cut the City's losses or dig into Lloydminster tax dollars and finish the project without lottery funding. Letters to the Editor poured in as never before.

"Why do our city leaders want to pretend that we have the money to live so flamboyantly," wrote Kevin Ramsay in the September 29, 1993 edition of the *Lloydminster Times*. "Why do they want to push through a project that is so clearly against the public's best interest?"

Another letter from Bruce Macdonald argued that "... if City Council had waited until funding was assured and irrevocable, this wouldn't have happened."

On Wednesday, September 22nd, City Council voted 4-3 in favour of completing the project. Mayor Pat Gulak and Aldermen Joe Rooks, Barb Foster, and Rod Pillman voted in favour of completing the project as

The Story of the Lloydminster Public Library

The Lloydminster Library was first established in 1929 with the help of the Ministerial Association, Kinsmen Club, and Rotary Club. The town was canvassed for donations of books and $1 membership fees were sold to provide start up capital. 180 people signed up, and over 600 books were collected. Edith Duke offered the use of the Garbot Business College, which she operated, as the home of the library at the rent of $15.00 per month. It remained there until October of 1930 when it moved to a small room on the first floor of the Town Hall, which the town provided rent free. Jenny Killen became the librarian in 1931 and remained until 1957. Many credit her for the library's survival through the difficult depression era.

The first of many children's story hours was held near the end of 1930. Library fees were raised and hours were increased to three evenings per week and Saturday afternoons. In 1944, the library changed its name to the Mechanics and Literary Institute in order to acquire Saskatchewan grant money. In 1948, it became

Photo courtesy Provincial Archives of Alberta PA4297

Inset photo by Foster Learning Inc.

After several moves over the years, a Canada Centennial project gave the library a home at the corner of 49th Ave and 46th St. (above). In 1991, it moved to the Atrium Centre (interior in inset).

known as the Lloydminster Public Library.

Elaine Gunderson, known as "the story lady", was the Children's Program coordinator until she retired in 1991. Beloved by all who frequented the library, she was honoured at the library's 65th anniversary.

In 1986, the Lloydminster Public Library affiliated with the Lakeland Library System (Saskatchewan). In 1989, the library was one of the founding members of the Northern Lights Library System (Alberta), in which it retained membership until 2000. For those eleven years, it functioned in both systems, receiving some funding from both provincial systems and acting as a reference library.

Ron Gillies became head librarian in 1989, and continues to serve into the 21st Century. He has led several upgrades in service including a dramatic shift to computerization of the card catalogue and the provision of Internet service.

planned. Aldermen Bill Kondro, Ilston Plant, and Herb Flieger voted in opposition. It was argued that it would take almost two-thirds of the project's cost to repair the damage made by the construction that had been so abruptly halted. Instead, the City would use the 1993 budget surplus to complete the project and Mayor Pat Gulak stated that taxes would not rise. Public opposition continued and the long dormant Lloydminster Ratepayers Association reappeared. The group sought, unsuccessfully, to force a plebiscite on the issue.

The controversial project was finally completed in the spring of 1994, and the four large red towers, which had caused one of the greatest debates in our history, stood tall over the city. Some warmed up to them over time; to others they remained one grand expensive joke.

On April Fool's Day in 1995, the *Meridian Booster* published an altered photograph that pictured one of the markers having fallen into Colonel Saunder's large bucket of chicken across the street. It was less funny than some believed. In 2000, one of the markers was removed so that engineers could study how to make the towers stand more firmly as their oscillation in the wind alarmed residents.

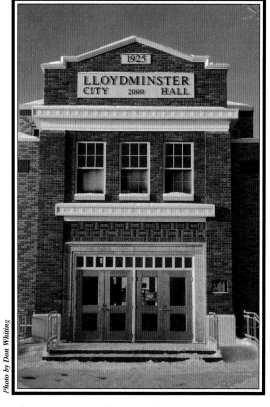

Photo by Don Whiting

The Cost of Progress

Several important issues face Council as Lloydminster nears its 100th anniversary. One of the most noteworthy is traffic flow. For years, citizens have complained about the backlog of traffic due to the many rail crossings. Lloydminster's prosperity has also led to a larger number of vehicles on the streets. Ring-roads and by-passes may be the answer, but progress is never cheap.

Alderman Duff Stewart, first elected to Council in 1994, notes the difficulty in working with two provinces with different financial means: "The Saskatchewan side of Lloydminster is not funded in the same proportion as the Alberta side. Consequently, we have a real 'have' and 'have not' city, and that is one of the challenges that council must continue to address."

Where the province of Saskatchewan has not been willing or able to put up funds, the City and the Province of Alberta have often underwritten projects on the Saskatchewan side for the benefit all.

Councils have faced great obstacles over our first century, many involving "border issues". Since 1905, when the border arrived, these issues have been part of our daily life here in "Canada's Only Border City".

The new City Hall opened in 2000. There had been protest over the demolition of the Meridian School which had stood on the spot since 1925. It was a case of too little too late, unfortunately, as the building was not in a state that it could easily be repaired. City Council agreed to a proposal to incorporate the design of the Meridian School into the central entry way of the new building. Some of the bricks from the old school were even preserved to recreate the front facade in the style of the historic building. So, with this nod to our past, The City of Lloydminster eagerly moved into a new facility which could house all of their departments under one roof.

Photo by Don Whiting

Chapter Five

Health Care

Research by Sheila Bennett and Ian Goodwillie; with draft writing by Ian Goodwillie

Above: The first hospital building in Lloydminster was built in 1912, after years of medical care being provided in private homes. Matron Alice Hunter (in white) and others unidentified pose in front of the 10 bed facility.

Below: This 1924 photo of the interior of the Lloydminster Hospital shows a semi-private room, available at an extra cost over general ward care.

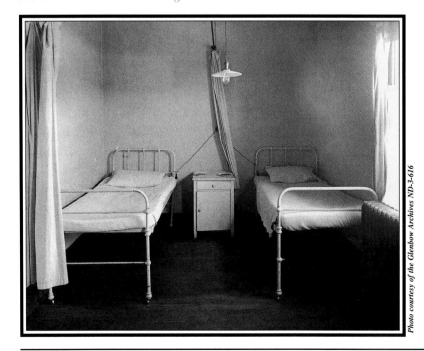

Photo courtesy of the Provincial Archives of Alberta A1242

Effective health care, compassionately and competently delivered, is what people desire in a community. The absence of such care can be a frustrating, fearful, and ultimately deadly. Naturally, the question of health care was high on the list of concerns of those who founded our community.

Isaac Barr responded with the idea of a "medical co-operative", a scheme which may well have been the earliest prepaid health care program in Canada. Each family that paid its fees to join the co-operative was told it would receive full hospital care, although there were some rather significant exemptions, such as maternity care, for which there would be extra fees. As well, Barr promised that medical doctors and nurses would accompany the colonists, that there would be medical stations along the line of their trek from Saskatoon, and a full fledged, military style field hospital once they arrived at "headquarters camp".

Some $350 was subscribed to the medical co-operative. However, the two medical doctors whom Barr had recruited fled from the site of the throngs crowding onto the S.S. Lake Manitoba before it even left Liverpool. A few hard pressed nurses, assisted by some of the calmer mothers, had to attend to the colonists' medical needs. There were no signs of the medical stations along the prairie trails. Isaac Barr departed the "Colony" in haste and disrepute and when the crate was opened which contained the equipment for the headquarters field hospital, it was found to contain a three legged cot, a straw mattress, and a feather pillow. Some might say this foreshadowed what was to come, that is, there was never a doctor when you needed one, the equipment was meager, and nurses did all the work!

Photo courtesy of the Glenbow Archives ND-3-616

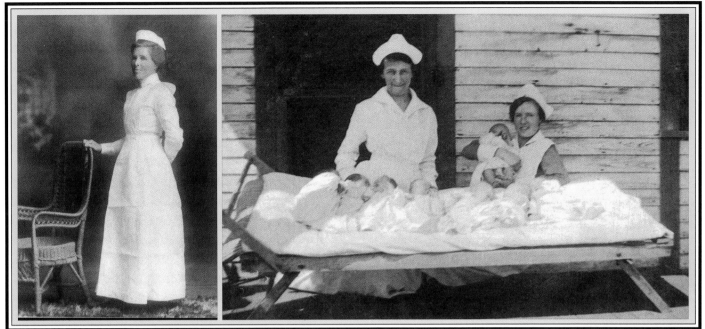

Photos courtesy of Lynn Manners

Florence Mary Lampitt (above left, at graduation, and above right, seated with baby) began nursing training at the Lloydminster Hospital in 1913. Her only time away from Lloydminster was during the Flu Epidemic in 1918 when she was in Drumheller. When she returned to Lloydminster, she did volunteer practical nursing for both family and neighbours, delivering babies and caring for accident victims. In 1923 Florence married Headley James Manners, whom she had met while nursing. They farmed and lived in the Southminster community until 1982, when Headley Manners passed away. Florence continued to reside on the farm until 1983 when she moved into Pioneer Lodge. In 1985 she moved to the Jubilee Home, where she passed away on July 30, 1990.

In response to their situation, the settlers put up their own field hospital. Fortunately, there was a Miss Still among the group who had received training as a nurse in England. Other dedicated women such as Mrs. Tom Bevridge and Miss Mabel Drewe supplied nursing services from their own homes to the community in the early years.

It was these nurses who recognized the stop-gap nature of the care they were providing and led the drive to establish a more permanent hospital. Lacking government support, by 1905 a community fundraising effort was in full swing, with the proceeds from events such as concerts going to the hospital fund.

In 1904, the earliest physician, a Dr. Keating arrived in Lloydminster. He was soon able to convince Dr. W. W. Amos, a young graduate of Queen's University, to make the trip to Lloydminster to join him in his practice. Dr. Amos received $50.00 a month plus $11.25 for room and board. Shortly after his arrival, Dr. J. T. Hill, a former classmate of Dr. Amos, arrived. Dr. Hill left in a few years to do post-graduate courses in Scotland, then reputed to have the finest medical schools in the world. He returned in 1909 but left again in 1914 to serve in World War I. On his return, he resumed practising medicine, served as mayor on four different occasions, and won agricultural prizes in the 1920's.

Below: The influenza epidemic of 1918-1919 caused more Canadian deaths than did World War I. Pictured here on the veranda of the Lloydminster Municipal Hospital are the medical staff in the recommended isolation uniforms of the time.

Photo courtesy of the Glenbow Archives NA-1422-7

Photo courtesy of the Lloydminster Hospital

Above: The Lloydminster Municipal Hospital shortly after it opened in 1917. It was built right beside the previous hospital. The five nurses on the veranda (in white hats) are identified as: P. Chapman, F. Lampitt, V. Bolton, K. Massey and M. Young. The others are unidentified although the Model T is said to belong to Eddie Howell.

Dr. G. L. Cooke (below) arrived in 1912. In addition to serving patients in both the village and town, he travelled extensively in the rural areas tending to the sick and injured. At first he used a horse drawn buggy but as soon as they became available he hired various automobiles and even an experimental snow plane to cover distances more quickly.

By the 1950's, doctors were no longer making the rounds of house calls. Patients were expected to come to the doctor's offices. It was more efficient for several doctors to share office expenses and so the idea of the clinic was born. (Bottom right): In 1955, a medical clinic opened at the corner of 51 Ave. and 48 St. It featured eight qualified doctors, one physiotherapist, three graduate nurses and one nursing aide.

Finally, in 1912, the first proper hospital in Lloydminster was complete. It was a ten-bed frame structure staffed by Miss Alice Hunter, the matron, and one other nurse. This hospital was the main medical facility until 1917, when a new, brick hospital was built on 46th Street, with several additions to follow.

It was also in 1912 that Lloydminster gained its next doctor, Dr. G. L. Cooke, another graduate of Queen's University. He was soon joined by his brother, Dr. A. B. Cooke. Also from Queens, "A. B." had interned at the Norwegian Lutheran Hospital in Brooklyn, New York and had served as a medical officer during World War I.

The two Cookes, Drs. "G. L." and "A. B.", as they were known around the community, maintained an office in the village of Lloydminster, Alberta. They purchased the first x-ray equipment in the area in 1921. The machine remained in their offices until 1927 when it was transferred to the hospital in the town of Lloydminster, Saskatchewan. The two brothers continued in practice until Dr. A B. Cooke's death in 1947. Dr. G. L. Cooke was honoured at a banquet in 1954 for more than forty years of service to Lloydminsterites. Rather ironically, in view of later health concerns, he was presented with a solid silver cigarette case.

In late 1918, many Lloydminster residents were struck down by the deadly Spanish influenza epidemic. Entire families became ill, leaving no care giver able to carry on. The hospital was so crowded that Mayor H. Huxley appealed in the November 7, 1918, *Lloydminster Times* for help in dealing with the epidemic. Those doctors and nurses who were not taken ill themselves were exhausted from working long shifts for days on end, caring for the sick.

Photo courtesy of the City of Lloydminster

Photo courtesy of Don Whiting Collection

From "Hospital Aid" to the "Lloydminster Health Care Auxiliary"

The Hospital Aid program formally began in 1932. In reality, it was a continuation of the central role of women in supporting the provision of health services. Disbanded in 1940 due to the demands of war, the effort was reorganized in 1949 as the Lloydminster Hospital Auxiliary. In 1975 it was again retitled the Lloydminster Health-care Auxiliary.

Members of these organizations donated their time and talents to provide additional comforts to patients.

Photo courtesy of the Saskatchewan Archives Board 40061-73

The Lloydminster Hospital Auxiliary Executive, 1962.
Back row: Miss Bertha Archer, Mrs. Reid, Mrs. Nelson.
Front row: Mrs. Ruby Bellward, Mrs. Bullock, Mrs. Hoage.

They did mending and sewing of hospital linens, and sponsored bake sales, card parties, and talent contests to raise whatever money they could. One of the most successful ventures of the Auxiliary has been the volunteer-operated gift shop. The Lloydminster Regional Hospital Foundation today operates the newly expanded gift shop with one paid staff member and volunteers. The showcase of items for sale is kept full by volunteers who donate items they have knitted and crocheted.

For their many years of service and contributions to the Hospital and the community, the Lloydminster Health Care Auxiliary was honoured with the Lloydminster Lions Club "Citizen of the Year" Award in 1999, the 50th Anniversary of the Auxiliary.

The Many Faces of the Lloydminster Hospital

Photos, left and centre, courtesy of Don Whiting; right, courtesy of Ken Gillis

Above: In the early 1940's a new structure was built beside the old Municipal Hospital but still fronted 46 St., east of 48 Ave. The Municipal became known as the Old East Wing. Another addition was started in 1949 and called the New West Wing. It had two operating rooms on the second floor where all surgery was done. The upper floor of the east wing was then exclusively devoted to maternity. The New Wing contained a new main entrance which now faced 48th Avenue (above left).

In 1965, the hospital was expanded yet again giving it 92 beds with 12 bassinets in the maternity ward. The new addition updated the facilities in the wards, operating rooms and laboratories. The out patient service was also upgraded so that it could offer 24 hour service. (above centre) There was a staff of approximately 150 people.

In 1988, construction began on a new hospital on the eastern fringe of the city (above right). Lloydminster's newest "new hospital" was said to have updated medical technology as well as the capacity and staff to meet Lloydminster's needs.

Soon after this opening, all the previous hospital buildings were demolished despite objections from historic preservationists. The site of Lloydminster's hospital for over 70 years is home today to a condominium complex.

W.A. "Slim" Thorpe Recovery Centre

Slim Thorpe was known around Lloydminster as a drinker who seldom drew a sober breath. However, in 1950, Slim heard about a movement called Alcoholics Anonymous (A.A.). At that time, there were no separate treatment facilities and hospitals would not accept alcoholics as patients. Members of the Edmonton chapter of A.A. welcomed Slim into their homes and introduced him to the philosophy of the movement.

Slim returned to Lloydminster a changed man. He was sober, and would remain so for the rest of his life. Once home, he started Lloydminster's first chapter of Alcoholics Anonymous.

Eleanor and "Slim" Thorpe (centre) at the ribbon cutting ceremony for the Walter A. "Slim" Thorpe Recovery Centre in 1975. Inset: Until 1987, the Centre was on the second floor of the former nurses' residence for the Lloydminster Hospital.

When special treatment centres for alcoholics began to spring up across Canada, Slim and other members of A.A. in Lloydminster proposed that the hospital board allow alcoholics to be admitted as patients. They promised that if the hospital provided the space, the A.A. members would provide the manpower. The hospital board agreed and a treatment process was begun. The results were disappointing.

Alcoholics would join A.A. and be admitted to the hospital under the supervision of other A.A. members. They would remain in hospital for three or four days and become sober. After that, they were discharged from the hospital. Unfortunately, many would fall back into their old ways and need to be re-admitted.

To counter this "revolving door" problem, it was argued that closer supervision for longer periods of time was required. However, the hospital could not provide the time or the space. Thus a committee of Slim, other A. A. members, and doctors went to the two provincial governments as well as to other groups in the community for funds to create a full-fledged treatment centre.

Both provinces eventually agreed to provide funding and, finally, in 1975, the second floor of the former Nurses' Residence beside the old hospital was converted into a Detoxification and Recovery Centre. A Board was founded to manage the facility. The Centre was named the Thorpe Recovery Centre in honour of the man who had brought Alcoholics Anonymous and the Recovery Centre to Lloydminster. After six years of service, the Centre needed to expand. More staff members were hired and the service was expanded to become a full treatment centre.

On June 22, 1987, ground was broken for the new Thorpe Recovery Centre by Eleanor Thorpe and various officials. The land was purchased from the Auxiliary Hospital Board for the price of one dollar. Money to build the new location came from various businesses and service groups around the city. As well, a rental agreement was hammered out with the two relevant provincial commissions. On June 16, 1988, the new Centre was officially opened.

Unfortunately the needs the Centre meets have continued to grow. Now there are active programs not only for alcoholics but for assisting those with drug and gambling addictions as well. However, a plaque still hangs in the Thorpe Recovery Centre, dedicated to Slim Thorpe for his pioneering work. It reads, "Named in honour of Walter A. "Slim" Thorpe for his sincere and relentless dedication in helping the alcoholic in the Lloydminster district."

Throughout the course of the epidemic, the *Lloydminster Times* was filled with influenza related announcements. Moxley's Drug Store described how to avoid getting and spreading the flu, as well as the products they carried which could effect a cure. Insurance companies ran advertisements stressing the importance of having a sickness policy. More sobering though were the pages crowded with obituaries, often attributing the cause of death simply to "the prevailing epidemic".

Lloydminster's Bi-Provincial Status Creates Difficulties

As was the case in education, so in health care, Lloydminster was required originally to have two separate hospital districts, one in Alberta and the other in Saskatchewan. Obtaining funds for the Lloydminster Hospital required working with the two provinces, each with different regulations and requirements. The frustrating problems eased somewhat in 1948 when a special Act was passed by both provinces allowing for the hospital districts in Lloydminster to be amalgamated into one.

Dealing with the two provinces was complicated by the continual changes each has made over the years. On top of this, the introduction of successive hospital care, health care and medicare schemes has increased the complexity of the issues right into the recent era.

In the fall of 1993, Saskatchewan overhauled their system, creating 29 health districts, and in June of 1994, Alberta created 17 new Rural Health Authorities. The Alberta portion of Lloydminster was placed in the East Central Regional Health Authority, but the Saskatchewan side was not immediately included in a health district because of the border issues. Until a final decision could be made, a temporary board was put in charge of Saskatchewan health services in Lloydminster. As a result of discussions between the local stakeholders and the two provinces, the Lloydminster Health Care Act finally resulted, bringing about one health care system for the Border City.

Photo courtesy of the Saskatchewan Archives Board 40061-76

James Whitbread (above), Lloydminster's first chiropractor, was born April 7, 1868, in Wilton-near-Marlboro, Wiltshire, England. He came to Lloydminster in 1903 with the Barr Colonists. After trying his hand at a variety of trades, including blacksmithing, Whitbread decided to become a chiropractor at age 56. In the fall of 1924, he traveled to Chicago, to take the course of studies leading to a Doctor of Chiropractic degree. Chiropractic treats musculoskeletal and neuromuscular conditions related to the spine and all of the joints of the body. Despite his lack of previous formal education, he did well, earned his degree, returned to Canada in February of 1926 and began his practice in Brandon, Manitoba.

Whitbread returned to Lloydminster in 1932 after his first wife's death and set up a practice which continued until he died of a heart attack in 1942.

Dr. Whitbread was followed by many other chiropractors in Lloydminster. Two of the longest serving were Dr. Orville Berg and Dr. Fred Murray, both associated with what is now known as the Lloydminster Chiropractic Clinic. Dr. Berg opened his clinic in 1956 and Dr. Murray joined him in 1971. Dr. Murray purchased the practice in 1980 and while he remains active, Dr. Lee Atkinson purchased the practice in 1997.

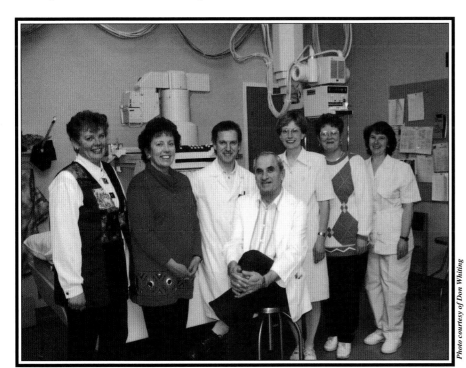

Photo courtesy of Don Whiting

The newest hospital had up-to-date x-ray equipment, shown to the left with staff: (l-r) Debbie George, Barb Moir, Dr. Brian Baitz, Jerry Markowski, Pat Bakker, Myrna Jalbert and Charlotte Kerelchuk .

After Almost 100 years, Lloydminster Dentists Continue Reminding us to Floss

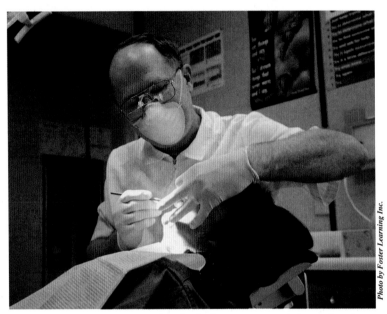

Above: Dr. Dennis Polischuk began practicing dentistry in Lloydminster in 1966. As of 2001, he was the longest serving dentist in practice in the Border City.

In 1905, Lloydminster residents in need of a dentist had to travel to Lashburn to see Dr. Robert Holt. In 1913, Holt moved to Lloydminster, and, until his nephew Dr. Sid Holt moved to the city to join the practice in 1927, he was the only dentist in the city. Dr. Robert Holt stayed in practice until 1930, Dr. Sid Holt until 1974.

Unfortunately for the two Holts, the 1929 fire that ripped through Lloydminster destroyed their clinic. Though they did manage to save some of the equipment, the building was entirely destroyed and had to be replaced. From 1950 - 1985, Robert's son, Dr. Pat Holt, practiced dentistry in Lloydminster. The three Holts accumulated more than eighty years of dental service.

Dr. Gerald Charles, Dr. Vic Stelmaschuk and Dr. Dennis Polischuk are other dentists with long service in Lloydminster. According to Dr. Polischuk, the greatest change during his 34 years in dentistry has been in its philosophy. Years ago, dentistry was about removing or fixing problem teeth. Now, the emphasis is on prevention. Another change is the increased demand for what are essentially cosmetic procedures.

Dr. Polischuk believes, as well, that personal dental habits have improved. More people are brushing and flossing more regularly, and starting at an earlier age.

Over the years, the training required in dental services, and the technology available has increased substantially. Most practices employ several individuals with complimentary skills. One result is that the cost of a visit to the dentist has increased.

However, an additional benefit of good preventative practises is that when dental work is needed it is usually the less expensive procedures that are required. Many of the cosmetic procedures, though, can be expensive for those without dental benefits in their health care coverage.

Over time it became necessary to revamp the management and budgeting structures to integrate Lloydminster's health services to better meet the needs of the citizens. The community approach to health care actually began before the provincial reforms were in place. The elderly, for example, received a variety of services from a variety of agencies such as home care, public health, community health, and other organizations. The problem was that agents from each organization would visit elderly clients without knowing what the other agents were doing. In addition, individuals did not know how to access the services or even what services were available.

In the early 1980's, the separate boards that ran the home care, the ambulance service, the Dr. Cooke Extended Care Centre, the Jubilee Home, and other organizations started to meet. The meetings culminated in January of 1992 when the Lloydminster Health Planning Group was formed. The group worked with the various boards and the two provincial governments to make sure that the coming reforms did not fragment health care services in Lloydminster. The co-ordination of the various boards in Lloydminster to create a single health unit was one objective. Another was to ensure that health services were organized to benefit the entire community.

Finally, in 1994, the Lloydminster Region Health District Board was incorporated. The hospital, home care, ambulance and special care boards such as the Jubilee Home and Dr. Cooke Extended Care Centre came under its jurisdiction. Currently, the board remains responsible for providing acute care, home care, long-term care, and community health programs to all of Lloydminster.

From G.P.'s to Specialists

Dr. John Skene and Dr. Ron Nattress were medical school classmates who graduated from the University of Saskatchewan in 1949. Dr. Nattress arrived in Lloydminster in 1951 and the next year convinced Dr. Skene to come to Dr. G. L. Cooke's clinic. Both doctors remained in practice here until the early 1990's.

Photo courtesy of Dr. John Skene

Above: The staff of the Lloydminster Clinic shortly after it opened in 1954. Back row (l-r): Marg Arneson, Annie Ingram, Jean Milne, John Wesley, Lois McIntosh, Wendy Reynolds, and Grace Steele. Front row (l-r): Dr. Jim Hemstock, Dr. Ron Nattress, Dr. John Skene, Dr. G. L. Cooke, Dr. Jack Dickout, Dr. Bill Jenson, and Dr. Elmer Smith.

Both noticed specialization becoming more pronounced over the years. When they began, almost every doctor was a general practitioner. However working as colleagues over the years, each developed a particular expertise. In addition to their general practice, Dr. Nattress handled anaesthetics while Dr. Skene became known for anaesthetics and obstetrics.

Today doctors are specialized in one type of disease, or one area of the body or one procedure. Because of this increase in specialists, referrals between doctors have increased. Another result of increased specialization has been a symbiotic relationship with technological development.

Another thing that they noticed about the early days was that all the doctors knew each other. They all spent time together, worked together, and co-operated as a team and a family. As the city grew, its health services expanded and with that expansion, some of the familiarity was lost. It may be a good thing for professional reasons, but those who remember the old days would say not. There was a level of camaraderie and support that is not there any more. That is one of the costs of progress.

Specialization is also impacting nursing. Anne Willard graduated with distinction from the St. Boniface Hospital Nursing Program. She began work in Lloydminster in 1964. Willard notes that the specialization of nurses now extends to such areas as: intensive care, surgery, and chemotherapy.

For much of our century, medical care has been heavily based on institutions. Hospitals were seen as factories that conveyed health care to passive patients whose only responsibility was to obey the god-like doctors. Nursing, more intimately related to patients as real people, was one of the first areas to challenge this paradigm. Now nursing reaches out into the community through treatment and educational programs. These new programs are especially important to Lloydminster's seniors, helping them stay in their own homes longer by making them more independent. Home care has expanded to include physiotherapy and many other so-called helper professions.

Even more of a departure from the days when doctors and hospitals supposedly had all the answers about disease treatment has been the revolutionary growth of so-called alternative therapies. There was a time as late as

Below: Anne Willard, R.N.

Photo courtesy of Anne Willard

In the Days of the Family-Owned Pharmacy

Above: The Medical Hall was Lloydminster's first drug store. In this 1910 photo, it can be seen to also house a Land Office and upstairs the offices of Dr. W. W. Amos. Dr. Amos is thought to be shown above on the left wearing the white straw hat.

One of the longest running local businesses, and a Lloydminster landmark on the corner of 50th Street and 49th Avenue, was the Medical Hall Drug Co.

In 1907, when the business was two years old, it was purchased from Dr. J. T. Hill by Spurgeon Aston and Alex Miller. Spurgeon was the druggist and Alex the salesman. It was the only drugstore in Lloydminster for the first decade.

Spurgeon's brother Claude, and nephew Harold, bought Spurgeon's part of the business in 1923. Disaster struck in 1929 when the Medical Hall burned to the ground along with most of downtown Lloydminster. The store was rebuilt and during the 1930's diversified into many unusual lines, including: sporting goods, radios, Gramophones, Victrolas, and records. Following World War II, the Medical Hall carried a range of household appliances.

Harold's brother Cecil and sister Elsie were both Pharmacists and on staff at one time. Bob Baynton, brother of George Baynton Sr., was a partner in the Medical Hall for several years before taking over Moxley Drugs in the early 1960's.

Above: (l-r) : Harold Aston, Rex Scott (a salesman for Rexall Drugs), Claude Aston and Alex Miller. The store carried a wide variety of goods including a fine selection of comic books.

Harold's son, Doug Aston, grew up in the store, working there after school and later serving his apprenticeship upon graduating in Pharmacy from the U. of A. in 1957. He bought into the store in 1962. Doug's interest in cameras and darkroom work led to the store's camera department becoming the largest in Lloydminster, following an expansion of the store in 1978.

The Medical Hall had been in the Aston family for over 80 years when it was sold to Ron Lane in 1989. In 1992, the drugstore was closed, the end of an era.

In "retirement", Doug Aston (left) offers his expertise at the Camera Expert, owned by Charles Lamb.

Charles Moxley operated Moxley Drugs from 1913 until his death in 1959. Earl Ingram, owner of Ingram Drugs and a former employee of Moxley's, and Bob Baynton, then with the Medical Hall, bought shares in Moxley's to keep it running. A few years later, pharmacist Bill Kondro bought it, eventually moving to the Lloyd Mall and transforming it into a Value Drug Mart. Shopper's Drug Mart bought Kondro's store in the early 1980's, along with securing its prime site in the Mall..

Another early drugstore was Ellis Pharmacy, opened in 1939 by H. A. Ellis. He was known as "Pop" in reference to the fact he had graduated pharmacy and optometry in 1905 and had run drug stores in North Battleford and Lashburn for 34 years before arriving in Lloydminster. "Pop" was an active, athletic man who had won bicycle races and high jump events as a youth in P.E.I. He immediately became involved here, umpiring ball games and refereeing hockey. He also served on Town Council from 1940 - 1944. He was a life member of the Masonic Lodge and a 60 year member of the Foresters. He turned the store over to his sons Ronald and Robert but remained active well into his nineties.

Above: Lloydminster Cancer Society volunteers, Mary Laursen, secretary (left) and Shirley Aston, president, meet with Steve Fonyo during his cross Canada run to raise funds and awareness for cancer research. Volunteers work thousands of hours and raise millions of dollars and while there are successes still cancer remains a common killer of Lloydminsterites.
(for more on the efforts of volunteer groups to combat disease, see Chapter 13)

Today, Shopper's Drug Mart is one of the busiest drug stores in the city. In addition to its pharmacy, the chain store also houses a post office and sells confectionary, groceries, and cosmetics.

The store eventually became a Bi-Rite Drugs. Its final owners were Ron Lane and Art Mickelson in 1987. Mickelson would later open the Sprucewood Pharmacy & Home Care in the Lloydminster Clinic and Sprucewood Pharmacy 2 in the Family Medical Clinic.

The trend today is towards chain pharmacies, such as Shopper's Drug Mart. In addition, Superstore, Safeway, Wal-mart and Zellers, all operate pharmacies.

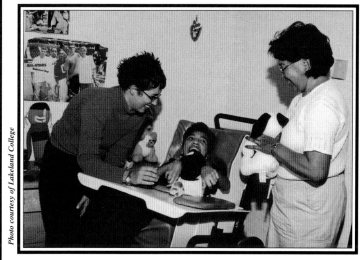

In 1989, an education service related to health was introduced to Lloydminster when a Rehabilitation Practitioner program was introduced at Lakeland College. The two-year diploma program provides students with knowledge about a wide variety of disabling conditions as well as ways to help individuals, families and communities live more inclusively. Currently, practical nursing and other health related programs are being expanded at the Lakeland College Lloydminster Campus.

the 1970's when taking vitamins, minerals and herbal supplements was viewed as foolish and was actively opposed by the medical establishment. During the last twenty years, many voted with their after-tax dollars for a better alternative.

The use of vitamin, mineral and herbal supplements is now widely practised. Where once one had to visit a "health food" store, now varieties of these products are sold even in traditional pharmacies. Lloydminster supports two health products outlets. Wallace Sangster has operated Sangster's Health Centre in the Lloyd Mall since 1975. Back to Basics Health Foods is located downtown. As well, several multilevel marketing programs featuring "natural" health care alternatives are active.

The growth of this dimension of health care is largely a result of more individuals taking responsibility for their own health care. Put off by the impersonal nature of the institutional approach, or victimized by mis-diagnosis or the side effects of prescribed drugs, individuals seeking to be better informed and treated as a whole person have joined the search for a better way. This has led many well beyond taking their daily vitamins.

One of the leading practitioners in the natural health area is Ron Sand of the Therapeutic Massage Clinic. Massage Therapy aims to rehabilitate or augment physical function through manipulation of the soft tissues and joints. Their treatments facilitate healing and ease pain.

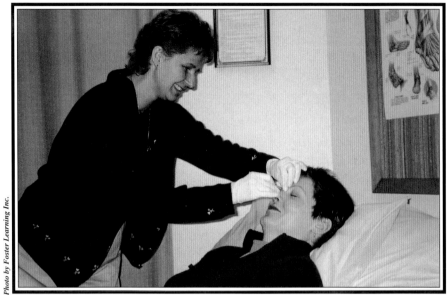

Joyce Salzl-Borzel (above left) has operated Salzl-Borzel Physiotherapy & Acupuncture Ltd. since the fall of 1997. She works with those injured in accidents, sports, or at work. A qualified physiotherapist, she is also trained in acupuncture, a therapy alternative that seeks to balance the body's systems, especially the energy flows. A measure of its increasing acceptance is that some 30% of her clients now request acupuncture treatment.

Below: Ron Sand and Kirsten Cutsforth are both Registered Massage Therapists. At their clinic they treat the whole person, constantly teaching and learning about how our physical, mental and spiritual systems are interrelated. This wholistic approach may mean pressure point massage, application of essential oils, dietary adjustment, specialized exercises, cleansing, and yoga.

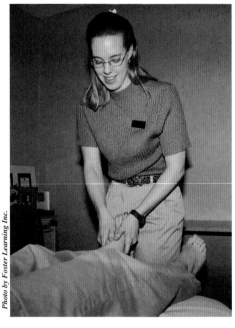

Andrea Kaye (above) of Alta-Sask Resolution Rehabilitation & Sports Physiotherapy came to the realization that the city needed more practitioners as there was a huge waiting list for rehabilitation services. Alta-Sask provides physiotherapy, exercise therapy, sports conditioning and comprehensive rehabilitation services.
Private practitioners help to alleviate the strain on outpatient services at the hospital. As well, more Lloydminster residents are seeking alternative treatments to help them deal more effectively with injuries or simply improve their overall health.

Along with the broader acceptance of alternative therapies has come more emphasis on physical fitness and exercising for health. One of the reasons for the unexpectedly high usage of Bud Miller Park has been the numbers of people walking, jogging, biking or skiing for health reasons.

Attitudes to health issues have changed markedly in recent years as well. Where 50 years ago, smoking was common and fashionable, now (slowly in Lloydminster) non-smoking areas are common and accepted. Many public facilities and private homes have declared themselves smoke free, requiring smokers to indulge their habit out-of-doors.

So we see then that there has been a remarkable trend over our first hundred years. The meaning of health care has changed from professionals treating our diseases in large expensive institutions, to a growing understanding that health is something we need to care about as individuals. Many are informing themselves, seeking alternative therapies, and accepting responsibility for life-style choices. In these ways, many have come to see that caring for our health is one of our key responsibilities.

Dr. James W. Hemstock (lower left, inset) spent some time as medical officer near the end of World War II. He came to Lloydminster in June of 1946 to replace Dr. Gordon for six months. Dr. Gordon soon decided to retire and Dr. Hemstock stayed on, practicing in Lloydminster until 1985. As did many doctors in those days, he had to cover most areas of medicine, however, he did specialize somewhat in obstetrics. It was for his service as a physician, and to the community generally, that his friend, Ray Nelson, urged the naming of Lloydminster's newest health care facility after him - (under construction below) the Dr. James W. Hemstock Assisted Living Residence.

Photo courtesy of Bay Van Photography

Photo courtesy of Foster Learning Inc.

Chapter Six

Education

Research by Alan Griffith

Above: A crowd, including many active, happy children, attends a gymkhana exhibition in the fall of 1915. In the background, the building that would serve for the next 33 years as the Lloydminster High School.

Photo courtesy of Marjorie Brooks

The Barr Colonists and other early settlers were part of an era that placed paramount importance on education. They were a generation that looked back on unprecedented technological progress. Entire new industries had sprung up, such as: electricity, telecommunications, automobiles, and even the wondrous emergence of the "aeroplane".

This remarkable progress undergirded the attitude of optimism and anticipation with which the English-speaking world ushered in the 20th Century. Many believed that science had unlocked the secrets of the physical world and now would solve the problems of the human condition. Psychology and later sociology were heralded as the sciences which would revolutionize human behaviour and achieve the long sought goal of humanity living peacefully and prosperously. Some believed, almost literally, we were within sight of establishing heaven on Earth.

The key to preserving the gains of the past and achieving the goals of the future was education. Because education was so vital, it had recently been recognized that it should be universal. All boys, and now girls, should be able to attend regardless of family finances. Education was so important that society, or at least ratepayers, should pay the cost as a way of contributing to the building of the better world of tomorrow. One way to express all this was in the construction of a building. This was the generation which saw the school replace the church as the dominant social institution as signalled by it often being the largest physical structure in the community.

> *"The commissioner of education intimates that the present School District must be divided before the 31st inst., as after that date, a part of it will be in each of the two new Provinces, and neither Department will be in a position to deal with the matter."*
>
> *The Lloydminster Times*
> *August 8th, 1905*

S.D. Clark

The one time Lloydminster student became the founder of Canadian Sociology

One of the earliest students at Lloydminster's imposing new schoolhouse was Samuel Delbert Clark. Unknown to most in Lloydminster, S. D. Clark became a prominent figure in the development of Canadian Sociology.

Born in 1910 near Streamstown, Clark went on to a long career as a professor at the University of Toronto. His career began in 1938 as a lecturer in the Political Economy department. At the time, no Sociology department existed. It was through Dr. Clark's efforts that the new department was established on July 1, 1963. Clark served as department chair until 1969.

Clark wrote numerous books, his most well known being, *Church and Sect in Canada*, published in 1948.

Photo courtesy of University of Toronto and S. D. Clark

Canadian sociologists today credit Clark with opening the field of Sociology in Canada. He was named honorary president of the Canadian Sociology and Anthropology Association in 1967. He was president of the Royal Society of Canada in 1975-1976, and received an honorary Doctor of Laws from the University of Toronto in 1988.

Professor Deborah Harrison of the Department of Sociology at the University of New Brunswick, states "...he is generally acknowledged as the father of the Canadian approach to [sociology].... For reasons of both his scholarly engagement and his articulation of a 'Canadian' sociology, Clark is the most important sociologist Canada has yet produced."

A School-house is Built

So it was that the Barr Colonists moved quickly to see that their children were educated. Before a school-house had even been built, classes were held in the Anglican Church and later the Medical Hall Drugstore. In June of 1905, the trustees invited tenders for the construction of a permanent school building in Lloydminster.

The creation of the new provinces of Saskatchewan and Alberta, in 1905, created difficulties for the school board however. Since one portion of Lloydminster would be located in Alberta, and the other in Saskatchewan, the school district was ordered to divide itself. The trustees complied and Lloydminster School District No. 1036 for Saskatchewan and Lloydminster School District No. 1753 for Alberta were created. However, to preserve a common community approach, a joint board was created with three representatives from Alberta and five representatives from the Saskatchewan side (which had the greater population at the time). Plans proceeded for the construction of a two room schoolhouse. In 1906, the building was complete. Now all that was needed was a teacher. It was not an easy chore. The trustees were finally able to secure a Mr. Hartley, who commenced teaching duties on February 26th, 1906 with 35 students.

By 1912, the growing number of high school students led to a new, imposing four room brick school on the town's east side. At first, there were elementary classes on the lower floor but by the end of World War I, it was entirely a high school and would serve until 1949. Long after it was demolished, it was still known as "the old high school".

> *"...with the greatest scarcity of teachers, and the non-desire to accept positions in the new district of the Northwest, the task of securing a suitable man has not been an enviable one."*
>
> **Albert Curtis, Secretary treasurer**
> *Lloydminster Times,*
> *February 20th, 1906*
> *Letter to the editor*

Above: 1950-51 staff of the Lloydminster Public School: Back row l-r: Laurie Simpson, Earl Pfeifer, Lorraine Pope, Ruth Ostrom, Eva Ellis, Io Riddell, Alf Lampitt, Mo Price, Lou Codling, Ray Matheson, Effie Pollock, Chester Avery (Principal). Front row l-r: Ruth Bexsfield, Sheila Goble, Marilyn Meagher, Theresa Hoegel, Ellen McNab, Katherine Demaer, Eileen Graham, Gwen Brownridge, Rosemarie Taylor, Ruth Deines, Hazel Matheson, and Bertha Archer. The school, built in 1925, was the community's pride. It symbolized the tremendous progress, from bare prairie to this imposing structure in little more than 20 years. It also represented the struggle to build one community in the face of its division into two provinces. The co-operation in education established a momentum which led to municipal amalgamation in 1930. Finally, it expressed the determination to build a better future by providing first class education to the succeeding generations. Later known as the Meridian School, the building was demolished in 1999. However, the architectural style of its entry way is recaptured in the new city hall, built on the site in 2000.

Post-War Growth

As Lloydminster grew, so did the need for better educational facilities. As early as 1945, the school board discussed establishing a new composite high school to provide "… greater facilities and a wider range of subjects than now available." (Lloydminster Public School District Minutes, 1945). Three of the trustees, Dr. G. L. Cooke, H. C. Messum, and W. Street, were appointed as a committee to look into the matter.

In 1949, the new Lloydminster High School opened its doors. Less than three years later, four classrooms and an auditorium were added. With the addition came a name change: Lloydminster High School became Lloydminster Composite High School to reflect the greater academic and technical range of the new school.

Until this time, the high school was governed separately by the Lloydminster High School Board. However, the board recommended its own amalgamation with the Lloydminster Public School District in 1953. Administration of all the various schools in Lloydminster by one board seemed more efficient and effective for the community. On January 1st, 1954, the high school board was disbanded and its members voluntarily resigned from their positions.

While high school students had a new building, the growing population meant many elementary students still attended make-shift classrooms in places such as the Central Tire Shop and Grace United Church. Keeping pace with population growth was to be an ongoing challenge.

Jean Doyle O'Neill - A "Special" Educator

In 1959, Jean Doyle O' Neill came to Lloydminster to start a school. However, this was not just any school; it was the start of a new era in Lloydminster for education for people with disabilities.

Mrs. O'Neill had been hired by the Lloydminster Retarded Children's School Board, which formed in 1958 to establish a school in Lloydminster for students with mental disabilities. Jean and her husband Henry Edmund Doyle O'Neill immigrated from England to Canada in 1957, coming to Lone Rock in 1958, where Mr. O'Neill was a teacher.

Jean O' Neill was persuaded by board member Hank Bestvater to offer her skills and compassion as a special education teacher in Lloydminster. It was agreed she would be paid $300 a month and school would begin on February 2nd, 1959.

Mrs. Jean Doyle O'Neill (right), the first special education teacher in Lloydminster, is pictured with students at a Hallowe'en party in the first of a series of houses and buildings which the school rented.

Fiona O'Neill, Jean's daughter, describes her mother as a woman who greeted challenges enthusiastically and was innovative as a teacher. At a time when few teachers sought such a position, Mrs. O'Neill put her heart into her work.

In less than one year, the school moved three times. The one constant from the beginning was the teacher, Mrs. O'Neill. O'Neill and Joyce Kemp, also a teacher at the school, offered a rich program which incorporated music, art, and physical education. Their educational goals were to teach civic responsibility, human relationships, self-realization, and economic efficiency. A fabulous artist and painter, Jean shared her love for art with her students. Regular arts and craft sales were held showcasing student work. The community was often amazed at what the students accomplished. With Joyce Kemp's training in music and Jean O'Neill's dedication, the students were able to compete at a high level in local music festivals.

In June of 1966, a field day was organized for the students and the *Saskatoon Star Phoenix* took notice: "The field day was organized by the principal and senior room teacher, Mrs. Jean O'Neill, and the other teachers who believed the children should participate in the same activities as [other children] when possible."

O'Neill ignored the public attitudes of the day and took her students out into the community as often as she could, to playgrounds, out for lunch, or to the gymnasium at the Lloydminster Composite High School twice a week for physical education.

There were difficulties. The initial budget for the school in 1959 was $4360, of which $3600 was reserved for Jean O'Neill's salary. Still, O'Neill persisted, and made continuing requests for equipment, supplies, and additional funding. "She had always insisted on having a kitchen in the school," notes her daughter Fiona. She believed in the importance of teaching the students life-skills to allow them to live independently in the future.

Jean and her family moved to Sardis, British Columbia in 1970, where she continued to teach students with disabilities at a special education elementary school, and eventually at a high school. She was well loved by her students, and she kept in touch with many of them after her retirement, even employing some of them to do chores and odd jobs for her.

A true pioneer of special education in Lloydminster, Jean Doyle O'Neill passed away in 1990. Her life-long dedication to her work and her students will always be remembered.

Photo courtesy Lloydminster Regional Archives

Above: A new Lloydminster High School was under construction in 1948. It opened the following year. By 1951, it had become "Lloydminster Composite High School". A much used auditorium/gymnasium and later a wing of classrooms was added. In 1968, when Lloydminster Comprehensive High School opened, the building became Neville Goss Elementary School. In 2000, the school was demolished.

Changing times brought changing attitudes toward students with disabilities as illustrated by the unveiling of the newly named Parkland School in 1966 (below left).

Below right: When Rendell Park School opened in 1987, it was the first public school intended to include students with disabilities. Today, students with disabilities are accommodated in all Lloydminster schools.

Special Education takes shape in the Border City

The dawn of special education in Lloydminster began in 1958 when what was then named the "Lloydminster Retarded Children's School Board" was formed to establish a school in Lloydminster for students with mental disabilities. Teacher Jean Doyle O'Neill was hired in 1959 (see page 65) and a small house was rented on 55th Avenue and 47th Street for $65.00 per month. In 1966, the Lloydminster Public School District assumed responsibility for special education and built a new school, soon re-named Parkland School – a reflection of growing community sensitivity to students with disabilities. "With the establishment of Parkland School, there were deliberate efforts made to provide for students who were developmentally delayed," comments Dr. Donald Duncan, Director of Education for the Lloydminster Public School Division. In addition, requests, by the Lloydminster Association for Community Living, for greater integration in the schools, were supported by the local school divisions.

Rendell Park School was a unique facility which opened in 1987. Named after the Barr Colonist Rendell family, the school embraced a mainstreaming philosophy. Students of all abilities were integrated into the school in an effort to create understanding and co-operation. The school was initially intended to accommodate all students with disabilities irrespective of their ages, but as the division made the transition from a mainstreaming philosophy to one of "inclusive education", students were placed in age-appropriate schools. By the 1990's, Bishop Lloyd Junior High and Lloydminster Comprehensive High School were including all students to a much greater degree than previously.

Today, all schools are involved in the integration of students with disabilities, clearly marking the path of progress which has been made in both educational and community attitudes toward inclusive education and true "community living".

Photos courtesy of the Lloydminster Public School Division

Lloydminster's Business College Flourishes

The first business college in Lloydminster was Garbot Business College, which operated in the 1920's. Classes were conducted upstairs in the Town Hall. In the early 1940's, Hazel Miller responded to the wartime need to train new office workers by opening Miller Business College. Classes were held in a building at the corner of 52 St. and 48 Ave. which had once served as the business education building for the Lloydminster High School. In 1961, Clayton Reeves, a former teacher and office manager, bought Miller Business College.

The new Reeves Business College was soon expanding. In just a few years, enrolment increased from 25 to 75 students. Reeves Business College would at one time operate branch schools in North Battleford and Red Deer as well. The College maintained a reputation of producing quality office workers, who were employed quickly after graduation. Students were prepared on the current technology of the time whether typewriters or computers, spirit duplicators or photocopiers. Other subjects taught included shorthand, typing, English, and, at Mr. Reeves insistence, on the job skills such as deportment and personal grooming.

In 1992, Clayton Reeves retired and was bought out by his son and son-in-law, Clinton Reeves and Ken Coleman. Shortly thereafter, the new owners moved the College to the newly developed Atrium Centre.

Photo courtesy of Clayton and May Reeves

Clayton Reeves bought Miller Business College in 1961 and built the reputable Reeves Business and Career College, still in operation today.

Left: In the 1960's, Clayton Reeves took his students on an annual trip to Edmonton via CN Rail to tour offices in the city.

Photo courtesy of Clayton and May Reeves

School Buildings and Additions

1905	In June, the trustees invited tenders for the erection of a permanent school building
1906	The first school (two classrooms) opened on 50th Ave. near 45 St..
1912	Lloydminster High School opened on 47 Ave. near 49 St.
1925	Lloydminster Public School (later known as the Meridian School) opened
1949	New Lloydminster High School (later known as Neville Goss School) opened
1951	A resolution was made to add four rooms and an auditorium to the Composite High School.
1954	Queen Elizabeth School opened
1956	Avery School opened
1959	The first school for mentally challenged was a rented house at 5511-47th St Lloydminster Catholic School Division was established
1960	Lloydminster Junior High (later re-named E.S. Laird) opened as well as St. Thomas, the first school for the Lloydminster Catholic School District
1963	Barr Colony School was built on 45th Ave. St. Mary's School opened
1968	Lloydminster Comprehensive High School opened
1976	Barr Colony School was moved to its present location on 31 St.
1977	Father Gorman School opened
1979	Bishop Lloyd Junior High opened
1982	St. Joseph's School opened
1983	The Queen Elizabeth School addition was completed.
1985	The second floor was added to the Comprehensive High School Holy Rosary High School opened
1987	Rendell Park School opened
1990	New Lakeland College Campus building opened
2000	Jack Kemp Elementary School opened
2001	New Holy Rosary High School opened

State of the Art Comprehensive High School a Catalyst for Change

Above: Martin Browne, long time school caretaker and friend of generations of students, was honoured by having a school named after him.

Centrefold: The Lloydminster Comprehensive High School opened in the Spring of 1968, embracing a comprehensive educational philosophy to better serve the academic, technical, and vocational needs of its students.

Bev Henry, who served the Lloydminster School Division for 38 years in various positions including treasurer, remarked that "the district grew in student numbers, but also, it grew in opportunities." One of the greatest opportunities came into play when the Technical/Vocational Act was passed in the mid-1960's allowing for federal funding of high schools which offered a greater range of technical and vocational courses. The Lloydminster Public School board superintendent, J. J. Giesbrecht, and the County of

Vermilion River and Separate School boards all co-operated to make the building of the Lloydminster Comprehensive High School a reality. In 1968, the state of the art facility was opened for students from grades 10 to 12.

The school adopted a new philosophy of secondary education. The school would serve the academic, technical, and vocational needs of the majority of the student population rather than catering primarily to the ten to fifteen percent of students going on to university. Al Dornstauder, first principal of the new school, stated that "the idea was to teach in breadth and depth." The school offered 27 different courses, including: Agriculture, Automotives, Welding, Electricity/Electronics, Visual Art, and Band; plus the traditional core academic subjects.

Photos by Alan Griffith

Alex Sokalofsky came to Lloydminster in 1952 and taught sciences in both the Lloydminster Composite High School and the Lloydminster Comprehensive High School.

Mayson Abraham, (left) former Humanities teacher, and Al Dornstauder, (right) the first principal of L.C.H.S. at the 30th year re-union in 2000.

Jim Berry was the valedictorian for the class of 1970, the first class to complete all three years of their schooling at L.C.H.S. He later returned to the school as a Computers/Sciences teacher.

The opening of the new high school was a catalyst for many changes for education in the Border City. The Lloydminster Composite High School building became Neville Goss School for elementary students who had formerly attended the Meridian School. With Meridian School Empty, the Division decided to renovate it for use as their central office. Prior to this, they had rented a small two room office on the second floor of the Skinner Motors Building on the corner of 49 Ave and 49 St..

Llue Hanson, Superintendent of Business and Administration for the school division at the time and later a long serving board member, remarked, "All citizens were proud of this very fine school. To this day, it continues to provide quality education to the teenagers of Lloydminster."

Photo courtesy of The Lloydminster Public School Division

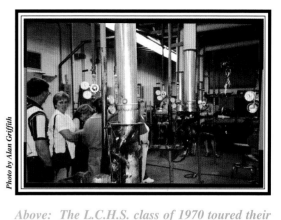

Photo by Alan Griffith

Above: The L.C.H.S. class of 1970 toured their old high school at their 30th year reunion in the summer of 2000, visiting the high school's many new shops used for technical/vocation instruction.

Below: The high school began offering cosmetology in 1998 to add to the range of technical courses.

Photo by Alan Griffith

The Lloydminster Catholic School Division

In 1960, Father Gorman organized a meeting of Roman Catholic parents in Lloydminster to discuss the establishment of a Catholic school. Of the 187 people present, 184 voted in favour of the proposal. St. Thomas School was the result, named to honour Father Thomas Dobson and Thomas the Apostle.

The separate division's student enrolment grew as Lloydminster prospered and the division continued to build schools to facilitate the swelling school population. One of these schools, St. Mary's had been a high school, but when a new public technical/vocational high school was proposed, the Catholic school board's support was sought. According to former director of the Lloydminster Catholic School Division, Jim McLoughlin, the only way to get a federal grant for the ambitious project was to have the separate school division on side as well. The Catholic School Board backed the plan, and handed over the education of their grade ten to twelve students to the Lloydminster Comprehensive High School. Students would benefit from the increased opportunities which the new school offered. St. Mary's became a junior high school.

Photo courtesy of The Lloydminster Catholic School Division

Above: Holy Rosary High School became a reality in 1985.

As the years went by though, there was a growing desire among Catholic board members to "keep their students at home" and re-establish a system which would educate Catholic students from kindergarten to grade twelve. The establishment of a Catholic High School was met with resistance. Influenced by lobbyists, the Alberta government did not support the new school. An impressive technical/vocational high school already existed in Lloydminster and, by some, a new Catholic high school was seen as competition. Even some Catholic parents opposed the idea, fearing they would be obligated to take their children out of L.C.H.S. These parents sought a court injunction against the construction. The resistance was eventually unsuccessful as it was the Catholic Division's constitutional right to build.

The Catholic board persisted, despite the opposition. In particular, Board Chairman, Bob Dunham was determined to see the new school built. "Without Bob, I'm sorry to say, we probably wouldn't have had Holy Rosary High School today," comments Dr. Jim McLoughlin. Under Dunham's leadership, it was decided to build the school on the site of St. Mary's school. There was not enough money to purchase a new site. In 1985, Catholic students began attending the new Holy Rosary High School.

In the same year, the separate school division sought areas of specialty to enhance the services which they were offering. St. Thomas School, became the first and only school in Lloydminster to offer a French immersion program.

The Golden Shovel

With the plans finally in place to build the school, the official sod turning approached. Dr. McLoughlin wanted the event to be special. A visiting friend, Roman Kwasnica, encouraged McLoughlin to make the most of the day. An ordinary shovel would not do. Unfortunately, the hardware stores of Lloydminster did not see the need to keep golden shovels in stock. "We just had to turn the sod in style. We bought that Canadian Tire shovel, then, sanded off the trade mark, varnished it up a bit more and spray painted the metal with gold paint. I remember telling Bob Dunham to scratch around carefully (it was February, after all) and not disturb the three coats of gold we had on there too much," McLoughlin remembers. The official sod turning took place one February morning in 1984, with Bob Dunham at the helm of the precious garden tool.

The shovel hung in Holy Rosary High School's display case, until it was used again for the 2000 sod turning of the new Holy Rosary High School, being built near Bud Miller Park.

Photo courtesy of the Lloydminster Catholic School Division

Left to right: Bob Dunham (with shovel), Mayor Pat Gulak, and Dr. Jim McLoughlin at the 1984 official sod turning for Holy Rosary High School.

Lakeland College is Born

By 1971, Vermilion College's declining enrollments in agricultural and other programs had brought it face to face with imminent closure. James Foster, Minister of Advanced Education for Alberta, and deputy Ministers Peter Jenner and Dr. R. Rees, visited Lloydminster on December 17th as part of a fact-finding mission to explore ways to maintain a community college in the region.

A decision was made to explore the concept of a new regional college. Dr. Walter Worth of the University of Alberta led a task force to flesh out the details. By 1974, Saskatchewan and Alberta had both agreed to finance a new college to serve north-east Alberta and north-west Saskatchewan. Reflecting its status as the largest population centre in the region, and its potential for continued growth, the corporate offices of the new Lakeland College were placed in Lloydminster. The assets of the old Vermilion College were assigned to the new college. Meridian School was leased from the Lloydminster Public School District in 1976 and Lakeland College classes began that autumn. Administrators moved their offices from Nelson House behind the Lloyd Mall to the Meridian School building later in the year.

The first president of the newly founded Lakeland College was Dr. Robert Olsen. He faced tremendous pressure. The community of Vermilion deeply resented the loss represented by placing the central offices for the new college in Lloydminster. A College yearbook of the time does not even acknowledge the existence of Dr. Olsen but instead contains a message from Vice-President Bob Campbell. Public and political pressure would take its toll, and the central offices were soon moved to Vermilion. History would also be rewritten to present Lakeland College as simply one more stage in the evolution of Vermilion College which dated back to 1913.

Over the years, the focus of the College changed. The original intent was to offer educational opportunities in existing community facilities. However, plans were made in the mid-1980's for a new building in Lloydminster. The persistence of the Board of Governors, the hard work of MLA Doug Cherry, a donation of 30 acres of land from the City, and financial assistance from both provincial governments led to the construction of the 12,450 square meter facility beside Bud Miller Park.

In 1990, the Board of Governors, under chairman Ed Jenson, was able to enter into a joint venture with the Bi-Provincial Upgrader to build a housing complex beside the college. The residences were first used by the 3,600 upgrader construction workers. The complex was then turned over to Lakeland College for students.

Photo courtesy of Lakeland College

Lakeland College - Lloydminster Campus was a $23 million dollar facility which opened in 1990.

Below: Among other programs, students at Lakeland College can take the first two years of a university degree program. Here Dr. Franklin Foster reviews for students of world history some of the intricacies of the Danish-Prussian dispute over Schleswig-Holstein.

Photo courtesy of Lakeland College

Lloydminster teacher Linda Nykolaychuk (right) received many awards for her contributions to Art Education over the years, including the 1987 Crayola Art Education Award for Excellence in Art Education (above).

A Look into the Future

One of the greatest changes in education is the greater openness to the public. For example, until the late 1980's, the phone numbers of the public schools were not even printed in the telephone book. Now, as Dr. Don Duncan, Director of the Public School Division notes, the Division is working hard to involve the public in the schools. In 1999, over 400 volunteers worked in the system. The City of Lloydminster contributed $150,000 to the construction of the gymnasium at Jack Kemp School. The School's design allows greater community access to its facilities during the evenings.

While the Public system grows, the Lloydminster Catholic School Division also demonstrates its vitality as construction of the new Holy Rosary High School is completed in 2001. Lloydminster's rapid growth means student numbers have swollen for both jurisdictions.

Jack Kemp School - What's in a Name?

Jack Kemp Elementary School, 2000. Inset: Jack Kemp, in the two room office which the school district rented from Skinner Motors in the early 1960's. Kemp shared the space with secretary Bev Henry and Director J. J. Giesbrecht.

The Lloydminster Public School Board has named a number of its schools after people who have served the division and community well. Martin Browne School was named after a caretaker who started working for the Lloydminster Public School District in 1913 and retired at the age of 83. Avery School was named after Chester Avery, the elementary school principal in Lloydminster from 1925 to 1959. J. J. Giesbrecht, who retired as Director of Education in 1974, was honoured by having his name attached to Lloydminster Comprehensive High School's Auditorium. Neville Goss School's name came from a World War I veteran who served the district as Secretary-Treasurer from 1948-1960. The school which replaced Neville Goss School in 2000, is named after Mr. Goss' replacement, Jack Kemp.

Jack Kemp was born in England in 1912. Jack's mother's step brother was J. G. Willard, publisher of the *Lloydminster Times* who had come to Lloydminster in 1905. On a visit to England, J. G. Willard's wife convinced eighteen year old Jack to come to Lloydminster to work for his uncle at the newspaper.

In the Spring of 1931, Jack arrived in Canada and made his way to Lloydminster. He began working for the *Lloydminster Times* although he had no prior experience in the newspaper business. Kemp learned every inch of the trade. In exchange, his uncle allowed him board and room in his home.

Jack put his newspaper career on hold when he joined the army in June 1940. Today a proud veteran, Kemp saw his share of action in World War II. (See chapter 16)

When Neville Goss retired in 1960, Jack Kemp became the new Secretary-Treasurer for the Lloydminster Public School District. He served the Division well in this position, retiring on July 31, 1978, the day Queen Elizabeth II visited Lloydminster. "It was awfully nice of her to make the trip for me," Jack jokes.

But Jack did not stray very far. He was elected to the first of three 3 year terms on the school board in 1979. He embraced his new duties as he had his position of Secretary-Treasurer. "No two days were ever exactly the same," he remarks.

Jack Kemp is well remembered for his contributions to special education. Involved from the inception of the what became Parkland School, he and his wife, Joyce, a teacher at the school, strongly supported educational opportunities for students with special needs.

Given the contributions that Jack Kemp has made to the Lloydminster Public School District, the community of Lloydminster, and to his country, "Jack Kemp Elementary School" is indeed a most suitable name.

However, not all parents opt to send their children to the school systems. In 2000, an estimated 50 students were registered as home-schooled. More parents are choosing to educate their children at home due to concern for moral and religious values and the desire for instruction catered more specifically to a child's learning style.

Lakeland College has evolved over the years. After the new campus opened, enrollment grew rapidly and the range of programs was expanded to include, for example, Heavy Oil Operations Technology. However, in the mid-1990's, Lakeland College endured both provincial and College based cutbacks, including the elimination of its centres throughout the region and some signature programs such as western horsemanship. Waves of restructuring led to declining morale as departments were closed or downsized and people had to reapply for their jobs. Some people were terminated and rehired three times in a two year period.

However, with the appointment of Bill Kondro as Chairman of the Board, the College began to show signs of rebounding. The hiring of Dr. Mark Lee as president added to the momentum. Even with that, government officials still felt it necessary to inform College officials that they had only two years to increase enrollment or Lakeland College would face closure. Thanks to the new attitudes, student enrolment in 2000 was up noticeably, especially at the Lloydminster Campus. In an effort to continue the trend, the College began to seek partners to establish a Heavy Oil Research Centre in Lloydminster, expanded programs in the health services, and in 2001 construction began on the Performing Arts Theatre.

The educational organizations of Lloydminster are increasing their outreach. For example, both school divisions, and Lakeland College, have hired native liaison officers to assist aboriginal students and parents.

As we enter the 21st century, the educational organizations of Lloydminster are determined to continue to offer quality education but with a greater emphasis on those who have been overlooked in the past.

Photos courtesy of Lloydminster Public School Division

Above; The Lloydminster Public School Division acquired its first computer, which was shared by all of the schools in the division, in the 1970's. Today, there are networked computer labs in every school in the city. Both divisions have also established a wide area network which will connect every computer in the system. High speed internet and other innovations create new opportunities for teachers and students to further their education.

The construction of the new Holy Rosary High School began in 2000. The facility opened in the Fall of 2001.

Photo by Don Whiting

Chapter Seven

Crime and Calamity

Research and draft writing by Ian Goodwillie

W hile the constitution of the United States specifies that its purpose is to protect "life, liberty, and the pursuit of happiness", the comparable declaration in the British North America Act provides for "peace, order, and good government". Prime Minister Macdonald was determined that the settlement of the Canadian West would be peaceful and orderly. Not least in his plans was the establishment of a police force. So it was that the North West Mounted Police (NWMP) was created in 1873 adopting such terminology as constable and superintendent from the British police to un-

Photo courtesy of Glenbow Archives NA-4721-2

A crowd of Barr Colonists poses proudly with a visiting bicyclist and two members of the North West Mounted Police. Summer 1904.

derline the difference between the Canadian approach and that of the United States which had seen what was effectively a military occupation of their western plains by the U.S. Army. An even more symbolic borrowing from the British tradition was the red serge tunic of the old British army, an icon familiar to native people who had fought side by side with the British in the War of 1812 and had seen British troops again during threats of American invasion in the 1840's and 1860's.

These symbols of the British Empire were even more familiar to the Barr Colonists. Many commented in their diaries and letters home how reassuring it was to see the North West Mounted Police in Saskatoon, along the trail, and among them as the new community of Lloydminster and District grew. As they commented, the scarlet tunics reminded them that despite the great distances they had travelled and the enormous emptiness and loneliness of the new landscape, they were still within the purview of British law and order. In fact, many of the Colonists had worn the red serge in the British armies in South Africa. Others had served in India.

The Lloydminster R.C.M.P. Musical Ride performed at the Lloydminster Exhibition in 1930.

Now it was a reinforcement of their essential notion that they were transplanting the best of Britain into the heart of the Canadian North West. They heartily endorsed the move in 1904 to declare the NWMP a royal force, thus changing its name to the Royal North West Mounted Police. (In 1920, the name changed again to the present Royal Canadian Mounted Police.) As our first century unfolded, Lloydminsterites did their part to ensure that our community was characterized by peace, order and good government.

Policing

As the Colonists arrived, policing was provided by extra patrols from the Battleford and Onion Lake detachments. Soon, given the large number in the new influx, a separate Lloydminster Detachment was opened in the summer of 1903 under the command of Inspector T. McGinnis of Battleford "C" Division.

Early policing reflected the needs of the early settlers. In September of 1904, for example, two horses "strayed away" from a local farmer and were taken in by a man working at a railway camp. A warrant was issued for the man under the charge of running off strays, but he had left the vicinity. Two years later, though, he was captured near Dundurn and brought back to Lloydminster for trial. He was taken before a Justice of the Peace and charged with working stray horses. He was found guilty and fined $50.00 plus costs and another small footnote was added to the legend of the Mounties always getting their man.

Below: R.C.M.P. officers pack up after a successful show at the 1930 Lloydminster Exhibition.

As the population continued to grow, the focus of policing grew and changed as well. In 1908, the Lloydminster detachment was given additional responsibilities under the Immigration Department. This formalized duties they had already been doing, especially for the Barr Colonists, such as advising them how to survive the winter, look after their livestock, construct their houses, and avoid prairie fires. The new responsibilities charged police with providing needy settlers with relief supplies such as provisions and fuel. The Lloydminster Detachment continued to be manned by the R.N.W.M.P. until 1917, when the Saskatchewan Provincial Police were formed and took over responsibility for law and order in the province.

On February 1, 1920, an order-in-council changed the Royal North West Mounted Police into the Royal Canadian Mounted Police. Then, on November 1, 1925, the Onion Lake Detachment was closed and moved

Photo by Don Whiting

In December of 1959, the R.C.M.P. moved to their new headquarters on 44th Street. By 1979, the police had outgrown the facility and a new detachment was constructed on 47th Ave.

to Lloydminster because it was a more central, accessible location. Corporal F. B. Pearson, formerly of Onion Lake, was put in charge of opening the new detachment, which located in a six-room building on Church Street. J. G. Willard leased the building to the force at a rate of $30.00 per month. They stayed at this location until June 24, 1931, when the detachment took up residence in two rooms above the newly reconstructed Post Office building.

Even in the early days, Lloydminster had its fair share of criminal capers such as the one detailed in the August 30, 1934, *Lloydminster Times*: "Dillinger 2nd Attempts to Hold Up Bank". The man in question was a local who entered the bank manager's office and handed him a note asking for one thousand dollars. It also stated that if he was not out of there in fifteen minutes, two more men with guns would enter the bank. He then gave Mr. Rowland, the bank manager, a quick view of his gun.

Mr. Rowland responded by hitting him in the head with an ashtray, wrestling him to the ground and calling for help. People entered his office

Hallowe'en 1979

Lloydminster was fortunate to have two television stations serving it and the surrounding area in 1979. However, anyone wanting to watch television on November 1st was in for a shock. Both CKSA and CITL were off the air. Most people assumed at first it was their television sets acting up. It was much more than that.

Photo courtesy of Don Whiting

The damage to the tower kept both stations off the air until a smaller tower was erected to service the immediate Lloydminster area. Full coverage of the original area did not resume until a new tower was erected 16 days after the incident.

Because the tower was located on the Alberta side of the border, Kitscoty RCMP were in charge of the investigation. At the time, six full-time investigators were put on the case and were aided by RCMP officers from Edmonton. The exact method by which the tower was destroyed was never released, nor was a culprit ever caught. There have been many theories and rumours ever since as to who the guilty party or parties might be, but no one has ever been charged. The identity of those involved remains one of Lloydminster's unsolved mysteries.

Believed to be an act of Hallowe'en vandalism, the 625-foot transmission tower, located eight miles north of the city, had collapsed like a telescope and lay crumpled on top of the technical equipment building. The unusual way the tower collapsed was fortunate. If it had fallen across the nearby highway it would have blocked traffic and possibly injured someone. As it was, the wreckage was more than dangerous enough as the high voltage wires were still live.

---

to assist him while another person summoned R.C.M.P. Constable Cookson, who was in charge of the detachment at the time. He arrived with two other officers and took control of the situation. The man was disarmed and it was discovered that his gun was only a wooden facsimile. It was also discovered that he was acting alone, though he did claim that he was forced into it by the two gentlemen mentioned in the note. He was taken to Battleford to be tried and was sentenced to 16 months in jail for attempted robbery.

The R.C.M.P. headquarters remained in the two rooms above the Post Office until December 5, 1959, when they moved to the newly constructed detachments quarters at 4801 - 44th St. Unlike the quarters occupied by the detachment before that, these premises were owned by the Police.

After the 1959 move, the R.C.M.P. Detachment continued to grow and many renovations of their 44th St. location took place. It was 1968 when the Detachment was finally reorganized into a municipal detail and a rural detail. However, a new problem then arose; they did not have the space to house both. The city had the responsibility of housing the municipal detail, but existing policy prevented the renovation of the rural detachment for more than six new men. This policy was reviewed and renovations were eventually undertaken.

As time went on, other renovations were performed on the 44th St location, but the time was coming when another move was needed. On January 17, 1977, Sgt. Ross Alexander went before the Lloydminster City Council to request the approval for new headquarters. He

Below: Unfortunately, one of the most common policing duties is investigating traffic mishaps. Over the years many of our families have been stricken with the tragedy of fatalities or serious injuries. At such times, the assistance of police and other emergency personnel is greatly appreciated.

Photo courtesy of Don Whiting

Photo courtesy of Don Whiting

At approximately 4:21 AM on July 19, 1998, a passer-by phoned the R.C.M.P. after seeing suspicious activity at the local Safeway store. Crooks had backed a pick-up truck through the glass entrance to the store and loaded the ATM into the back of the truck. Police rushed to the scene, arriving only seconds after the incident. A quick search located the criminals in the northwest corner of the city attempting to transfer the ATM. A chase ensued with both the criminals and the police vehicles shoving each other for position on the road. As the chase continued, the ATM fell off the back of the truck. However, the criminals rammed the police car, damaging it enough that the R.C.M.P. could not continue the pursuit. One of the culprits attempted to escape on foot. He was captured with the assistance of the North Battleford Police Service dog section. Police also recovered no less than five stolen vehicles that were believed to be related to the crime. The one man apprehended was convicted and served a jail sentence but no one else was ever charged in the case.

reminded the city of their responsibility under the agreement with the R.C.M.P. to provide an adequate headquarters. He recommended that the city build a headquarters for twice the number staff members in order to prepare for the future expansion of the detachment. The current headquarters, he pointed out, had no interview room, no photo room, no room for extra drug operations, no equipment room and the garage was designed for two cars when the Detachment had twelve. The staff had grown to the point that there were 50 people working out of offices designed for 15. The Mayor and Council agreed there was a problem and plans for a new building were approved on September 6, 1979.

Shortly after, work on the new building on 47th Ave. was started. The new structure added two more interview rooms, more cells, and a badly needed identification section. Previously, any forensic work needed was done by the North Battleford detachment because the Lloydminster detachment did not have the space to house the identification section. The new building was opened and still serves as headquarters for the Lloydminster Detachment. On May 20, 1982, the 44th St. quarters were declared surplus and transferred to the Department of Public Works.

Lloydminster has its share of crime. The number of offences fluctuates but many of the problems relate to alcohol abuse. In 1997, Lloydminster recorded the highest number of impaired driver convictions per capita in Canada. In recent years, the Detachment has received help patrolling the streets from the dedicated volunteers in the Citizens on Patrol (COPS) group and the Auxiliary Constables. They receive training similar to the R.C.M.P. officers, especially in arrest procedures. Once training is completed, each Auxiliary Constable is sworn in as an officer and has the same authority when out with a regular member. The uniform is essentially the same, but they do not carry firearms. The last time the R.C.M.P. advertised for one new Auxiliary Constable, they received 35 applications from which they selected three new Constables.

Right: The dangers of the job. On its way to a roll-over this R.C.M.P. cruiser slid into the ditch and found itself in the same situation.

Photo courtesy of Don Whiting

Firefighting

When Alberta and Saskatchewan were formed in 1905, Lloydminster was divided into two separate communities, each with its own municipal government and separate provincial police constables. Each side also had its own fire brigade, equipped with a hand drawn chemical cart. In the early twenties, the Alberta brigade purchased a Model T Ford which they used as a fire truck after transferring their chemical tanks to it. By 1927, Saskatchewan followed suit by buying a Chevrolet chassis and placing their chemical tanks on it.

Then, on August 19, 1929, Lloydminster suffered what that papers dubbed the city's "Waterloo". A fire that began in the back of a local pool hall spread across the downtown, destroying 53 buildings on the Saskatchewan side. Total losses in the fire were estimated to be in the range of one million dollars. The devastation was overwhelming; Lloydminster was still recovering from the $25,000 loss of the Lloydminster Milling Co. Ltd. flour mill to fire as well.

Photo courtesy of Don Whiting

Above: The local R.C.M.P. holds an annual Dress Ball which is a hot ticket on the Lloydminster social scene.

Victim Services in Lloydminster

The RCMP have a primary responsibility to solve crimes and deal with criminals but over the years a need was recognized for someone to follow up and deal with the plight of the victims.

The Victim Services Branch was formed in September of 1998 with Ross Pluss as Director. The branch responds to the needs of victims of crime and trauma. Volunteers at Victim Services must provide intervention, referral and support in times of crisis. Most importantly, they provide information, regarding victims' legal rights and recourse, and give them appropriate referrals to other agencies such as the Sexual Assault and Information Centre and the Lloydminster Interval Home.

Since 1982, the Lloydminster Sexual Assault and Information Centre has provided intervention, support and education to the victims of crisis situations. Contrary to popular belief, the centre does not only deal with women and children. It is also used by men who come from abusive backgrounds.

The Lloydminster Interval Home was first conceptualized in 1979 when Dolores Cummine and Marge Nattress recognized the need for a safe home as well as counselling and assistance for women in crisis situations. Local church and service groups were very supportive of the idea, but it was more difficult to get support from the two provincial governments. Saskatchewan Social Services was already funding six Interval Houses across Saskatchewan while Alberta had no department to cover such issues at the time. Though funding from both governments was eventually received, the shelter began thanks to a donation of a house and money from Nelson Lumber, as well as assistance from other individuals and groups. The shelter has since moved to a new, larger location. They have increased their paid and volunteer staff and are now better equipped to handle the needs of abused women and children.

The Interval Home provides temporary shelter from abusive situations. Stays can be anywhere from several hours to several days or longer. The Home also provides many other services to help clients leaving abusive situations. Transportation can be provided to attend appointments and job interviews as well as take children to school. Clothing can be provided if the situation requires, such as for a job interview. The Home also provides legal assistance in addition to a range of emotional and practical counselling services. One of their most important roles is to provide education regarding the issues of abuse in the home.

Each organization has paid positions but they are all dependent on volunteers. The dedication of the countless volunteers in these organizations has helped Lloydminster victims of crime, trauma, and abuse to better cope with their situation.

Photo courtesy of Barr Colony Heritage Cultural Centre

From the earliest days of Lloydminster the need for fire protection was recognized. The brigades began with hand-operated water pumps, later moving to hand-drawn, chemical extinguishers. When there was a fire, a bottle of Sulphuric Acid was poured into the 100-gallon water tank. This created Carbon Dioxide gas which propelled the water solution at the fire.

Below: The Lloydminster Fire Department in 1949. Throughout its history, down to today, ours has been a volunteer fire brigade. Too often overlooked is the fact that this means ordinary working people donate their time and risk their lives simply to serve our community. In so doing, they also save Lloydminsterites many thousands of tax dollars that it would cost to support a full-time paid force.

Photo courtesy of Mary Shortell

"The Great Holocaust", as it came to be known, along with the flour mill blaze and another huge fire, which engulfed an entire city block in January of the same year promoted some changes to the two communities. One of these changes was the amalgamation of the village and town on May 20, 1930.

The fires also left quite an impression on the local fire brigades. Though they had fought valiantly, they were overmatched by the inferno of August 19. They realized that new equipment and tactics were needed to prevent a recurrence of any such calamity. A second-hand truck was purchased and outfitted with a new 250 gallon per minute (gpm) pump and a 500-gallon water tank, an improvement from the old Model "R", which was retired from service.

However, only a few years later, the new arena went up in flames. The fire was first noticed in the front portion of the building at 4 AM on December 27, 1934. By the time the fire brigade was alerted and on the scene, the building was too far-gone to save. The roof of the new arena caved in within minutes of the brigade's arrival.

The City purchased its first custom built fire truck from A. E. Hickey & Son's in 1949. The truck had a 500-gallon water tank with an impressive 500 gpm pump at midship, twice the pressure of any before it in Lloydminster. Another important addition was that the truck now carried ladders. In the same year, a new fire hall was built at 5011-49th Ave., the present location.

Even with the many advancements the Fire Department made over the years, there were still many serious losses due to fire. One of these was on March 3, 1977. The destruction of the Alberta Hotel resulted in the loss of one of the city's oldest buildings and the deaths of five people.

Another spectacular blaze in 1977 was the explosion and fire at the Husky Oil Refinery. At 8:50 PM, on August 16, an Asphalt Exchanger Shell split. This allowed the hot product within to come into contact with the air, igniting the explosion. Damage was minimal and no one was injured, but the refinery was forced to run at 50% capacity until repairs could be completed. A third explosion occurred on September 19 at Domtar Roofing Materials Ltd. when an asphalt storage tank blew its top. One man was injured but the Fire Department contained the fire quickly. This did not make it any less spectacular for those in the three-mile radius who heard the explosion and felt the shock.

"Lloydminster's Great Holocaust"

That was the front page headline of the August 22, 1929, *Lloydminster Times.* Only three days before, fire had destroyed 53 businesses and caused one million dollars damage, a devastating loss at the time.

At 12:30 that morning, the westbound train pulled into town to the sound of a siren blasting. A fire had broken out at the back of the Boyd & Waddell Pool Hall. All night the fire raged across the business district destroying virtually everything in its path. Most buildings were made of wood and thus were susceptible to the ravages of fire. Only the Royal Bank building, made of brick, survived on the 4900 block of 50th St.

Photos courtesy of Sylvia Baynton

Above - top: Street scene of downtown Lloydminster in 1926 (left - looking north on 50 Ave. and right looking east on 50 St.) Above - middle: Same view but shortly after the August 19, 1929 fire. Above - bottom: View from on top of Town Hall looking south west. Log church on extreme left; in the distance on the right, businesses on the Alberta side are seen still standing.

The business district of Lloydminster, Saskatchewan was virtually lost to the fire, but the Lloydminster, Alberta business district was left mostly untouched. This was not due to fate or good fortune but to the efforts of residents. The fire brigades of both communities fought to the bitter end armed with only two chemical engines and their tenacity. Alberta business owners soaked blankets and draped them over the front of their stores. Then, they stood atop their buildings using the limited amount of water available to keep the blankets wet while across the street flames leaped into the air and sparks flew from collapsing structures. On the Saskatchewan side, only a few businesses such as Shortell's Workshop and the new Town Hall, survived.

Despite the destruction some counted their blessings. For all the damage done by the fire, there were no fatalities. Even though the Post Office was destroyed, mail service continued. Many surviving businesses offered space in their buildings for the victims to continue operation until new buildings could be built.

The other upside to the fire was that it pushed ahead the amalgamation of the two Lloydminsters into one town. Part of the difficulty controlling the fire was due to the lack of a water supply, and to the outdated equipment of the fire brigades. Public opinion demanded an improvement. A second-hand truck was purchased and equipped with a proper pump and water tank. A town bylaw was passed requiring new buildings to be made fire proof. This meant increased use of brick instead of wood. The Royal Bank building still standing seemed to justify the by-law.

Most of the businesses stricken by this disaster recovered. It served to bring the community together and strengthen it. While much had been lost, Lloydminster and its residents had learned some valuable lessons. Their response to these lessons would ultimately result in a more unified community. We had come through the fire and emerged the stronger for it.

Always evolving and changing, the Fire Department's most recent acquisition was in 1995 with the purchase of a new truck. It increased pumping capability to 1050 gpm, and possessed a 500 gallon water tank. The most recent addition to the fire hall was in 1991, when the hall was renovated in three phases, with two new drive-through bays added.

Below: A series of photos of the Lloydminster Fire Department in action at various calls.

Photos by Don Whiting

Emergency Services

The R.C.M.P. and the Fire Department have the support of three other important groups. These groups are the Britannia/Wilton Fire Department, the Lloydminster Rescue Squad and the Lloydminster Ambulance service. The Lloydminster Rescue Squad began in the mid-Eighties when the Ambulance Service became privatized and a need was recognized for this service.

Photo by Don Whiting

It is not only the technical aspects of the Fire Department which have changed, but the philosophy as well. Fire Chief Todd Gustavson, (above) one in a long line of Gustavson fire fighters, sums up the Fire Department in the phrase "pro-active, not reactive." In his time as Fire Chief, many programs designed to prevent fires have been instituted. The Department performs about 1200 residential inspections a year around Lloydminster checking for fire prevention issues. The Tot-spotters program, which puts reflective stickers on the bedroom windows of children so that fire fighters know where children are in the house, began in 1990.

Fire safety booklets are also published and distributed through the schools in Lloydminster. The distribution is accompanied by a presentation by a member of the Department who first arrives in normal clothes and then in full gear to lessen children's fear.

It has evolved from meager beginnings into one of the most effective units of its kind (see page 84).

The Ambulance Service was a hospital-run unit until October of 1985 when Rod and Karen Westman took over the service when it was privatized. Alan Kendel, an EMT since 1986, is the current operations manager for the unit. He is in charge of the maintenance of equipment

Photo by Don Whiting

Above: Members of the Britannia-Wilton Fire Department pose while at a training session. In order to respond effectively at fire calls, fire fighters must undergo rigorous training.

and vehicles. His responsibilities also put him charge of the staff of eight full time Emergency Medical Technicians, (EMTs), and a few casual employees, who are trained as drivers and assistants.

In the first years of the service, the average number of calls ranged from 65 to 80 a year. Now the average is up to 100 calls per year. The main duty of the service is to respond to emergency calls dispatched from the hospital.

The presence of EMTs at local events is required to deal with injuries to citizens and participants. The other important capacity in which the EMTs serve Lloydminster residents is as a transportation service. They are often called upon to move patients from one hospital to another.

One Summer Evening...

Photos courtesy: (top left) - Wilf Kenyon, (bottom left) - Glen Rusling, (bottom right) - Don Whiting, (background) - Bob Hayes. Diagram based on a sketch by Glen Rusling.

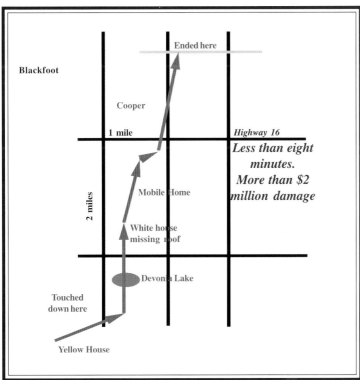

Blackfoot

Cooper

1 mile

Highway 16

**Less than eight minutes.
More than $2 million damage**

Ended here

2 miles

Mobile Home

White house missing roof

Devonia Lake

Touched down here

Yellow House

When you grow up on the farm, you learn to watch the sky. If it's hot and humid, you have an additional incentive - tornado watch. The tornadoes of 1912 and 1934 had long since faded from memory when the 1980's brought tornadoes back into mind. On August 11, 1982, a tornado caused extensive damage to a local farm. Less than a year later, on July 8, 1983 a large tornado was clearly visible to the west. Many Lloydminsterites climbed on roof tops or drove out into the countryside for a better view. Fortunately for them the tornado didn't swerve toward them. (See map below) It did injure one man, caused over $2 million property damage and destroyed farm buildings and killed animals. The 1987 tornado in Edmonton captured headlines and increased the number of locals watching the dark skies closely on hot summer days. A violent thunderstorm on July 28, 2000 spawned several tornadoes. One passed over Lloydminster but did not touch down. Another did touch down to the north. The Tupper brothers took shelter in their basement and escaped serious injury but when they emerged they found their entire farmyard had been shredded into rubble in a matter of seconds. When the clouds gather on a hot summer day - it pays to keep watch.

Lloydminster Rescue Squad

When tragedy strikes, it is often the Lloydminster Rescue Squad that literally, comes to the rescue. They have attended everything from airplane crashes to cars colliding with bulls. The Lloydminster Rescue Squad deals with these emergency situations in a competent and professional manner.

The Squad formed after ambulance service in Lloydminster was privatized in the 1980's. Until then, ambulance personnel performed rescue duties on an as needed basis with minimal equipment and little specialized training.

In May of 1985, Graham Howie began the Rescue Squad with a donated old oilfield truck and a small grant from the Hospital Board.

Many of the incidents which the Lloydminster Rescue Squad attends involve extraction using the "jaws of life" as pictured above. Squad members are volunteers who donate their time both for rescue calls and for the extensive training their work requires.

Since the beginning, the Lloydminster Rescue Squad has been an entirely volunteer organization. It began with eight individuals whose only motive and reward was helping other people in times of crisis. Two of those original members, Don Whiting and Norm Namur, are still with the Squad. In the early days, members had to scrounge equipment and try to operate a service that was literally homeless. Its first headquarters was the parking lot of the old hospital.

Norm and Don recall the procedure for answering calls in those early days. The first person to the parking lot would have to take the tarp off of the truck and get it started. Only three people could travel in the truck at the same time; the other members would have to follow in their private vehicles to the accident scene.

Depending entirely on volunteer time, money and resources made operating the service extremely difficult. There was never enough money for suitable equipment, let alone a permanent facility. Since they began in 1985, the Squad has moved seven times. Finally the Rescue Squad took up permanent residence in a building on 50th Street donated by the City and shared with the Britannia-Wilton Rural Fire Department. Today the Squad has 15 volunteer members and operates two mobile units.

Each unit is equipped for a variety of rescue situations, including a snowmobile for winter rescues and a boat for water rescues. In their first year, they answered approximately ten calls. Even though they now serve only a 50 kilometer radius around Lloydminster, they responded to 60 calls in 1999.

Not only do the volunteers respond to some horrific trauma situations, they also donate a considerable amount of their time to training and developing their skills.

Although the Squad has had to survive on private donations, the dedicated volunteers of the Lloydminster Rescue Squad continue to offer an invaluable service which enriches the quality of life in our Border City.

Another way the Squad contributes is by making presentations emphasizing the importance of safety. Don Whiting (left), travels to many schools and organizations stressing preventative measures such as using seatbelts and avoiding drinking and driving. His graphic photos of injury and death at accident scenes may shock some, but Don hopes they may also save a life.

Photos by Don Whiting

The border in Lloydminster creates many legal issues. Lawyers who practice in Lloydminster must be called to the bar in both provinces in order to serve all clients. There are two separate provincial courts. Judge Kim Young presides over the Saskatchewan court and Judge R. Tibbit presides over the Alberta court. In 1990, George Baynton became the first Lloydminster lawyer appointed to the Court of Queen's Bench, in Saskatoon.

Despite the many challenges presented by the Alberta Saskatchewan border, our police officers, firefighters, and emergency technicians work hard to keep us safe in our community. This is the same challenge that protective services personnel have confronted ever since members of the N.W.M.P toured the camps of the Barr Colonists that first winter of 1903.

Photo by Don Whiting

Chapter Eight
Oil and Gas

Research by Franklin Lloyd Foster

There's an old saying around the oil patch that "before you can find some oil, you have to find some money."

The heady excitement of the early finds often deteriorated as quickly as the oil production. Wells sanded in or watered out. It took awhile before we realized we had a special type of oil; a black, thick, smelly, highly viscous crude - now called heavy oil. For more than 70 years we've been responding to its challenges. It's generated more work than conventional oil, prompted more inventive technologies, and fostered a greater spirit of innovation. Now, in the 21st Century, our expertise and innovations are sought after throughout the world. Our heavy oil community has contributed to a significant expansion of the recoverable energy reserves of planet Earth. Not bad, eh!

It all started with Charlie Marren's cows. Like any farmer, Charlie worried about having enough water. Sloughs dried up in the hot summer sun. His cows couldn't eat snow all winter. So he was pleased that summer of 1926 when, after six weeks of laborious effort, he and his helpful neighbours struck a good body of water at a depth of 160 feet. Then the cows refused to drink the water. A visitor in the district, about 10 miles south of town, took a sample to the laboratory at the University of Alberta and a few weeks later the reply came back. The water contained significant amounts of petroleum distillates.

It didn't take Charlie and his neighbours long to put two and two together. They had almost struck oil. Now there's an old saying in the oil patch that "before you can find some oil, you have to find some money." Charlie was soon involved with promoters raising money for the brand new Marren-Lloydminster Oil and Gas Company.

There was great excitement in the *Lloydminster Times,* about having our very own oil field. The excitement spread and, in the heady days of the late 1920's, people pushed their money forward and sub-

Below: A derrick at the Dina field towers over the Battle River Valley one hot summer day in 1937.

Photo courtesy of Barr Colony Heritiage Cultural Centre

scribed $100,000 in the Company which had little to offer beyond some discontented cows.

Whatever became of the $100,000, or the promoters, or even Charlie Marren, are questions still waiting to be answered but the oil bug had bitten and soon other reports were coming in. Oil was reported down along the Battle River near Ribstone Creek. That was a fair distance from Lloydminster in those days but it kept the topic hot. Other discoveries were made and producing wells brought in, some out west, near Borradaile.

Other wells were disappointing. When the drill hole was baled there were definite signs of oil, in fact, oil itself; but it didn't come gushing out of the ground. You couldn't even pump it out. It was black and sticky and looked more like tar than crude oil. Reluctantly, such wells had to be abandoned and the search continued for a "real producer".

Above: O. C. Yates (pictured here with his wife Helen) was for many years the "main push" behind the exploration and development of the oil and gas industry in Lloydminster. He went on to a long, successful career as President of the Lloydminster Gas Company.

Caught up in the excitement but recognizing the need for solid business organization behind the search for oil was Lloydminster's C.P.R. agent O. C. Yates. "O. C." had been bitten by the oil bug for some time. He had followed local water well drillers all over the country trying to get a better understanding of the underlying geology of the area. In February 1933, he called a meeting of community members who might financially support developing local oil or gas wells. The upshot was the Lloydminster Gas Company.

Professor Frank Edmonds (left) was the principal geologist in the early years of Lloydminster's oil development. Lloyd Clinch (right) was one of those described as a "promoter", a person who raised the money and enthusiasm to make projects viable.

Soon, that company had a rig drilling just north east of town, manned by the most experienced driller in the area, Charlie Mills. Being so close to town, the project attracted a lot of interest. The mayor, Dr. G. L. Cooke was out at the site on November 20, 1933 to man the controls for the official "spudding in" ceremony. The large crowd contained a goodly number of shareholders as the Company was entirely financed by local subscribers.

All winter long, drilling progress was the prime topic in the homes and cafes of Lloydminster, and the *Times* kept its readers informed with "breaking news" headlines. Cold temperatures and heavy snows slowed progress but as winter eased, optimism grew. Then, early on Good Friday morning, March 30, 1934, natural gas was struck at 1200 feet and the well blew in.

Up close with heavy oil. Its high viscosity is illustrated above as it barely flows from drill stem to bucket.

Above: the introduction of gas kitchen ranges like this repelled some of the gloom of the Great Depression

By noon a large crowd had gathered and some claimed they could hear the roar of the gas escaping the hole up to 14 miles away. All weekend, the crowds gathered to watch in amazement. The nervous entrepreneur, O.C. Yates paced among the crowd pleading with people not to smoke. It being Easter, many had lunches of hot cross buns with them. There was great excitement about the gas being able to supply the heating needs of the town.

Sure enough, by "Fair time", in July, a makeshift pipeline had been run the short distance to the Exhibition Grounds. Some gas burning stoves had been brought in, and the mayor was on hand again to join in demonstrating that Lloydminster was now "cooking with gas". By November, over 200 homes were connected, most with an unusual meter in which one inserted coins for a timed period of gas delivery.

Meanwhile, other companies were springing up and exploration continued apace all around Lloydminster. Colony Oil and Gas Company brought in two producing gas wells in 1935. However, Lloydminster Gas Company No. 2 hit only salt water, proving that oil and gas exploration was still far from an exact science.

Finally, in May of 1937, the Dina Oil Company Limited, back along the Battle River, brought in a well that produced a good flow of good quality oil. Soon three other wells were drilled and a small refinery was set up after shares in the new Dina Oil and Refining Company Ltd. had been heavily subscribed. O. C. Yates was the president of this new company and its Field Superintendent was the intrepid driller, Charlie Mills.

Above: Real oil at last. (l-r) Jack Brown, Bob McKay, Ken Djuff, and driller Charlie Mills celebrate the bringing in of Dina # 1, May 26, 1937.

The first Dina Refinery was so small it did little more than heat the crude in hopes of encouraging some of the impurities to leave. As well, the site, while near the new Dina wells, was so far out of Lloydminster it was inconvenient for workers and for the still curious spectators.

All this while, Charlie Mills, and others, had been grappling with the problem of recovering the heavy oil. So it was that Charlie was the one to introduce, in 1943, the new drilling technology of the rotary rig. The old cable tool rigs actually

Cable tool bits on rack - 1937.

involved punching a hole in the earth's crust. The rotary rig, which rotated a three headed drilling bit, could drill more easily and to greater depths. With the new rotary rigs, more producing wells began dotting the countryside prompting the desire to build a larger refinery, this time at Lloydminster.

Husky Oil Comes to Town

The oil industry really became a significant part of Lloydminster's economy with the construction in 1946 - 47 of a refinery on the town's northern outskirts by Husky Oil Limited. Glenn E. Neilsen, principal owner of the company, had vessels and other refinery parts moved from a wartime refinery in Riverton, Wyoming. Colourful "Husky Bill" Williams supervised the refinery construction and many of those who got involved with the company at this stage became stalwarts of the oil industry.

In the late 1940's and early 1950's, a big market for Lloydminster oil was what was called Bunker Fuel, used by the railways. Almost anything qualified as Bunker fuel, including waste oils. There was no concern about sulphur content. A second market was asphalt for road construction. Since the late 1940's, up to today, Lloydminster has been a major source of road asphalt for Western Canada.

Bunker fuel lost its market when the railways switched to diesel engines in the mid-1950's. Husky refocused and started producing

Photo courtesy of BCHCC

The rotary drilling rig, introduced in the 1940's, made drilling easier and faster, thus making possible the ambitious drilling schemes of the 1950's.

The Excelsior (later Kodiak) Refinery - pictured below in the 1940's - was on Highway 16 west at about 66 Ave. From the late 1930's until the late 1950's it operated as a competitor of Husky Oil.

Photo courtesy of BCHCC

Photo courtesy of Lloydminster Regional Archives

Above: Rail cars loading bunker fuel in the early 1950's.

"Husky Bill" Williams (right) supervised the construction of the original Husky Refinery which went on stream July 10, 1947. It marked the beginning of the oil industry as a major part of our economy.

Below: Some young ladies watch closely as crude oil is dumped into a storage pit. Archie Miller (right) looks on.

diesel with a maximum .5% sulphur content. Husky ran raw diesel through a "Huskyfiner" to reduce sulphur content. A "Reformer" was used to produce car gas. They fed raw gasoline in, added the maximum lead - 3 ml. per gallon for regular and 4 ml. per gallon for premium to achieve the desired octane level. In 1963, new process units, called "Catformer" and "Unifiner", allowed Husky to produce higher octane gasoline as well as a diesel fuel with a lower sulphur content.

In the early days, Bob Chapman ran a bulk fuel dealership not far from the refinery. Among the products sold was something referred to by the public as "skunk gas". It was raw gasoline with added casing head gas. Some lead was thrown in and it was dyed purple and used in tractors.

Around 1950, the Sidney Roofing Company established a plant to produce asphalt shingles. Later Domtar and then Northern Globe operated the plant. The asphalt for their roofing products was delivered via pipeline from the Husky Refinery.

The first Husky Truck Stop was here in Lloydminster. The service station was run by Helmer Thorsen and George Reinholt. Jim Chaley operated the restaurant. The concept of a large parking lot, with phones and sleeping quarters available was quickly accepted by truckers. Later, wanting a symbol for their truck stops which could be seen from a distance, Husky came up with the 100 ft. pole with the 20' X 40' flag.

Photo courtesy of Grant and Billiela King

The Royal Cafe and Phillip's Men's Wear were two of the businesses in town that prospered when the "oil men" moved here. Workers usually went to Phillip's on Fridays to cash their cheques because they got off shift after the banks closed at 3:00 PM. As well, the store supplied clothing for the roughnecks and refinery people. To many, the store was the one stop bank and shopping centre. The Royal Cafe beside the post office was a popular spot for meals and socializing.

Main Street, 50th Avenue, was the

Photo courtesy of BCHCC

first street in Lloydminster to be paved. Workers had to dig down 9 feet and fill with gravel as parts of it had been a bog. What is now 55 Avenue, then referred to as "Husky Road", was the route on the edge of town that crude oil trucks took to the refinery. There was lots of oil on the road but it was still very dusty. The drips of crude oil were very stringy. Eventually the trucks got drip pans under the dump valve so they didn't drip oil onto city streets.

It was very common in Lloydminster, but a novelty to visitors, to see signs on doors which said "Please remove oily footwear". It became common practice for people to take their shoes off at the door of any businesses or homes they were visiting.

Another common practice was to run the waste oil at the refinery into open outdoor pits and every day set fire to the pits. There was a "gentlemen's agreement" that the pits would not be burned off on Mondays because that was "Wash Day". When a newcomer, unfamiliar with the local routine, set fire to the pit one Monday, Husky had a public relations fiasco and had to apologize profusely "to all the ladies". Contaminating the environment and air pollution weren't even discussed.

Safety precautions weren't great in the oil field in the early days and fires and explosions seemed to be part of the normal work environment. Over the years the focus has switched to where safety is the absolute first priority versus production as in the old days.

Glenn E. Nielsen, the founder and president of Husky, had the tremendous foresight in the early 1950's to put together a deal acquiring the mineral rights to millions of acres of CPR lands. This turned Husky into a major oil producer. Another dream Husky pursued for years was of a pipeline extending from Lloydminster to the Interprovincial Pipeline System to the south which would carry the heavy oil to the newly found markets in the north central U.S.

There was yet another challenge. Heavy oil was not likely to flow through a pipeline, especially in winter. In the spring of 1962,

Photo courtesy of the Der family

The Royal Cafe, located east of the old post office - now the Heritage Building, was a popular spot for meals and socializing. There was a story that "Husky Bill" Williams once rode a horse into the cafe.

Photo courtesy of BCHCC

Cloud of thick black smoke drifts over Lloydminster as waste oil pits near the refinery are burned off circa 1953.

Ditching for a pipeline from Blackfoot to Lloydminster, early 1950's.

Right: Blow out and fire at Commonwealth Drilling site just north-west of Lloydminster, April 1, 1948

representatives from Williams Brothers Pipeline Company arrived to test various pipeline systems. They designed and built various sized lines, and tested different pressures and temperatures. The key proved to be mixing the heavy oil with a light natural gas liquid called condensate. Various percentages of condensate and crude were tried to see if the two would simply separate in the pipeline and clog the system. Fortunately, a blend was found and that solution still is what makes it possible to pipeline heavy crude to distant markets.

Construction of the original line from Lloydminster to Hardisty commenced in 1963. It consisted of one 6 inch diameter line, termed the "yo-yo" line because the plan was for it to be used for two-way service. Although the yo-yo line was workable, it was cumbersome and soon a separate line was built to move condensate north from Hardisty and the 6" line already in place moved blend south.

With the advent of a working pipeline system to deliver crude oil blend from Lloydminster to the markets to the south, things really started to heat up in the black oil patch. Secondary recovery methods started to emerge. Husky experimented with a type of water flooding which was all the rage in the U.S. at the time.

Hamish Garland: "In Lloydminster, oil doesn't gush: it drips!"

"Hame" came to Lloydminster in November 1948 to work at the Husky Refinery. Later, he joined the Production Department, when Husky was in the midst of a 100 well drilling program, running a fleet of six company-owned drilling rigs.

In 1955, Hame was promoted to Production Foreman where he was part of pioneering such enhancement techniques as water-flooding and fire-flooding. He was also involved in battery construction and such innovations as using horizontal treaters at battery locations.

In 1973, Hame joined Murphy Oil as District Production Manager. He retired on October 31, 1986 but remained active, assisting in developing the OTS Heavy Oil Science Centre. After almost 40 years in production, battling sand, he marvelled at the shift during the 90's to sand production. The old enemy - sand - had become a friend!

In 1964, they first experimented with thermal recovery. That year they also commenced drilling some pattern wells and installed the area's first horizontal treater, in the Dulwich area. Husky pioneered steam flooding and constructed the first steam plant in Lloydminster.

In 1965 things really took off. Markets for the heavy crude south of the border were excellent. Husky's first battery at Aberfeldy was constructed and a total of four more steams plants complete with attendant batteries and treaters were constructed in the Aberfeldy area east of Lloydminster.

Photo courtesy of Keith Wright

From 1965 to 1970 new batteries were built in the Lloydminster area. As the pipeline capacities increased and new markets were added, the push to get more oil from existing wells became a shove. Waterfloods were initiated in almost all areas, as that was considered the way to go at that time. Along with waterflooding came experimenting with various types of bottom hole pumps and lifting mechanisms. Lloydminster, as always, remained a hotbed of experimental work.

Above: Four stalwarts of the Lloydminster oil industry pose behind an "electric survey truck" (seismic) as fields expand rapidly in the late 1940's. L-R Mel Coons, Don Cleal, O.C. Yates and Stuart Wright.

Far left: early field storage tanks were elevated on platforms to provide gravity drainage.

Photo courtesy of BCHCC

Grant King spent 50 years in the oil business, the last 35 with Gibson Petroleum. He culminated his career as President of Gibson's whose trucks, terminals and pipelines move millions of cubic meters of oil daily.

Grant King, born in Lloydminster, began his career right out of high school with Husky Oil, mostly in drilling and production. In 1961, he joined Gibson's. At the time, large volumes of oil still moved by rail tanker cars, but Grant was part of the trend toward truck transportation. He was responsible for their truck's distinctive yellow colour that they still bear today. He also supervised terminals, large collection points where oil is introduced into long distance pipelines, such as at Hardisty, Alberta, the point that receives the production of the Lloydminster Upgrader.

Photo courtesy of Bay Van Photography

Vic Juba

Vic Juba answered an anonymous ad. in the *Edmonton Journal* seeking a lab tester. A job offer arrived from Husky Oil, of which he had never heard, in Lloydminster, where Vic had never been. Fresh from a year of Graduate school after a Bachelor of Science degree in Chemistry from the University of Alberta, Vic packed his bags and headed for the border city in the Spring of 1953.

Juba had only been working for Husky for six months when his supervisor suddenly resigned. Although there were other testers in the lab who had been there longer, Vic was asked to fill the supervisor's shoes.

"I was as green as grass," Juba remarks. He took on the challenge though, and stayed in the position for several years. Eventually Vic worked his way up to Process Manager, where he was responsible for refinery operation. In 1976, he became Refinery Manager.

Juba alerted Husky to the the refinery's decrepit state. "We're putting patches on patches, and I'm running out of haywire," Juba wrote to Husky's president. Juba suggested building a new refinery and gearing it to produce asphalt, for which Lloydminster Heavy Oil is particularly suited. The refinery was built in 1982 and is still operating.

Vic Juba remained in the position of refinery manager until 1988, when he had intended to retire.

However, Husky president Art Price asked him to take on a newly created position for one year - Community Relations Director.

Juba had served the community extensively for years, and was then completing his work as chair of the Lloydminster Indoor Swimming Pool Project. Husky had noticed his efforts and made him an offer he could not refuse.

"The president, Art Price, said 'We'd like to give the community of Lloydminster *you* to work for *them*. It was tailor made for my lifestyle," recalls Juba. "When I left the office, I took the elevator down, but it felt like I was floating."

Barely three weeks into the job of Community Relations Director, it was announced that the megaproject Upgrader was going to be built. Vic was asked to plan a signing ceremony. When the day came, there were 1000 people present, and more television cameras than covvered the announcement of the Hibernia project.

A year passed and Juba set his sights on retirement, but then, Senior Vice-President Murray Peterson

Husky Refinery in the early 1950's when Vic Juba first arrived. Note, centre left, Husky Road (now 55 Ave) crosses the railway track. Upper right of photo shows the competing Excelsior Refinery in the distance. It was on the north side of Highway 16, near the present Cornerstone Shopping Complex.

Vessels at the Husky Refinery in the 1950's

approached him with a proposal. Stay on while the Upgrader was being built, as communications coordinator - a broad title which encompassed housing, communications, and labour relations.

Everyone knew that housing 3500 construction workers was going to be a challenge. Juba had learned from past mistakes though. When the new refinery was built in 1982, Husky erected an on-site camp for construction workers where they lived, ate, and played. Local business people were irked by the move, feeling they had not fully benefited from the refinery construction. "When the Upgrader project was announced," Juba remembers, "local business people said 'I hope you're not going to do the same thing again.'"

At the same time, Lakeland College board chair Ed Jenson approached Juba with an idea to have the joint-venture Bi-Provincial Upgrader collaborate on the building of residences for Lakeland College. During construction, the workers would be housed, and when the project was complete, the residences would be turned over to the College. The $7,000,000 project was fast-tracked, with the support of the federal and provincial governments. The construction workers were housed, business services were used more fully, and Lakeland College had a residence, a drawing card for out-of-town students.

Finally in March of 1993, Vic retired. At his retirement banquet in Calgary, Art Price joked, "Are you sure we haven't done this before?"

For more on Vic Juba's community work, see Chapter 13

The Husky Lloydminster Upgrader, which opened in 1992, has done much to improve the economics of both heavy oil production and the Lloydminster community.

Photo by Don Whiting

Bottom left: one model of the Progressing Cavity Pump: one of the innovations which has revolutionized heavy oil production in our area.

Bottom right: The bi-annual Lloydminster Heavy Oil Show recognizes Lloydminster's contribution to the industry. The three day event is well attended by people from all over the world.

The Upgrader

The challenge of making full use of heavy oil had been around for a long time. For years, the major application was as asphalt for road construction. This meant that demand dropped drastically in winter and wells had to be shut in. With ever declining reserves of light crude, it became increasingly important to find a way to have heavy oil contribute to the demand for transportation fuels. The concept of an Upgrader developed which could convert heavy oil by "cracking" it into light petroleum products, with useful by-products such as sulphur and coke. It was an on again off again proposal which finally came to reality through a combination of local and national political leaders and industry initiatives. When the Bi-Provincial Upgrader (now Husky Lloydminster Upgrader) finally opened in 1992, it seemed to usher in a decade of revolutionary change in the heavy oil sector. The Upgrader's technology and processes made heavy oil far more useful. The use of condensate to create a "blend" had solved the difficulties of transportation by pipeline.

Photos by Don Whiting

Now, production seemed to be the limiting factor. This was revolution-ized by some new technologies and a change of attitude. The important new production technology was the progressing cavity pump but that was only because of the changed attitude about sand production. After decades of trying to prevent the "enemy" sand from infiltrating pumps, well-bores and treaters, now, in a method called cold production, sand was literally lifted to the surface. The new methods allowed significant increases of production in many wells.

Of course, the challenges of heavy oil were not solved so easily. There are still ongoing efforts to perfect ways of enhancing recovery such as steam assisted gravity drainage (SAGD). However, heavy oil seems well on the way to losing its status as the ugly duckling of the petroleum industry. At the 2000 Lloydminster Heavy Oil Show, the keynote speaker claimed heavy oil was the most profitable sector of the industry. Constant improvements in technology and process have driven down production costs per cubic meter to historic lows. Greater success in cost control has meant greater success in coping with the periodic downturns that come with the cyclical nature of producing a commodity for sale on world markets. With ongoing innova-tion, Lloydminster proudly retains its title - Heavy Oil Capital of the World.

Photo by Don Whiting

Chapter Nine

Business Industrial and Manufacturing

Research and draft writing by Dorothy Foster

(Foreground below) The Electrical Supply Plant, (one block east of current Fire Hall) was operated by William Johnson and supplied the town with D.C. electrical current generated by a steam electrical plant from 1910 to 1930 when Canadian Utilities Ltd. purchased his plant and obtained the franchise. Canadian Utilities then built a Diesel-electric plant to generate A.C. current. This plant supplied the town until transmission lines entered in 1955 to supply three phase, 60 cycle power from a steam-electric plant in Vermilion. Later, hydro-electric energy flowed to Lloydminster from plants in western Alberta.

It has been an ongoing challenge in Western Canada to diversify the economy. While primary industry such as agriculture, and oil and gas are still the basis of our local economy, Lloydminsterites have been remarkably energetic and successful in broadening the base of our economy through industry and manufacturing. Many of these enterprises were based on home grown innovations which started small and, in some cases, went on to become well established companies with a large number of employees and a global reputation as leaders in their field. Lloydminster should be proud of the many entrepreneurs who have overcome technical, engineering, financial, and political challenges to provide our area with a solid and growing base of economic activity in our community.

Photo courtesy of Jack McGuffie

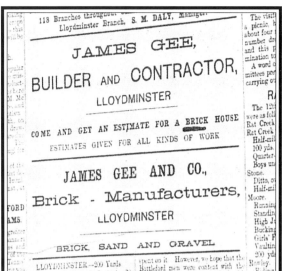

James Gee Sets Up Shop

James Sidney Gee first came to Canada in 1881 and worked in early land surveys of the West. He returned to England to marry Elizabeth Wiltshire and brought his family back to build summer homes in the Ottawa area from 1894 to 1899. Even though they liked the Canadian way of life, James was lured back to his homeland.

In 1903, when Rev. Barr was organizing his plan to settle farming lands in the Northwest Territories, James decided to let his two elder sons, Sid and Cecil go. Not very long after, James, his wife Elizabeth, sons Bernard and Stanley, and daughters Mabel and little Kathleen, born in 1901, notified the older sons that they were coming too. Cecil and Sid travelled by ox team to meet them in Saskatoon.

James, a skilled builder, supervised the building of the log church, St. John's Minster. He did not like farming and in 1905 he found a good spot just a mile and a half from Lloydminster to start a brick yard. The plant ran a soft mud process. The remains of the operation are still in evidence where the Lloydminster Packers Ltd. is today, just east of Highway 17. All of the early brick buildings in Lloydminster were made from these bricks.

One of Gee's most notable projects still stands today - the St. John's Minster Anglican Church. Gee and his son, Barney, were present at the ceremony of the laying of the cornerstone in 1910 (see page 27). James and his family moved into Lloydminster in 1911, and Gee served as town mayor for one year.

In 1912, the Gee Family moved to Edmonton where James established a contracting business from which he retired in 1943. Other notable structures that Mr. Gee built were St. Stephen's Church in Edmonton and the Tighnduin farm near Lashburn.

Left: The James Gee and Company horseshoe could be found on every building that Gee built. Right: An advertisement from a 1905 issue of the Lloydminster Times for Gee's services.

The Gee family of eight (below) first settled into a newly built log barn, which was to house two other couples, the Belwards and the Paynes, as well. It was divided using tents as partitioning for the privacy of twelve people. A large cook stove in the centre was for heat and cooking.
In the spring a new house, "Glenhome" was built, consisting of a large living room, a bedroom for the boys, one for the girls, and one for James and Elizabeth. The boys worked on the farm and gathered wood for the stoves. Mabel and her mother worked keeping the family clean and fed.

Photo courtesy of Lloydminster Regional Archives.

Photos courtesy of Ben Sproull

Blacksmiths

In the era of horse power, it was important to have a blacksmith available. This was even more the case given Lloydminster's early isolation. So, a blacksmith shop was among the first businesses established in 1903. Blacksmiths shod horses and fabricated and repaired parts for farm machinery, wagons and literally anything brought into their shops. Herb Elkington and Art Lower operated a shop near Immigration Hall into the 1920's and 1930's. First the disappearance of the draft horse and later the prevalence of standardized parts reduced blacksmiths to a niche market.

The Lumber Yards

The first lumber yard emerged in Lloydminster in the early 1920's, owned by Hayward and Harris. Beaver Lumber, under their subsidiary, Superior Lumber Yards Ltd., purchased the yard in 1928. The first local manager was Phillip Fretwell in 1934. In 1946, Ray Nelson arrived to manage the lumber yard before leaving in 1949 to start Nelson Lumber with his brother Austin (See feature on pages 102 and 103). There were sceptics, who believed that Nelson Lumber would not stand the test of time, but it soon established itself and, locally, far surpassed its main competitor Beaver Lumber. In 1958, Nelson Homes was established, and was soon building and transporting homes across Western Canada.

The company also played a vital role in enticing other industries to set up shop in Lloydminster. When the Sidney Roofing and Paper Company in Victoria, BC decided to shut down its shingle operation, Ray Nelson of Nelson Lumber urged the company to relocate to Lloydminster. Nelson

Photo courtesy of Lloydminster Regional Archives.

Photo courtesy of Jack McGuffie

Lumber was the roofing company's largest customer, and Sidney Roofing agreed. The plant was built in the winter of 1950-1951, and it was ready for operation by summer. The plant's first shingles left Lloydminster by rail on August 24th of 1951, with products shipped throughout Western Canada. The factory was good for the town, providing additional employment and a boost to the economy by way of local transport firms, retail outlets, and machine shops.

In 1962, the plant was purchased by Dominion Tar and Chemical (Domtar), a large national company. In its final days, the roofing plant was operated by Northern Globe, which closed the plant in the early 1980's due to rising costs.

An Industrial Supply House

The Wright family came from England in 1905 to settle on a farm a quarter mile east of the present site of the Upgrader. Stuart Wright was one year old and Colin, his brother, was three at the time.

In the thirties, the Wright brothers and other farmers, decided to join O. C. Yates, to start the Lloydminster Gas Company. They drilled one well, Lloydminster # 1, and when it blew in they quickly developed a plan to distribute natural gas to local homes. It was a challenge to convince home owners to use gas for heating and other uses due to its new technology and safety concerns. However, distribution began, and they were able to give continuous service from the one well until more were drilled. Success led them to organize The Lloydminster Development Company. In 1936, The Oxville Oil & Gas Co., situated on the bank of the Battle River, went bankrupt and the Development Co. bought the refinery, which became known as the Dina Oil and Refining Co. with three producing oil wells. Stuart, a director, managed the refinery in the summer and travelled to Victoria in the winter to work in the shipyards, through World War II.

A skilled welder, Stuart Wright eventually set up a welding business in a shack under the water tower. Wright was self-educated, and became an expert pipe fitter and petroleum engineer.

Photo courtesy of Lloydminster Regional Archives.

Sidney Roofing and Paper Company located a roofing plant (above) in Lloydminster in 1951 at the request of its largest customer, Nelson Lumber.

Stuart Wright (bottom right) gave his employees initial guidance and then stepped back for them to figure out the rest. Stuart's nephew Keith remembers Stuart as a blunt man who didn't mince words. "Get on with the job!" he would say. Jack Allen, a friend, remembers him as an excellent petroleum engineer who could make his ideas a reality. A genius with a slide rule, the oil men depended on Wright's judgement. "He couldn't be stumped," Keith remarks. While operating his business, Stuart attended Alberta College to take business administration and accounting.

Bottom left: Heavy oil provides many challenges but these in turn generate many jobs. Well servicing is a major part of our economy. Here a Lloydminster Development Company service crew (l-r:) Ed Preston, Walter Simon, Amos Goheen, and Fred Schwandt pose in 1959.

Photo courtesy of Norma Ricard

Photo courtesy of Keith Wright

Nelson Lumber

Ray Nelson arrived in Lloydminster on April 23, 1946, discharged from the Canadian Army and ready to assume his new job – Manager of the local Beaver Lumber outlet. After three years learning the business, and becoming convinced of Lloydminster's potential, he persuaded his brother Austin to join him in starting their own lumber business. So it was that the two purchased a block of land from Les Rendell, which had been part of the original Rendell homestead of 1903. The nay sayers said the site was too far out of town to succeed but the Nelson brothers were ready to meet the challenge and, through bad times and good, built Nelson Lumber into one of the top 75 privately held companies in Canada, while still maintaining its head office in Lloydminster.

Good people are always part of any success and in 1949 Ab Truss was hired as Vice-President of Marketing and in 1953, Axel Foght became Vice-President of Finance and Administration. The two would be with Nelson's until 1986. In 1954, Austin Nelson moved to Edmonton to manage a Nelson Lumber outlet there. It was part of an expansion that would eventually see Nelson's with a presence in Bonnyville, Slave Lake and Grande Prairie as well. From these outlets, Nelson's would supply and service all of northern Alberta and beyond. At its peak, Nelson's would employ over 400 people.

Above: Ray Nelson poses with a restoration of the first Nelson Lumber delivery truck. From the 1960's to the 1990's, the distinctive plaid Nelson Lumber trucks (below) delivered more than 35,000 homes to every corner of Western Canada.

In 1958, the first brochure featuring "Nelson Homes" appeared with two plans: the Nelson "Standard" was 768 sq. ft. at a price of $2550, and the second, the "Elmwood", for $2995. "We looked at the construction scene," Mr. Nelson said in an interview, "and we thought there was a big vacuum in help available for people who wanted to build homes, especially in the rural areas." Nelson's would go on to sell over 35,000 "manufactured homes" in what, at the time, was a unique concept of building components in the factory in Lloydminster, and then delivering them for assembly at the site. These sites ranged all across Western Canada, and, as Nelson's reputation for quality homes at affordable prices spread, Nelson Homes were sold into Ontario and British Columbia and beyond. At one time Nelson Homes were exported to Japan, the United States, Germany and even Iceland.

Nelson's first factory, built in 1958, burned in January 1961 due to a gas explosion. Almost before the ashes were cool, a larger and more up-to-date facility replaced it. A second fire on Victoria Day 1975 caused only a few days setback in production. Not only was the facility replaced but it was expanded and a warehouse was added. Production of this scale required a large operation. As much as 300,000 board feet of lumber was shipped in a single day from the 16 acre plant. Convoys of the distinctive plaid trucks transported home packages to places such as Whitehorse and Fort McMurray. The Lloydminster market was not neglected through all this. At one time it could be said that 85% of the homes here had been either built by Nelsons or that they had supplied the materials to build them.

A construction division was formed which went beyond homes to apartment buildings, light industrial and commercial buildings and seniors' lodges.

In 1988, Ray Nelson purchased Austin Nelson's 50% interest in the company giving him 100% ownership of Nelson Lumber Company Ltd. In 1991, Ray Nelson was a central part of the negotiation which brought the Real Canadian Superstore to Lloydminster. There were some sharp critics of this move claiming it would destroy many of Lloydminster's businesses. The reverse has seemed to be the case. Superstore was a large

step in the direction of Lloydminster strengthening and broadening its role as a regional shopping and service centre.

In 1994, Nelson's acquired the Horizon Village trademark and continued to build developments for active seniors which focused as much on life-style as housing style. Another recent innovation is the Dr. James W. Hemstock Assisted Living Centre which will bring a new dimension of living to Lloydminster. The $5 million Phase I, constructed in 2000-2001 will supply rental accommodation while a later Phase II, also valued at $5 million, will provide condominium type living, both with access to assistance for daily living.

Photos courtesy of Nelson Lumber.

Above: Nelson Lumber was an innovator in business management, initiating one of the first annual company wide professional development conferences. Here long time employee, Eric Collins, leads a fun-filled learning session.

Above: Co-CEO, Glenda Elkow helps lead Nelson Lumber into its second 50 years of business.

Raymond J. Nelson

Ray Nelson grew up in a Christian home in Frontier, Saskatchewan. He has always tried to exemplify high moral and ethical principles in his daily life. He established the Nelson Family Foundation in 1962. Each year, five percent of the company's profits go into the foundation to aid charitable endeavours. The Foundation supports World Vision, Christian college bursaries, and many other community and regional projects. Ray Nelson was mainly responsible for bringing the American Management Association's youth workshops called "Operation Enterprise", first to Canada and then to Lloydminster. It is actions such as these, and many others untold, which demonstrate Ray Nelson's values. "My testimony is not what I say from the many platforms to which I have been invited to speak. My testimony is what I do, day by day," is how Mr. Nelson sums it up.

Nowhere did his faith play a larger role than bringing him through his becoming the oldest heart transplant recipient in the world in 1999. He credits this achievement to the "Grace

and Mercy of the Lord" and sees it as a contribution to breaking through arbitrary age barriers restricting access to medical care.

Ray Nelson's vision, planning, hard work and faith have allowed him to make major contributions to Lloydminster and beyond. However, he is the first to declare that, "My experience has been that it is very clear I did not do this alone. Over the years, my life has been enriched by the many people I have worked with who shared in the effort to provide quality products and services. Without their cooperation and faithfulness, very little could have been accomplished." Mr. Nelson also sites the support of his wife, Marie, through the busy years when the Company was consuming a lot of his time, and more recently through his health tribulations. As well, his four children, Allyson, Glenda, Tannis and Scott provided reason and reward for his efforts and additional cause, as Ray Nelson puts it, "To thank God and Our Saviour for the success that we have had."

Photo courtesy of Bay Van Photography.

Photos courtesy of Stuart Wright Ltd.

As industry grew in Lloydminster, Wright saw that there was a need for a "supply house for industry". In 1944, he set up business on 49th Avenue, between 50th and 49th Street. Stuart supplied 32 volt power plants, insulation and power tools. He soon grew out of the space and moved to the corner of 49th street and 50th Avenue.

Emil Lychak, joined the company in 1960, and worked his way up from shipping/receiving, through sales to management. Stuart's son, Bill, left the navy to join the business in 1963. Starting at the bottom he learned the various aspects of the business and was managing the company a year before his father died in 1974. Together they expanded the operation to supply not only to retail but wholesale customers. In 1981, Emil Lychak joined Bill Wright as a partner in the company.

In 1991, Emil Lychak and Rick Lyon joined forces to purchase Bill Wright's shares. Today customers such as Husky Energy can access Stuart Wright inventory via computer and place orders quickly. The computer also handles price changes automatically, and prepares invoices. Emil and Rick though, still keep a close eye on the figures to remain competitive and fair to the buyers.

Stuart Wright Ltd. is recognized to be one of the largest independent industrial supply houses in Western Canada. It has been serving the Lloydminster area since 1948, and it specializes in oilfield, agricultural and industrial equipment. Stuart Wright Ltd. has achieved a remarkable feat in maintaining its independence, without being affiliated with buying groups or franchisees, in these times of mergers and acquisitions.

On-going expansion has seen Stuart Wright Ltd. occupy a number of buildings, from downtown to their current facility (inset) on 48th Street and 51st Avenue which opened on November 29, 1976.

Below: The ADM Canola Plant. Canola is used to produce edible oil products, such as salad dressing, cooking oil, and margarine. Canola's erucic acid has many non-food uses such as oils for chain saws, hydraulic oils, and agents used in lubrication, in the manufacture of plastic wrap and bags, flotation agents for potash mines, high temperature oils for iron casting, and ingredients for the soap and cosmetic industry.

Lloydminster's Canola Crushing Plant Further Diversifies Local Economy

One large step in drawing industry to Lloydminster was the construction of Lloydminster's first industrial park, Hill Industrial, in 1973. Prior to this, industries were scattered throughout the city. An industrial park allowed Lloydminster to grow by means of an orderly urban plan.

United Oilseeds Products built a canola crushing plant in the industrial park in 1973, creating seventy-five new jobs. Canola was a relatively new cash crop to farmers, and the operation added greatly to the local economy. Jack Smyth was hired as the General Manager. United Oilseeds was a leader in the industry, building export markets for canola oil and canola meal. The industry also developed new and better varieties of canola.

When the cooking oil markets tightened, the plant had limited options, as it produced only raw unrefined oil. The Crow Rate, a government subsidy for the transport of grain, did not apply to processed materials. In addition, importing countries placed higher tariffs on imported oil. It was cheaper to export raw canola as opposed to crushing and shipping it from Lloydminster. Due to these problems, the plant had several years of successive losses in the eighties. The City of Lloydminster took an active role in lobbying the federal govern-

Photo by Don Whiting

Bob Jack's Sheet Metal

Bob Jack Sr. had worked with metal in high school in England before coming to Canada as a young teenager in 1947. He was eager to continue working with metal. "Pattern drawing was my thing. I was a bench man," he commented. By age 19, Bob Sr. was the youngest journeyman in the province, working with George Bodards, and then, opening his own business, Bob Jack's Sheet Metal, in 1959. He rented a small shop from the Co-op, near the old Co-op lumber yard. As the metal operation grew, Bob made two more moves in four years ending up in the present location on Highway 17. It was not long until more space was needed, and the small shop was expanded to 5200 sq. ft. in 1969. This building included a drafting/design room and a manufacturing area.

Bob Jack Sr. also became an independent dealer for Lennox, a company which manufactures furnace and air conditioning equipment. Over the years, Bob Sr has won

Photos courtesy of Gladys Jack.

Left: Bob (Sr) and Gladys Jack have been in business since 1959. Over the years, Bob Sr. has won many awards, including Citizen of the Year, Sportsman of the Year, the Saskatchewan Volunteer Recognition Award. In addition, he was honoured as a Paul Harris Fellow by the Lloydminster Rotary Club. Right: Bob (Jr) and Gloria Jack have both been involved in the business for more than twenty years. Bob Jr. has followed in his father's footsteps in serving the community, especially in the area of sports.

several Dave Lennox awards, and has sat on the Lennox dealer advisory board in Edmonton.

Today, a total of 30 employees cover several departments, including: office staff, installers, a roofing crew, custom sheet metal manufacturing, and a planned service department which makes regular equipment checks. Many employees have stayed with the company for years; two long serving staff members recently retired at the ages of 65 and 70.

In the early days of Bob Jack's Sheet Metal, 90% of its business came from the housing industry, but as time passed, the commercial sector provided the bulk of their business. The Dairy Queen, Husky House, the Lloydminster Comprehensive High School, the Lloyd Mall, and the Atrium Centre were all local contracts completed by "Bob Jack's".

---

ment, and special meetings were hosted in Lloydminster where Deputy Prime Minister Don Mazankowski helped resolve the barriers to the successful operation of the plant.

With the death of the Crow and the passage of the Free Trade Agreement in 1988, there were fewer barriers to successful operation of the plant. Archer Daniels Midland (ADM) purchased the plant in 1991 and added an $800,000 refinery, allowing it to refine canola to edible oil standards. The canola crush increased from 750 tons to 2000 tons per day.

In 1993, a petition, signed by 401 Lloydminster residents of the west side of the city, was sent to Alberta Environment, asking them to investigate the odorous emissions coming from the canola plant. After investigating the complaint, Alberta Environmental Protection issued a control order, requiring the company to reduce the smells coming from the facility. The company enacted measures to comply with the order, which satisfied government although some residents continued to voice their opposition, including issuing an appeal against the construction of an addition to the plant by ADM in 2000. Despite all of this, ADM and Lloydminster continue to be an important part of what is now a three million ton per year canola crushing industry that contributes much to Lloydminster's economy.

Below: The Co-op Creamery was an important manufacturing facility for many years. Note the horse drawn delivery wagon, on the left, which would make the rounds delivery dairy products door-to-door. To the right is a rack of cream cans awaiting farmers to pick them up for refill back on the farm. As the number of cans increased, some painted colourful designs on them to make them easier to spot quickly.

Photo courtesy of Saskatchewan Archives Board.

Photo courtesy of Sylvia Fisher.

Agriculture, one of our major economic underpinnings, gives rise to two types of industries: those supplying farm equipment, and those processing farm produce. On the supply side, one of the key businesses is farm machinery sales and service.

Agland, Lloydminster's largest farm machinery dealership, can trace its ancestry back to the early 1920's when William Wesley Sloan moved here and set up shop on the Meridian just north of the CPR tracks, handling Oliver, Cockshutt and Caterpillar

Above: A colourized photo of the W. W. Sloan farm machinery dealership in 1930. "Not many people had telephones in those days," recounts Sylvia Fisher, (in photo as child with white top) "and I remember how the farmers would knock on our doors in the middle of the night, after working all day, until my Dad would throw open the upstairs window and ask what they wanted. If Dad had the part they needed in stock, he would dress and go to the shop and get it. If not, he would order it and tell them that he would hang it on the gate post by Friday night, or whatever the day. That old gate post saved us many disturbed sleeps. There was little money in circulation in the 1930's and the farmers paid their bills mainly in produce. I can remember going on collection trips with my Dad and we would return with the back seat of our 29 Chev load with milk, honey, butter, buttermilk, wood, meat, whatever was available that trip. Needless to say, we were never cold or hungry, like some families I remember."

The individuals in the photo are (l-r): Sylvia Sloan, W. W. Sloan, Doris Sloan, Mr. Rich and Harold Wilmot (in rear doorway, employees at the dealership) and Mr. Cottle, a salesman for the Oliver machinery company.

Above middle: John Tingley (left) was Lloydminster's John Deere dealer from 1957 to 1977. Solid product lines and innovative marketing via such things as the annual John Deere Day, featuring a free "picture show", supported Tingley as he grew the business into one of Lloydminster's leading suppliers of farm equipment.

Above lower: Cameron Kay (right) manages Agland today. For almost 80 years, the business, and its ancestors, has provided a line of green farm machinery. During that time, the size of machinery has increased considerably (inset left).

Photo courtesy of Ken Kay.

Photos courtesy of Foster Learning Inc.

equipment. Mr. Sloan suffered a stroke in 1935 and his son-in-law, John Davis, took over, converting to John Deere. John Tingley bought the business in 1957 and managed it for the next 20 years.

In 1977, Mr. Tingley offered partnerships to two employees: Bert Dyce and Ken Kay. Dyce soon left due to poor health and Ken Kay and his brother, Chuck, took over, renaming the business, Agland, and moving it to a location one mile west of Lloydminster on Highway 16. It grew to be one of the largest and most successful farm machinery dealerships in Western Canada, adding Vermilion and St. Paul outlets as well.

Ken Kay saw many changes in more than 40 years in the industry. One of the more obvious was the increased size of farm equipment. Field equipment went from 8 to 14 feet in width to 36 to 42 feet and beyond. Tractor and combine sizes increased proportionately. Another trend increased operator comfort by adding climate controlled cabs complete with radio, stereo and CD players. On board computers provide feedback on the equipment and can provide production statistics related to precise field locations derived from satellite generated GPS information. Today, Ken Kay's son, Cameron, manages Agland and like the farmers he serves, keeps a vigilant eye on commodity prices and the weather, two key determinates in their success and his.

Another key player in the farm machinery business is Agrifuture Equipment Ltd., established in 1976 by Vern Belsheim and Stan Parke. They began as distributers for haying equipment produced by Haybuster Manufacturing. Their first office was a rented ATCO trailer. Haybuster expanded into grain handling equipment and then an early "zero till" drill which surged in sales in the late 1970's and launched Agrifuture into the farm machinery business on a large scale. In 1979, Agrifuture took on the Ford tractor line and in 1982, shortly after Stan Parke had left the business to start a dealership in Vermilion, Agrifuture expanded again. When Massey Ferguson dealer, Sam Herman, retired from the business, Agrifuture added their respected line of tractors and combines. Unfortunately, Massey Ferguson ended in receivership in 1987, leaving Agrifuture with no product to sell.

As manufacturing companies went through mergers and acquisitions, and farm commodity prices rose and fell, Agrifuture expanded to a 17,000 square foot facility. They handled the Ford New Holland line until May 1999, when the industry was stunned to see Case IH (itself a merger of Case and International Harvester) merge with Ford New Holland, becoming the world's second largest manufacturer of farm machinery. The largest was John Deere, which intensified Agrifuture's cross town rivalry with Agland as Lloydminster's major farm equipment suppliers.

Above: Holt's Farm and Feed Supply's sign (left inset) drew attention to their business on 51 St. near 52 Ave. (centre) EXL Milling Ltd. opened their production plant in August of 1997. They produce all vegetable, all natural, protein and fat supplements for beef and dairy cattle, plus a new product for swine. Canola meal, purchased from the local ADM plant, is an important ingredient in the foods EXL produces.

Photo courtesy of Jack McGuffie

Above: A. F. Pals operated an early creamery, marketing milk and butter.

Photo credits: Top: Holt's Sign courtesy of Lloydminster Regional Archives, EXL plant by Foster Learning Inc.; cattle at Vee Tee Feeders, by Don Whiting.
Bottom: Background, Threshing on the Smith Rackham Farm in 1909, courtesy of Ronald Rackham; Foreground, combining on Hasting's Farm in 1999, by Don Whiting.

Tuplin's Sand and Gravel

In 1956, Frank Tuplin moved his gravel and excavating business from Maidstone to Lloydminster. The time seemed right as the town was growing steadily, and there was paving and excavating to be done. Among the projects was the construction of the Yellowhead Highway running through town, called "The Million Dollar Mile", by some local residents concerned about its cost.

Tuplin's business won contracts not only for work in the city, but also small government jobs and municipal road work. Tuplin's business kept growing, and his wife, Evelyn, remained a supportive partner, raising their family and helping to keep the operation running smoothly.

Despite the fact that Frank was in direct competition with Charles McKay, they worked well together. There was more than enough work for both businesses to stay healthy. When McKay sold out, Tuplin purchased some of the equipment, increasing his trucks to ten and loaders to five. The difficulty was finding enough drivers to keep up to the demand. Often, men were hired from the paving companies during slack periods or even in the morning before their regular shifts.

In 1975, the Tuplins sold their equipment at auction and Feldspar emerged as the leading company in the sand,

Photos (Inset) Frank Tuplin; (Background) Lloydminster Regional Archives.

Above: Charles McKay's operation (shown c. 1955) was on the north side of Highway 16 near the present 56 Ave. Inset: Frank and Evelyn Tuplin's success enabled them to purchase some of McKay's equipment and expand.

gravel and excavating business. Frank Tuplin, along with former employee Rod Sellers, and his father Jim Sellers, undertook another business venture. Bill and John Skinner were closing their Recreational Vehicle (R.V.) business so Sellers and Tuplin R.V. Centre was established on the former site of Tuplin's Sand and Gravel.

Universal Industries

During the oil boom of the 1940's, Hoskins and Gallagher was founded. In addition to their oilfield work, the company also manufactured snow ploughs, asphalt tanks, crude oil storage tanks, television masts, and playground equipment. In 1951, the company merged with Eastern Alberta Engineers, and it became known as Universal Industries Ltd. Well known driller, Charlie Mills was one of the key stockholders.

A series of presidents oversaw the company, with W. A. Thorpe assuming control in 1962. In 1971, Howard Geier, a Petroleum Engineer previously with Husky Oil, purchased the company from Thorpe and concentrated on serving the exacting needs of the heavy oil and tar sands industry. In 1972, Edward Brauer joined the company as a shareholder.

From 1972 to 1981, the company expanded greatly with a fabricating plant in Camrose, Alberta, and sales offices in Houston, TX, Denver, CO and Los Angeles, CA.

Photo courtesy of Universal Industries

Above: One of the hundreds of fabricated items produced by Universal Industries Corp., this one a 12 x 60 Fletcher Reverse Flow Free Water Knockout Unit, leaves Lloydminster for installation at a battery near Hayter, Alberta.

Revenue peaked at $48 million per year and total staff was approximately 400 personnel.

With the implementation of the so-called National Energy Policy, the company was forced to downsize dramatically emerging in 1982 with only a Calgary sales office and the Lloydminster fabrication facility and 250 personnel. Edward Brauer became the president and major shareholder. Upon the departure of F. W. James and retirement of L. A. Nordquist (a 35 year employee) in 1987, Brauer remained as the sole owner of Universal Industries Ltd. until 1998 when the company was sold to a group of private investors from Calgary.

Universal Industries is recognized as a leader in Western Canada, in design and construction of heavy oil treating systems, and in a wide range of industrial and oil-related equipment components.

Photo by Foster Learning Inc.

The Industrial Park

Although many residents were unhappy with the emissions coming out of the plant, the City had little choice in 1973 when Hill Industrial was developed. While the most desirable location was outside the city limits, the cost of installing sewer and water lines to service the plant was too high for a growing city with little money in the bank for industrial development.

However, Hill Industrial Park was only the beginning. When Universal Industries was looking for a location to expand its operation, it encouraged the City to develop another industrial park. The result was Glenn E. Nielson Industrial Park in 1979. The City bought and quickly sold 80 acres worth of lots at cost for industrial development. There were several phases to the development of the park, with phase 3 located on the south side of 62nd Street.

The industrial parks encouraged industry to come to town as there was now the necessary space and infrastructure. The development was overwhelmingly favourable for Lloydminsterites, because, with the growth of industry in the city, "the commercial/industrial tax assessment rose from 30% in 1972 to as high as 45% in recent years down to 40% in 2001," notes City Commissioner Roger Brekko. The growth of industry kept residential property taxes in check, and it allowed the City to accumulate a healthy reserve for future development and prosperity in Lloydminster.

The Heavy Oil Industry Encourages Innovation

Working with Lloydminster heavy oil has required a unique approach due to the multitude of challenges it provides. In many cases, small oil industry based businesses in the City have grown exponentially in size, because they are offering innovative solutions to dealing with one of our most valuable resources.

In 1975, for example, Larry Makelki and Ron Christie could see that there was a gap in the products and service that the heavy oil industry was receiving, and BMW Monarch became a reality. The business began with just the two partners doing oilfield sales during the day and repairing bottomhole pumps at night.

Above: Meridian Co-Generation Project . A joint project of Husky Energy and Trans-Alta Utilities, generates both electricity and steam which are used throughout the Upgrader operation.

In 1956, the U.S. firm, Greif Brothers Corp. established a steel drum facility inside the Husky Refinery compound to service the oil company's needs. A few years later, steel drum production expanded into the nickel and cobalt markets primarily for plants at Fort Saskatchewan.
In 1961, the local company entered the fibre drum market, primarily for food related products. Bob Simms was the original facility manager and in 1962, upon his retirement, John Knisley relocated from Ontario to take over the position.
The next major development took place in 1983, when the company purchased ten acres of land to construct a new fibre drum facility at the present site. In 1988, Deputy Prime Minister Don Mazankowski participated in a tree planting ceremony to mark a further $2 million expansion to include plastic drum production.
In 1996, John Knisley passed away, and John Acton, who had joined the local company in 1981, became the plant manager.
Pictured below is the steel drum facility shortly after it began operation in Lloydminster in 1956.

Photo courtesy of Lloydminster Regional Archives

Above: Metal lathe machining at a plant in Lloydminster in the early 1950's.

Below: Corlac Inc. patented the innovative Inclined Free Water Knockout System (the "Skud") -- its purpose to remove water from heavy oil, uses a unique incline to more efficiently accomplish the separation. Corlac Inc. also supplies a wide range of oilfield equipment, much of which is fabricated in their Lloydminster facility on Highway 16 west. (Inset top left: a Corlac manufactured field storage tank leaves for its assignment. Inset bottom right: Corlac head office staff with founder Dan Echino front centre, in light coloured pants.)

In the years that followed, their operation quickly grew to twenty-one stores serving Alberta, Saskatchewan, and British Columbia. The progressive cavity pump (see chapter eight) market was rapidly expanding, and, in 1992, Makelki and Christie decided to build a manufacturing facility to produce the pumps and develop innovative equipment specific to the heavy oil industry. Originally, a 5000 square foot pump manufacturing facility, the operation grew to nearly 100,000 square feet with two facilities, one in Lloydminster and the other in Medicine Hat. Weatherford Inc. bought BMW Monarch in 1997, making the company the largest single source of artificial lift equipment in the world. Of the 480 people employed by the artificial lift division in 2001, nearly half are employed at the head office in Lloydminster. Today, progressive cavity pumps are exported to many countries around the world including Brazil, Libya, and Russia.

Corlac Inc. has been another industrial innovator in the Lloydminster area. Dan Echino started the company in 1993 after working for PetroCanada for fifteen years. Corlac, a manufacturer, assembler, distributor, reconditioner and service provider of all types of production equipment to the oil and gas sector, provides patented items and products that are unique to their design, such as the state of the art Inclined Free Water Knockout, or the "Skud" as it became known.

In another example, Wayne King started his firm, Grithog Sand Control Systems, in his garage in 1986. King's intimate knowledge of the oilfield industry, from experience stemming back to his teens, allowed him

to quickly build his company, and develop a number of world class innovations in the heavy oil industry. Among the most revolutionary is a machine developed to clean sand out of oilfield tanks without disrupting production. The machine attracted attention around the world with delegates from Russia and Venezuela visiting Lloydminster in recent years to see the equipment.

Lloydminster has reaped the benefits of industry for years. A continuing flow of innovation and a solution oriented mindset have become characteristic of the local industrial sector. This heritage provides the Border City with a strong potential for future growth. The courageous entrepreneurs and the dedicated workers who have brought their dreams to reality provide a shining example of our community - bordering on greatness.

Photo courtesy of Stan Bugiera

Above: The old and the new. Custom built Peterbilt Trucks became a common site in Lloydminster over the years with the rapid advancement of industry and manufacturing. A local dealership was established in 1986 with Stan Bugiera as manager.

Feldspar Excavating & Redi-Mix has been in business in the Lloydminster area since 1978 under owner/manager Mark Kohlruss and his two brothers, Ed and Fred as partners. In the first years, the company had two front end loaders and three tandem trucks. The primary function at the time was to service the residential and commercial construction industry with excavation, grade work, and sand & gravel supply.
Their services expanded over the years to provide redi-mix concrete, concrete pumping, aggregate production, custom crushing, excavating, commercial and residential grade work, compaction equipment, snow removal, and a retail steel division. The fleet of trucks has grown to 25, along with 15 front end loaders and excavation trucks.
Below: Feldspar trucks at the construction site of the Upgrader in 1991.

Photo courtesy of Feldspar Inc.

Chapter Ten

Business Retail and Service

Research and draft writing by Dorothy Foster

Above: This photo taken in 1904 shows an early business outlet. The sign above the window reads: "LLOYDMINSTER: Hair Dressing, Shaving & Bath Room". To the left is a sign that assures patrons: "TEMPORARY PREMISES". Beside the door a sign reads: "Tobaccos, Cigars, Cigarettes, and Pipes; all of the best Quality". (Hall's Store is shown under construction in the background, just above the "Temporary premises" sign.)

Right: Scott Brothers Hardware and Hall's Department Store originally served the community as Hall, Scott, and Company. As shown here, the business was divided into two in 1906.

Right from its conception, "Lloydminster" was envisioned as a service centre for a large surrounding area. The sudden arrival of over 2,000 well-to-do settlers presented a wealth of business opportunities. This was recognized, even while the Colonists were in transit, by many a sharp eyed entrepreneur, from St. John to Saskatoon.

Locally, folks such as the Miller Brothers, and Hall and Scott, scurried to set up businesses to serve the newly arrived multitude. Lloydminster started faster and on a bigger scale than other communities and continued to promote itself as a major service centre for the growing numbers of farmers still arriving. In turn, there has always been a clear recognition that Lloydminster depends on the surrounding area for its success. Many organizations and businesses reflect this by naming themselves, "Lloydminster and District ...".

As we move into our second century, the idea of Lloydminster being a regional service centre is thought of as an exciting new prospect. Few of today's entrepreneurs know that it was an idea that began in 1902, as one of the dreams that Isaac Barr recorded in his initial publicity pamphlet, for a town he secretly hoped might be called - Barrview.

So, year after year, the businesses of Lloydminster have supplied goods and services. The presence of these retail and service outlets drew more settlers to the area and, in turn, provided a larger market allowing more businesses to establish themselves. Obviously, space does not permit a comprehensive review of the hundreds of businesses that have served our area in the first century but below are a few accounts of some of those businesses.

An Opportunity Presents Itself

Less than six months after the Colonists' arrival, the new Lloydminster had two large general stores, a post office, a telegraph office, a drugstore, a saddlery/harness shop, a carpenter's shop, three

Above: August 7, 1904 view of 49 Ave. looking north. Note sign for Minster Restaurant (right), the earliest established eatery in Lloydminster.

restaurants, and a livery stable - all established by business people eager to seize an opportunity and serve the colonists.

The Miller Brothers, accompanied by six-year old Archie, brought a skow load of supplies down the North Saskatchewan from Edmonton in June of 1903. Then, to prepare for that winter's trade, they brought 26 sleigh loads of supplies overland from Edmonton in October, a trip that took ten days.

Herbert Hall lived in Saint John, New Brunswick in 1903, and planned to take his family to the growing western town of Red Deer. However, his friend, Rev. George Lloyd, convinced him to join the trek to a brand new settlement. Originally Hall had intended to farm but the lack of supplies and services made him reconsider. Hall found

Above: (left) The Canadian Bank of Commerce had a temporary office until its pre-fabricated building was opened several years later (note - log church to the rear); (centre) the Medical Hall was the first pharmacy in Lloydminster; (right) J. E. Procter Boot and Shoe Maker, W. Johnson Butcher Shop, and Holmes and Griffiths farm implements were three early businesses

Left: Early issues of the Lloydminster Times carried many advertisements for "The Fill-Pot Store", a general store, and "Philpotts Store", a grocery store, both owned by J.S. Philpott. The shop was located in the space which had been previously occupied by the Canadian Bank of Commerce. Above: J.S. Philpott's son Dennis continued the family business into the 1930's.

The Lloydminster and District Co-operative Limited

Photo courtesy of the Lloydminster and District Co-operative Ltd.

Above: May 12, 1937 - Lloydminster, and the rest of the British Commonwealth, prepares to celebrate the Coronation of King George VI and his wife, Queen Elizabeth. The Co-op. has some elaborate displays. Centre left window display features a large replica of the coronation crown while behind the car on the right is a window display featuring the King's coronation monicker G VI R.

Organized co-operative enterprises dated back to 1844 in England. So it was that the Barr Colonists brought the idea of co-operativism to their new community. Nathaniel Jones and William Riddington organized Lloydminster's first co-operative, acquiring food, farm equipment, building materials, and other necessities for the settlers. Supplies were freighted from Saskatoon by oxen or horse drawn wagons. Soon the Miller Brothers and Herbert Hall opened private stores and the first co-operative ceased to exist. However, the idea of co-operative organization remained in the minds of the settlers.

In the early days, there were many complaints about grain and livestock marketing. The government was asked to implement a system but there was little response. Farmers began to band together, through the Saskatchewan Grain Growers Association and the United Farmers of Alberta, to jointly purchase farm supplies, such as binder twine, lumber, fence posts, nails and formalin. When the goods arrived, they were delivered to one farmer's yard, and everyone came to pick up their order.

Through the insistence of the Saskatchewan Grain Growers Association, the Agriculture Co-operative Association Act was passed in 1914. It provided the means by which co-operatively based businesses and organizations could be formed.

Twenty-four people at a meeting at the Greenwood School on June 12, 1914 committed to founding a local organization which continues today as the Lloydminster and District Co-operative Ltd. Stanley Rackham took the lead in explaining the advantages of a Co-operative to ship livestock and buy and sell goods co-operatively.

At the first meeting in Lloydminster, on August 7, 1914, Stanley Rackham was elected president and George Pensom, vice-president. Jim Almond, Ernie Burton, George Foote and Peter Sermuks were the first directors. T. A. Wright, a hard-working man of action, was the first manager

The first Co-operative building was the Billy Mackenzie stable, purchased for $100 and moved to the present site of the Home Centre, 5106 - 49 Ave., in 1915. Groceries and a complete line of supplies was stocked. In July, the Co-op bought the Northern Hardware Company building, "the best built store

Additions, Expansions, and Renovations

1914: Billy Mackenzie's stable purchased for $100 and relocated to the present site of the Co-op Home Centre.

1918: George Greening's store purchased; Northern Hardware Company Building purchased for $31,610.

1928: An addition to the Northern Hardware building enabled the Co-op to house all departments under one roof.

1929: The Great Fire destroyed all Co-op buildings except the Lumberyard; the Britannia Hotel property was purchased and used until a new building was constructed in 1930.

1934: A Hillmond Branch was established

1952: The Lloydminster store was re-decorated

1954: A new wing added for the sale of furniture and appliances.

1958: The Co-op Drug Department opened; a new building was erected for the lumberyard; a bulk fuel plant was established.

1960: The store building completely renovated: 10,000 square feet added to the basement to stock merchandise, more checkouts in the grocery department, and air conditioning added.

1962: The Barber Shop and Beauty Salon were added.

1973: The Noyes, McRae, Floor-On, Royal Café, and Locker Plant properties were purchased for the Co-op's expansion, including a new food store and parking lot, and enlargements and enhancements to the department store.

1980: The Co-op Parkade opened.

1983: Expansion of commercial space under the parkade and renovations to the Co-op Mall completed.

1986: The Legion Hall purchased and moved, and a major renovation to the shopping centre took place.

1987: The Co-op Shopping Centre renamed "The Heritage Centre"

2000: The grocery store moved to Highway 17 at 36th Street. Extensively renovated facility offered customers a modern shopping environment to meet increasing competition.

in town", giving the Co-op a solid store front presence.

After World War I, many problems surfaced within the organization. The pains of accounting, communication between the Board and manager, and employee benefits were hampering progress. T. A. Wright resigned and Howard Jones became the

Photos courtesy of the Lloydminster and District Co-operative Ltd.

After Davidson's retirement, James L. Kinney assumed leadership but by 1953 communication problems once again plagued the staff, administration and Board, leading to the resignation of several managers in succession.

On September 1st, 1957, Leon Doucet was hired as manager for the Lloydminster Co-op. He had been Operations Manager of the Saskatoon Co-op. for three years. Doucet quickly reorganized and modernized departments. Doucet stayed on in his post for twenty-eight years, retiring in 1985. He is well remembered for his contributions to the success of the business.

Continuing renovations and additions kept the Co-op departments modern. Technology was updated, with new cash registers, credit cards were accepted, computer systems installed, and the first bar code scanning system in a Western Canadian Co-operative was adopted. A decision in 1973 to keep the Co-op. downtown led to the purchase of several neighboring properties, opening the way for further expansions. Eventually, the need for more parking space justified the construction of a parkade. Mayor Matheson opened the facility by driving through the ribbon on June 12, 1980. One thousand people were there to show their support and enthusiasm for the Co-op's initiative.

Later in the 1980's, downtown businesses faced strong competition as the Lloyd Mall lured many shoppers to their stores. Then Superstore and later the Power Centre provided additional competition. In 2000, the Co-op. Board decided to take over the space previously occupied by the Canadian Tire Store on Highway 17 and 36th Street. Renovations were made and the Co-op moved into a modern facility, including a pharmacy, bakery, and deli, in addition to the spacious grocery store.

In 2001, Shirley Patmore succeeded Rudy Jurke as President, becoming the first female to hold that post. She plans educational efforts based on the ideals of co-operativism as a way of highlighting the current presence of the Lloydminster and District Co-operative Ltd., and the key part it has played in our unique history.

Above: Co-op. moments: (Top left): Doug Manners (left) and wife Helen receive a long service award from Ray Harmel for 19 years on the Board (1971-1990). (Top right): Joe Eddleston served 18 years on the Co-op Board (1969 - 1987). (Bottom left): (l-r) Alex Sokalofsky, Wilma Groenen, Art Gellert, and Doug Manners were all instrumental in the production of the local Co-op's "Reflections of 75 Years". (Bottom right): 1990 Board of Directors (standing l-r): Ray Harmel, Howard Barnsley, Alex Sokalofsky, Jim Long, Ilston Plant, Mary Holtby, Bill Rekrutiak. (Seated l-r): Harry Brudler (GM), Norbert Koch (President), and Ronald Rackham (son of first Co-op. President, Stanley Rackham (1914-1919).

new manager. Howard had been an administrator of the local hospital and was a whiz at numbers and finances. He re-established confidence quickly, and by giving a 5% patronage bonus, business grew steadily.

"The Great Fire" of 1929 decimated the Co-op. properties. Manager Scotty Davidson's dogged persistence was needed to acquire a loan of $15,000, from the Bank of Commerce in Regina, in order to re-build. The Co-operators of Saskatchewan would later honour Scotty for his leadership of the Lloydminster and District Agricultural Co-operative Association and his contribution to the Saskatchewan Co-operative Wholesale Society. Scotty retired from the local Co-op. in March 1948, aged 73.

Photos courtesy of the Lloydminster and District Co-operative Ltd.

The Co-op Parkade (background) opened June 12, 1980 with Mayor Kay Matheson (top inset) driving through the ribbon (bottom inset).

Photo courtesy of the Lloydminster and District Co-operative Ltd.   *Photo courtesy of the Lloydminster and District Co-operative Ltd.*   *Photo by Don Whiting*

The Lloydminster Co-op. underwent many facelifts over the years including the Co-op Centre in 1973 (left), the Heritage Centre in 1987 (centre), and the Co-op Marketplace in 2000 (right).

> Every public and semi-public service which a modern, progressive people will demand is found in the Town of Lloydminster.
>
> Day and night phone service with extensive rural and long distance connections, Municipal Hospital, modern new public school and high school, five churches, Dominion Public Building, Drill Hall. The up-to-date electric plant is operated by Midwest Utilities, a subsidiary company of the International Utilities of New York.. Adequate fire fighting apparatus safeguards the town. Six grain elevators, also a flour mill of 125 barrel daily capacity, two creameries, Weekly Newspaper, two chartered banks, and good hotel accommodations will be found here.
>
> All the lines of business required in the marketing centre of a thriving, agricultural district will be found in Lloydminster, while the facilities for quick repair and replacement of agricultural machinery and automobile parts are the envy of towns not so well served.
>
> **Lloydminster Board of Trade Promotional Pamphlet, 1928**

Photo courtesy of the Glenbow Archives PD-313-131

The Alberta Hotel opened its doors to travellers in 1906. Originally, a one story building, its first owners were Donald Irwin and Andy Hudson. The hotel was located on 50th Avenue and 51st Street where it still stands today. Unfortunately, the original building was burnt in 1977 in a tragic fire, but a new building was constructed. Today, the Alberta Hotel is the longest running business still in operation in Lloydminster. The above photo was taken in 1948.

Photo courtesy William Noyes

Above: R.J.R. Noyes Ltd. - winter 1955.

a partner in George Scott of Edmonton, and Hall, Scott, and Company opened a general store in early 1904. In 1906, Hall and Scott divided their business. Hall ran a grocery and dry goods store, and George Scott, and his brother Bert, operated a hardware store, under the name of the Scott Brothers.

The Canadian Bank of Commerce became the first bank in Lloydminster, opening on June 10, 1904, under manager Sam Daly. A bank was seen as a very important addition to the community. By 1910, the Commerce moved into a pre-fabricated structure, shipped from Vancouver, designed to provide the Bank identical buildings across the prairies. The Canadian Imperial Bank and the Royal Bank also established branches here in the early years.

The Family Business

Many local businesses were family businesses spanning a number of generations and becoming integral parts of Lloydminster's history. Samuel Noyes, for example, came as an 18 year old Barr Colonist and later urged his brothers, Herbert and Rowley, to come as well.

By 1921, Rowley decided to sell his homestead and go into the automotive business. In 1924, Rowley's 17 year old son, Bob (he shared his father's initials of R.J.R.) began working for his father as a mechanic and taxi driver. In 1929, Bob decided to go into business himself and established the North Star Service Station north of the tracks (50 Ave. & 54 St.). His business was known as S.O.S. No. 2 - the S.O.S. for "Sign of Service." In 1934, Bob leased the Texaco Station on the corner of 50th Ave. and 51st Street, and sold automobiles and J. I. Case farm machinery. In 1944, he purchased the lot and would operate the business there until 1974 when he sold the property to the Co-op. Noyes moved to a site on the Meridian south of the Yellowhead, which had been the farm yard of Barr Colonists William and Alice Rendell.

Bob married Bessie Jane Hickey, R.N., of Leduc Alberta, in 1933, and together they had two sons, Bob and Bill. From 1935 to 1945, Noyes had the Chrysler Agency, and in 1942, he took on the General Motors Agency. Having two agencies during World War II allowed

Bob to better meet the strong demand for automobiles as much factory production had been converted to producing military vehicles. Cars were effectively rationed to each dealer. Having the GM dealership was the highlight of R.J.R. Noyes' career. He was to maintain his association with General Motors for more than 50 years.

Sons, Bob and Bill, joined their father in the late 1950's. The business also created long term employment. Several employees served 30 to 40 years with the company. R.J.R. said of his employees, "They're the backbone of our business." R. J. R. Noyes Ltd. is now in its new location, on the corner of College Drive and Highway 17, which officially opened in July 2000. With a staff of forty, Bill, and fourth generation Dennis and Brent Noyes are proudly continuing the tradition of selling and servicing vehicles.

Similarly, brothers Ted and Irving Steeg began, "Smiling Serv-

Photos: Left courtesy of Lloydminster Regional Archives; Right, by Don Whiting

ice", a Texaco garage in 1951. The brothers later built a modern Esso with a two-bay garage, restaurant, and overnight sleeping quarters for truckers. Situated on the west end of town, the Steegs began selling Volkswagens in 1957 and those automobiles were a great hit.

Ted's oldest son, Bob, following in his father's footsteps, opened Steeg Motor Sales in 1979, selling used cars and trucks. In 2000, Bob closed his business and joined the team at Ulmer Chev-Olds.

Above left: Aerial view of the Ulmer Chev-Olds dealership opened in 1992 on Highway 17 south. The area has become an "auto-mile" with dealerships: Silverwood Toyota, Boundary Ford and R.J.R. Noyes Ltd. in the immediate area. Denham Dodge-Chrysler operates on Highway 17 north.

Upper right: Skinner Motors was opened in 1941 by Edward Skinner and his sons Bill and John. In 1946, they were appointed as the Lloydminster Mercury dealer by Ford Motor Company. In 1948, Skinner Motors moved from its location on the corner of Highway 16 and 17 to a new building shown here, at 49th Avenue and 49th Street.

Far left: R.J.R. Noyes speaking to a community group, c. 1955. Noyes gave more than fifty years of community service to Lloydminster, as an active Kinsmen member; Exalted Ruler of the Elks (three terms), President of the Alexandra Constituency Social Credit Association, and Town Councillor from 1946 to 1954 under Mayors G. L. Cooke and Robert Shaw. R.J.R. was on Council when the water and sewer system was installed, and when the curbs and gutters and the first street paving were done on the Meridian.

Left: R.J.R. Noyes congratulates Ross Ulmer at the grand opening of the new Ulmer Chevrolet facility in 1992. Ross and Doug Ulmer expanded their family business from North Battleford to Lloydminster in 1987, purchasing Cavalier Chevrolet Oldsmobile Ltd. which had been operated by Ed and Barb Gulka at the corner of Highway 16 and 59 Ave. since 1974. In 1993, the Ulmers, seeing no import dealership in Lloydminster started Silverwood Toyota to carry their popular lines. Today Ulmer's employs 45 people locally and carries an inventory of over 450 vehicles. The company also operates six auto dealerships across the mid-west and caters to the changing tastes in vehicle preference. Lloydminster has always provided a strong market for light trucks and they still account for 55% of sales. Mini-vans are another strong seller while luxury cars have almost disappeared, replaced in part by $65,000 9-passenger Suburbans.

The Phillips' Tradition

In 1927, John Christie, from Kitscoty, who owned Outfitter and War Surplus stores in Edmonton, Winnipeg and Lloydminster, retired and Roy Phillips, an employee, and Dr. G. L. Cooke bought the Lloydminster store.

Phillips had to extend credit to customers in the early days. Farmers, for example, had money to buy after harvest in the fall but by Christmas there often would be no money left. Mr. Phillips would carry their accounts until they could afford to pay them off. If a pair of boots was needed, a fellow would be fitted and the cost recorded as a receivable. People appreciated this considerate service and almost always honoured their debts. "The merchants, in those times were literally financing the country," George Phillips remarks.

During World War II, Roy had little part time help, and his sons George, Bob, Bill and Doug were expected to work in the store after school and Saturdays. George later decided to take a manager trainee session in Edmonton. This led to a job with the Hudson's Bay Co. in Port Alberni, B. C. in 1945. After a year and a half, George was offered a more lucrative job with the Woodward's store. However, in the fall of 1948, Roy asked his son to join him in the business back home in Lloydminster.

In 1949, George married Dorothy Rose from Lucky Lake, and he and his new wife became immersed in learning each element of the business. In 1965, Roy Phillips was killed in a car accident. George and Dorothy continued the business on their own, working diligently to expand by stocking a greater selection of merchandise.

George carried on his father's courtesies to his customers. It was usual for the store to have $20,000 on hand, ready to cash cheques for their customers who could not make it to the bank in time. The oil men would come off shift at 4:30, well after the banks closed. They would want to have their cheques cashed, so would stop in to Phillips', pay off their accounts, buy more items, and pocket the rest.

By the 1970's, George felt that the company needed a new image, and he opened another store, targeted at younger people. "Man's World" selling men's and ladies' sports wear, casual clothing, and formal dress, opened its doors with Norval Mallet as manager and three staff members.

George and Dorothy sold the business and retired in 1994. Their daughter, Joanne Berry, took on the challenge of continuing a Phillips' Clothing Store by taking over "Man's World". Her friend, Wendy Strilchuk, lent a hand and soon they yearned for more display space.

Joanne looked across the street at the corner building that her dad owned and she dreamed of setting up shop there. In a year it became a reality. The building was remodelled to have the same Phillips' friendly atmosphere, including her Grandfather's oak desk and chair, his oak filing cabinet with its shallow drawers and the famous pot-bellied stove. Joanne chose the name "Cornerstone." The stone structure was solid, had a local tradition, and was on a corner. "Cornerstone Clothiers" was just right for depicting the tone of the third generation!

Phillips' stores have journeyed through the changing times, following the many directions of fashion and fulfilling the needs of hundreds of customers, always keeping with the same level of friendly service and principles of good business. Today, Joanne Berry embraces them all, and they are firmly carved in the **"Cornerstone."**

Photos: b&w courtesy of George Phillips, colour by Foster Learning Inc.

Incorporated in 1929, R. H. Phillips Co. Ltd. carried items from work clothes to formal wear. Phillips' selection was one of the largest in Western Canada. Roy (centre in main photo) welcomed customers whether they came in to buy or just to chat. Many people, even today, remember people sitting on the long bench, while they visited by the warmth of the potbellied stove which had a central location in the store. Inset left: George maintained the courteous service of Phillips' menswear for almost 45 years. Inset right: Joanne Berry continues the tradition in her new store by preserving the past as symbolized by the proud role of the original pot bellied stove.

The Lloydminster Credit Union built its own buiding on the corner of 50th Street and 49th Avenue which opened for business on December 22nd, 1958. (Left inset): On June 1st, 1971, the Lloydminster Credit Union moved once again into new quarters at 4907 - 50th Street. (Right inset): Board of Directors in 1969 (back row l-r): Bob Jack, Llue Hanson, Norman Nielsen, John Hoegl, Jack Whiting. (front row l-r): George Baynton, Jr., Ernest Holman, Hardy Salt, Colin Wright.

Above: Serving over 30 years as General Manager, Peter J. Gulak (left) was instrumental in the formation and success of the Border Credit Union Ltd. Today, the Border Credit Union continues in the spirit of Gulak's community support with current General Manager Jeff Mulligan. In 2001, BCU took over the accounts of the local Bank of Montreal, a further sign of the remarkable growth of our local credit unions. Both Border Credit Union and the Lloydminster Credit Union contribute to a wide range of community projects, from the proposed Multiplex sports facility and the Vic Juba Community Theatre to student and club grants and awards.

The Credit Union

On September 21, 1943, (only six years after legislation permitted credit unions in Saskatchewan) the Lloydminster Credit Union opened its doors to the public. It began with only 25 members but grew rapidly and by 1944 loan limits had increased from $100 to $500. The institution was a leader in giving back to the community, and provided an example for other businesses to follow.

There were several moves in its first few years. Originally, the Lloydminster Credit Union operated out of the Co-op. store, and was open to the public only two afternoons per week. In 1947, the office moved to the Stuart Wright Building on 50th Ave. 49th St. before returning to the Co-op. and setting up a full time office in the basement.

In 1955, major changes happened at the Credit Union. Due to differing provincial legislation, a charter was obtained for the Border Co-operators' Savings and Credit Union Ltd. to serve Alberta side residents. However, the two Credit Unions continued to operate out of one building with one manager but two boards of directors.

The first Credit Union building was built in 1958, and both Credit Unions occupied one half of the main floor. As both continued to grow, the Border Credit Union moved to the basement. One of the Lloydminster Credit Union's early employees, Peter Gulak, became the first manager of the

When the Wager boys were called to war in 1942, Frank Long and family came to Lloydminster to take over their bakery on a temporary basis. Eventually, the Wager family sold the bakery to Frank and it was renamed "Long's Bakery and Confectionery." One of their largest jobs was to bake "dozens and dozens of loaves of bread" for nightly delivery via the C.P.R. to outlying communities. Clockwise from bottom left: 1) The original Wager's Bakery and Confectionery with David Wager; 2) Long's Bakery kitchen; 3) Frank and Millie Long in later years; Background: The bakery interior.

Photos courtesy of Sylvia Fisher

Photo courtesy of John Griffith

Border Credit Union in 1962. In over 30 years as Manager, Mr. Gulak recommended many people for loans on the basis of their character, even if their financial situation did not look promising at the time. He also stressed that the Credit Union should assist the community of which it was a part. With Peter Gulak's guidance, the Border Credit Union grew to be one of the largest and most successful credit unions in Canada.

Service Above and Beyond the Call of Duty

A long time landmark at the city's northern entrance, North Side Service was opened by Roland and Olive Lawson in 1954. When Mr. Lawson broke his foot in 1957, he approached a young neighbour - John Griffith, to help him by pumping gas.

In 1966, Dean Lawson bought the business from his parents and John, now a certified mechanic, became his partner. In 1969, they decided to sell motorcycles and the increasingly popular snowmobiles. Business was good, and in 1975, they added a Sporting Goods Shop that specialized in hunting and fishing equipment. Richard Pinske, who had a passion for outdoor sports, was the manager. For years, people enjoyed stopping in for supplies and a chat before they headed out to the lake.

In 1978, John Griffith and his wife Louise, who did the bookkeeping, bought Dean's share of the business. When the fifteen year lease with Shell expired, they bought the building, giving them more independence in operating the business. In December, 2000, John sold the business and retired. He was well known by his customers who appreciated the quality service and the honesty and integrity. "Making money isn't everything in life," Griffith remarked looking back on the many friends he and his wife made in business over the years. Shell Canada recognized John's 43 years at North Side Service with a simple plaque, while John's customers and friends remember the exceptional service above and beyond the call of duty.

Keeping Lloydminster Wired
Over 50 Years of Service from Harris Electric

Harris Electric began in Lloydminster in 1948.

Ron Harris (right) with a salesman. Alf Harris is seen in the background (far left).

Televisions went on sale in 1957, three years before Lloydminster even had a television station.

Alf Harris (left), Ron Harris (second from right), Gordon Harris (right)

All photos courtesy of Gordon Harris

In the original store, a wide range of 78 rpm records were displayed (above background), making Harris Electric Lloydminster's first record shop. A 1954 advertisement in the Lloydminster Times proudly proclaimed, "We have more ideas on music than the Public Library has books. Stop in, you'll find our selection of radios, records, record players and high fidelity equipment the most complete in Lloydminster."

Harris and Derraugh began operations in Lloydminster in 1948 with a contract from Shogust Construction of Saskatoon to wire 50 "war time" houses being built south of 44th Street on the Saskatchewan side. In 1950, Ron Harris purchased the shares of his partner, Doug Derraugh, and the firm became Harris Electric Co. Ltd. In 1957, brother Alf Harris moved to Lloydminster and joined the company to assist with the many rural electrification projects. By this time, a retail store at 4910 - 50th Avenue sold a wide variety of electronics. In the late 1960's, Alf and Ron divided operations into two divisions with Alf concentrating on Electrical Installations and Ron looking after Electronics and Retail.

Ron Harris Sr. was very much a part of his community and contributed significantly. He was a member of the Chamber of Commerce, a Rotary member and president (1981-1982), Lions' Citizen of the Year in 1987, Commanding Officer of the Lloydminster Air Cadets, and one of the founders of the Thorpe Recovery Centre.

In 1970, Ron's sons, Gordon and Ivan, became shareholders and concentrated on electrical contracting, providing quality service in all aspects of the electrical industry. In 1985, Gordon and his wife, Bev, bought Ivan's shares and became sole owners of the family business.

Since then, the company has expanded. In 1989, Gordon formed Teldata Communications to sell and install business telephone systems and computer network cabling, much of which has moved away from copper wires to fibre optics. Gordon and his staff have taken courses in Calgary, Vancouver and Winnipeg, in design and engineering for certification. Harris Electric has installed telephone systems for such businesses as: Nelson Lumber, Border Credit Union, and Weatherford.

The staff of 14 and the Harris family are a closely knit team. Together they enjoy social occasions, such as their summer barbecues. The rapid growth of Lloydminster continues to provide Harris Electric with opportunities to expand and grow with it.

Allen's Dairy Freez

It was the 1950's and the fast food industry was about to explode. Sellers' Dairy Freez was a popular Lloydminster eatery serving ice cream dishes, fish and chips, and burgers. One day a beat-up Nash station wagon pulled in off the highway. The driver came in and asked owner Jim Sellers if he would like to try some fried chicken. When Sellers agreed, the grey-haired man hauled in some pots and pans and cooked a chicken. Sellers liked the outcome and on a handshake with the stranger became only the second Kentucky Fried Chicken franchisee in Western Canada. The man was Harlan Saunders.

In October, 1967, Ilston Plant and Jack Allen purchased Sellers Dairy Freez. Three years later, the building was destroyed by fire caused by a lightning hit. A new building was erected and Plant and Allen were back in business again by November 29, 1970.

The new construction and equipment meant large personal loans. It was soon apparent that only by having one owner, drawing one salary, could the business remain solvent. In December 1972, Ilston Plant sold his share of the business to Jack Allen, and the restaurant's name was changed to Allen's Dairy Freez Ltd.

Jack and Elaine Allen began to monitor every phase of the business, seeing patterns in daily sales. This led to efficient planning and savings in the budget. The Allens built and maintained a business with the largest volume of sales in the West.

Above: Colonel Saunders poses proudly with the entire Allen family. L to R: Betty, Barbara, Elaine, Harlan Saunders, Jack, Shelley, and Brenda.

Above: (l-r) Gwenda Johnston, Brenda Allen and Pat Gallagher; ready to make your favourite shake. Jack and Elaine gave many young people a chance to learn and grow. Jack says, "It was good to see a person make something of his or her life."

Colonel Harlan Saunders returned to Lloydminster several times. He was a kind, gentle man, who loved people. When he died, eight franchisees from Western Canada, including the Allens, chartered a Leer jet to Louisville to attend his funeral.

In 1977, Jack built a second restaurant on Highway 16, but was ordered to sell only KFC products. The Allens met with other franchise holders and it was decided they would go to court to settle the matter, not only for themselves, but for the others. After 2 ½ years, they won the case, resulting in a more flexible contract for all franchisees.

In 1987, Jack bought the Esso Station adjoining his property. In 1996, after 29 years of serving the people of Lloydminster, Jack and Elaine retired.

The Allens are remembered for their dedication to a set of high principles that they shared with the Colonel and for guiding many young people to pursue those same principles.

On August 6, 1996, KFC was open for business under new operators, Wendy and Barry Gunn. They soon began constructing a new sit-in restaurant on the adjoining property, which opened April 1, 1997. At the official opening of the new KFC, the Gunns invited the Sellers, the Plants, and the Allens to join in celebrating a new chapter in the long history of serving a menu featuring some "mighty fine chicken".

Colonel Harlan Saunders made several visits to Lloydminster. A generous man, the Colonel contributed to many charities across North America. Left; Doreen Plant and Elaine Allen (perhaps Doreen had an even better recipe?? :) Centre, Jack Allen and cattle buyer Marshall Tindall (maybe the Colonel could try Kentucky Fried Beef-Kabobs?? :) Right: Jack Allen gets hands-on guidance from the Colonel as to how to make gravy.

Mert McCaw opened his funeral home (left) beside the Co-op Creamery in 1958. Since then, McCaw Funeral Service Ltd. has helped many Lloydminster families in their time of greatest need. Mert was killed in an automobile accident in 1959, and his wife Helen continued the funeral home until Dave McCaw (centre), who had been working for his parents for several years, purchased the business in 1964. After a fire destroyed the building in 1967, Dave purchased the Moore Funeral Home, on the Alberta side, from Walter Thorpe. The McCaws have helped people through difficult times for more than forty years. A third generation of McCaws became involved in the business in recent years. Right: Sons Glen and Dale pose with Dave (left) and Bob McCaw (second from left).

Harry Creech (2nd from left) has roots back to the Barr Colonists, his Grandparents George and Mary Creech. After operating a funeral home in Wainwright for many years, Harry and his wife Alva (3rd from left) opened a facility here with the help of their adult children, Todd (left) and Kimberly (right).

Photos: Top inset courtesy of Carol and Lloyd Doucette; others by Foster Learning Inc.

Lloyd and Carol Doucette took over a fur clothing sales and repair shop in 1976 but a 1983 fire destroyed everything. With hard work and dedication, the couple rebounded with 50th Street Fashions (top inset), recognized for style and service. Fashion Hut (background photo of window display) first opened in the Lloyd Mall on September 1st, 1980. Owner Marilyn Lowenberg has won the loyalty of customers with leading fashions and the respect of her staff, including store junior, Janice Lay, (bottom insert) with sixteen years of service.

Left: Hard work led to success for Amador and Theresa Lopez. When the couple arrived in Lloydminster from Spain, in 1976, they had little money, but their persistence paid off. Originally, the Lopez' owned the Lloydminster Motel. Over the years, they expanded their operations to include David's Steak House, Amigo's Night Club and Lounge, Arby's Restaurants, A & T Car Wash, and Family Garden Restaurant.

Above: Alex and Joyce Essar opened Essar's Jewellery downtown in 1954. Alex describes himself as "always a tinkerer ... No matter what kind of watch, clock, meter, or instrument, I had to try to fix it by taking it apart." The Essars' store closed its doors in 1991 after 37 years of faithfully serving their customers. More recent jewelry stores include Richardson's, owned by Juergen Schwenk who joined the company in 1981, and the recently expanded People's, managed by Wayne Fisher. Both stores are located in the Lloyd Mall.

Musgraves Find a Home

Bill and Ann Musgrave, with their young family, relocated from Shaunavon, Sask. in 1978 to continue their Real Estate and Development business. They wanted a community large enough to offer development opportunities and small enough that a credible reputation mattered. Otto Hvidston and his family, and Greg Hilderman, also from Shaunavon came to join the firm. Hilderman, managed the Insurance Department and later became a partner in the firm. "We're a one-stop place. We can identify your need, and we can take it from beginning to end," Greg remarks of the reason for Musgrave Agencies' success.

Musgrave Agencies Ltd. has remained a family business. After completing university, son Scott chose to return to Lloydminster to raise his family and run the real estate arm of the business. Son Kevin, after receiving his degree in Architecture, worked for four years in Dallas, Texas, before he too decided to return to work in the land development and com-

Photo courtesy of the Glenbow Archives NA-303-77

Above: One of the earliest real estate firms in Lloydminster was Johns and Thompson. Descendant Tom Johns was in the real estate and insurance business for over 50 years.

mercial construction division. The company first took on land development in 1983 as a result of the shortage of a consistent supply of residential lots for house builders. Their slogan was, "If we can't find it, we'll build it." They began providing well-planned residential neighborhoods and commercial sub-divisions as well as retail, commercial and industrial sites. Another arm of Musgrave Agencies, property management, services many of the developed properties. Southridge Mall, for example, is a large retail complex held by Musgraves and partners, and has maintained a high occupancy rate.

A highly successful entrepreneur, Bill Musgrave, sums up his business this way: "Lloydminster has and continues to provide as much opportunity as we are capable of handling in our family company. We feel very fortunate to have chosen Lloydminster in 1978. We have been blessed over the years with an excellent, long-term staff and a client base that has made the hours and the effort continually rewarding."

Photo courtesy of Charles Lamb Photography

The Musgrave Team 2000. Standing (l-r): Kevin Hauth, Lane Columbine, Dave Schobert, Larry McConnell, Brian Smart, and Ron Fleming. Seated (l-r): Leslee Coolidge, Kevin Musgrave, Eileen Heltman, Ann & Bill Musgrave, Laurie Kykkanen, Scott Musgrave, and Marion Piper.

Restaurants

Photo courtesy of the Glenbow Archives NA-303-78

Photo by Foster Learning Inc.

Photo courtesy of Lloydminster Regional Archives

Photo by Foster Learning Inc.

There is always a need to eat. (Above left) Behind the dark horse is the famous Minster Restaurant, operated by a Mrs Portemous, from 1904. (Above centre) Tim Hortons is a popular stop in modern day Lloydminster. (Above right) The Elite Cafe, operated by the Mah family. In mid-century, Chinese families dominated the restaurant sector, operating the Royal Cafe, the National Cafe, and the Prince Charles Cafe, all popular eating and social centres. (Left) The atmosphere and decor may change but the needs remain; good food served by friendly people, in a clean environment. Here hungry history researchers Alan Griffith (centre) and Dorothy Foster (right) give their order to server Gillian Summers (left) in Louis' Restaurant.

RV Dealers

The R.V. bug bit Rod Sellers at the age of eighteen when he travelled in Europe in a friend's Volkswagen Van. "As soon as I got home, I sold my sports car, bought a van, and camperized it," he recalls.

Above: Rod Sellers (centre, with white beard) poses with his sales and service staff. (Inset): One of many popular "fifth wheel" models which tows behind a truck.

Sellers, along with his father, Jim, and partner Frank Tuplin, founded Sellers and Tuplin R.V. Center in 1978. Sellers later bought Tuplin's shares and continued the business as Sellers R.V. Center, making annual buying trips to Louisville, Kentucky to secure the best products for his customers. Rod and his wife Anne have dedicated more than 22 years to serving customers in the Lloydminster area.

Hair Salons

Hair salons have existed from our earliest days (see pg. 112). Some have served a fiercely loyal clientele for years, while others come and go in what is sometimes a volatile business sector. Through it all, treating each customer as a special person has been the secret to success.

Paulette Williams of Stephen Raye Designers styles Abbey Dmyterko's hair.

Stephen Raye Designers, for example, opened in 1986 under Paulette Williams and Bonnie Campbell. The two set out to establish a stylish salon with a comfortable decor. In 1998, Williams opted to spend more time with her family. In 1999, Bonnie Campbell, with partner Tammy Edwards, re-acquired Stephen Raye Designers. Today, the salon offers a wide range of services beyond hair styling, including: tanning, aesthetics, electrolysis, and nail technology.

Travel Agencies

The Lloydminster outlet of Carslon Wagonlit Travel is the descendent of our first travel agency which was operated by Tom Johns Ltd. in the 1940's. That business sold Greyhound, Freight, and Whitestar Steamship tickets in those early years, in addition to selling insurance and real estate. The travel component eventually took its own name, Intra-Royal Travel, and was one of the first tenants of the Lloyd Mall on November 15, 1974.

When the Lloyd Mall completed Phase Two in 1979, Intra-Royal Travel moved to the west end of the shopping center. The office also became computerized with one terminal directly connected to Air Canada and other major carriers. It was a major concern of the staff that one might inadvertently cancel someone's reservation if you hit the wrong key," remembers manager Gerry Duhaime. "Fortunately, the system was not set up this way. At this time, all airline tickets, regardless of the number of flights, were written by hand."

Duhaime bought the travel agency from Tom Johns Ltd. in 1981, and shortly after, Intra-Royal Travel was one of the first to join the Independent Travel Retail Associated Organization. During this time, Intra-Royal Travel became fully automated with four computer terminals and an electronic ticket printer.

Above (left): Grace and Sandy Hill on board a cruise ship. Cruises and bus tours were popular with Lloydminster travellers. Sandy and Grace owned Hillcrest Travel at 4806 - 50th Avenue for 17 years in the 1970's and 80's. (right): A Hillcrest Travel escorted tour travels on a bus of Lloydminster operator Glen Dudding.

Carlson Wagonlit Travel merged with Intra-Royal Travel in 1999. While each office maintained independence and ownership, they were now backed by an organization with over 4000 travel offices worldwide.

In September, 1987, Beverly Old and Leslie Fulkerth opened Business & Leisure Travel in the Southridge Mall.. The Agency opened with up-to-date terminals to serve their customers well in every phase of their desired journeys.

Beverly Old bought Leslie's share of the business in 1993. With the advancement of technology came 'electronic tickets' which allowed travellers to present the ticket agent with one single piece of paper with all flight information on it; the problem of forgetting a folder of tickets at home was eliminated.

"With all of the travel options available to people now, the world is getting smaller, making it easier to travel for pleasure or business," remarks Beverly Old.

When the Power Centre opened in 1999, Marlin Travel, located in the new Wal-Mart. The growth in Lloydminster's population and economy attracted people from a broader area and another travel agency was able to compete in the market.

Photo courtesy of the Lloyd Mall

The Lloyd Mall Comes To Town

In the early days, the core business area was centred on 50th Ave. and 50th St. However, the Lloyd Mall established a new shopping area on 44th Street. Originally the mall's anchors were The Bay and Safeway. A variety of other tenants attracted many customers who could now do their shopping all under one roof. Downtown businesses felt the sting of the newly added competition. Merchants began to recognize that shopping malls were an important trend in retailing.

Charles Lamb Photography was one of the original tenants of the Lloyd Mall. After teaching in Hay River, N.W.T., Charles, originally from the Lone Rock area, decided to begin his own photography business in Lloydminster. Rent at the mall was competitive with downtown locations at the time due to uncertainty about the mall's success. Lamb believed the trend in business was moving towards large shopping centres so the Lloyd Mall was the perfect choice for him to attract customers to his store.

Photo courtesy of tCharles Lamb

Charles Lamb, one of the original tenants in the Lloyd Mall

In 1979, the Lloyd Mall completed phase two, doubling in size. The most noteworthy new addition was Zellers. The Canadian retail giant had made in-roads in larger centres due to its buying power. Its introduction in Lloydminster meant that Border City retailers faced stiffer competition than ever before. On opening day, Zellers was jam-packed with eager customers anxious to see what the discount department store had to offer.

Photo courtesy of Bay Van Photography, (Inset courtesy of Gerald Gagnon)

Gerald Gagnon was presented the 1993 Chamber of Commerce's Small Business of the Year Award for Jerry's Towing and City Centre Auto Body.

One of Lloydminster's more unique businesses is Potpourri Window Fashions and Home Decor. It is the Culmination of a business evolution which saw its owners, Peggy and Rod Baynton, begin in farming. "We both come from entrepreneurial families, willing to take risks," says Peggy. So, they were soon selling home made jams and sauces, then wool bedding from their own sheep. To market their growing inventory of crafts, they rented space in the Wayside Plaza in 1990. Next, they expanded into gift items and added custom draperies and opened a new store in the Atrium Centre. Growing business took them back to a new and larger facility (seen here) at the Wayside Plaza in 1996. As of 2001, they focus on home decorating accents and custom draperies to serve a rapidly expanding Lloydminster.

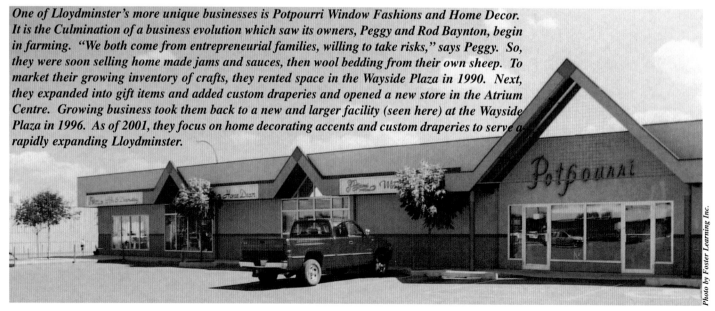

Photo by Foster Learning Inc.

Recession Hits The Border City

In the early 1980's, massive drops in crude oil prices lead to layoffs at Husky and other oil related companies in Lloydminster. Interest rates, inflation, and unemployment were at unnatural highs Canada wide, and Lloydminster joined the nation in recession. Due to high vacancy rates and high taxes, some businesses migrated out of the ailing downtown area to different locations such as the Lloyd Mall.

In the midst of this economic crisis, Cliff Rose came to town. After a stint as a developer in Texas, Rose, who originally hailed from Weyburn, Saskatchewan, was looking to return to Canada into a line of work with which he was most familiar - men's clothing. Cliff saw the opportunity for the success of such a store in Lloydminster. He opened Cliff Rose for Clothes in the Spring of 1986, just as the local economy reeled from a sharp drop in oil prices. While it made for a difficult start, Cliff's engaging personality and involvement in sports and community projects, along with the quality of service and clothing lines he offered, meant that his store was drawing customers not only from the Lloydminster area but from well beyond. Cliff Rose for Clothes countered the migratory trend of businesses and customers away from downtown. The business continued to flourish and in March 2000, long-time employee Dave Schneider became a partner.

In 1989, a small group of business people decided that there was a need for a downtown business improvement effort to deal with the serious issues that downtown was facing. The organizing committee consisted

Background photo courtesy of Provincial Archives of Alberta J4019 ; insets courtesy of Paul Douglas.

After construction of the Lloyd Mall, other businesses began to establish along Highway 16 on the Alberta side. Above: the Wayside Inn under construction in 1976, was soon offering modern hotel rooms and a full range of amenities such as saunas. In 2001, the Wayside affiliated with Best Western.

Photo by Foster Learning Inc.

Despite difficult times for local businesses, Cliff Rose (right) weathered the recession and built his business, Cliff Rose for Clothes, into a leading clothing store in Lloydminster. Long time employee, Dave Schneider (left) became a partner in 2000.

Photo by Don Whiting

The recession was cruel to the downtown businesses, and many stores closed leaving many vacancies along 49th and 50th Avenues. The Fisher's Department Store, Graham's Shoprite, Red Apple, Northgate Nissan, old May Theatre, former Beaver Lumber, former Royal Bank of Canada, former Safeway, and former IGA buildings were all empty to name a few.

Raymond Bailey, a former secondary school teacher from North Battleford, opened BayVan Photography in 1975. In order to preserve some of Lloydminster's photographic heritage, Bailey bought the negative collection of two former studios: Quarton Studio owned by Reg Quarton in the 1950's, and McRae's Photo House, owned by Harvey McRae from 1960 - 1973.

In 1998, the Rotary Club presented Ray with the Business Integrity Award. Bailey keeps up with photo technology. In 2000, he began offering digital photo effects (such as in the photo above) to his clients.

of John Vinek, long time General Manager of the Lloydminster Credit Union, as the Chairperson, Alex Robertson of Robertson Moskal Law Firm as Treasurer, and Harry Brudler, General Manager of the Lloydminster Co-op. The first meeting attracted nearly 150 business people to the Civic Centre. A strategic plan was developed with the assistance of Peter Vana, City Planning Director.

The plan incorporated a Business Improvement District with a by-law proposed by the downtown business people and passed by City Council assessing a supplementary levy on the business taxes in order to raise funds. The Streetscapes Company was formed in 1989, with a board of directors, consisting of ten people, including a City Council member and the City's Director of Planning as an advisory member. Pat Henry was hired as the manager.

Five committees were put into place: Executive Committee, Beautification and Physical Improvement, Business Development and Expansion, Marketing and Promotions, and Parking and Infrastructure. The Streetscapes Company enjoyed great success. An effective marketing and promotions plan was implemented with aggressive advertising campaigns and many community events, such as the Fringe and Children's Day, took place in the downtown core. The results of the organization's efforts were clear. Substantial decreases in property tax, increases in business development, major renovations to several buildings, continuously decreasing vacancy rates, and beautification initiatives such as corner bulbing, tree and flower planting, the addition of park benches, and the removal of the parking meters. All this led to a revitalization of downtown Lloydminster.

The Fisher's Building underwent major renovations in 1991 and became the Atrium Centre, a prime example of the Streetscapes Company's push for the revitalization and beautification of downtown Lloydminster.

The Service Area Expands Rapidly

By the end of the 1980's, the economy was on the rebound, and Lloydminster businesses were seeing increased traffic in their stores, due largely to several major local projects. The construction of the massive Bi-Provincial Upgrader brought large numbers of out-of-town workers into the city with plenty of disposable income.

Within three short years, from 1990 to 1993, Lloydminster's trade area expanded from 60,000 people to 150,000. A chain reaction was set off as the success of one large retailer or company led to the establishment of another. Sears Canada had long served Lloydminster with a downtown catalogue store, but in 1990, the company opened a full sized department store in the renovated Lloyd Mall. In 1991, I.G.A. moved from their downtown location to a new 35,000 square foot facility located on Highway 16, now home to a growing strip of shopping options, including Superstore and the Lloyd Mall.

As the service area continued to expand, American discount department store behemoth Wal-Mart opted to establish a location in Lloydminster in 2000. Springwood Development built a large "Big-Box Retail Site" on Highway 16 even further west, well outside of

The city's increased prosperity drew the attention of retail giant Real Canadian Superstore, and the franchise decided to open a store in Lloydminster, its first venture outside a major metropolitan market. Inset: Mayor Pat Gulak and Ray Nelson (right) preview plans for the Real Canadian Superstore prior to its construction. The Lloydminster Economic Development Authority and Nelson Lumber were major players in bringing Superstore to town. Nelson Lumber owned the land and building and leased it to Superstore on a long term basis.

Below: As was the case with Superstore, many merchants worried that the new Wal-Mart might well put them out of business by pulling customers from established Lloydminster business areas such as the downtown and the Lloyd Mall. It became obvious, though, that the new mega-stores were bringing more and more people to Lloydminster. Residents of Provost, Unity, Paradise Hill, and Wainwright, to name a few, were making regular shopping trips to Lloydminster, greatly expanding our market.

Entrepreneurs Amanda Block (left) and Koree Moline started "Kits for Kids" in 2000. The home based business sold custom school kits for students to save parents the hassle of hunting for school supplies.

Lloydminster's established business centres. Wal-Mart was the first confirmed tenant, and Staples and Canadian Tire, which re-located from its store on 50th Avenue and 36th Street, shortly followed suit. There was a total of 300,000 square feet of retail space spread over approximately 30 acres of land costing approximately $35 million.

No doubt, for smaller businesses, it is difficult to compete price-wise with the major buying power of the large retailers. The key to survival for the small business is in service and quality of goods. Even home-based businesses can compete as shown by entrepreneurs, such as Amanda Block and Koree Moline, who offer unique services to customers. In 2000, Block and Moline started "Kits for Kids", a service which custom prepares local children's school supplies all in one convenient package. The two keep their eye on prices and purchase in bulk to get the best deals. Block and Moline's home based business attracted media attention and achieves success through word of mouth and clever marketing.

"It's All about Service!"

Photo far left courtesy of Barb Gulka; others by Foster learning Inc.

How do you survive in Lloydminster with the growth of mega discount department stores? Local business people know that the special and unique services they offer will keep their customers coming back. **Left**: Barb Gulka renovated the Harvey Weaver home in 1993 and opened the Tea House, which attracts tourists from across the country as well as local residents. With life growing more hectic, Barb says, "I wanted people to come in, take the time to talk to each other, and leave their stress at the end of the driveway." **Centre**: A quilt on display at Patchwork Junction. Owner Marlene Kondro felt that the introduction of Wal-Mart in Lloydminster actually improved her business. More people were coming to town, and they soon realized that the larger discount department stores could not offer the expert advice in needlework, quilting, and sewing that she and her staff could. **Right**: Janice Lorenz, (left) owner of the Prairie Pedlar, with employee Bulah Rogan, broke away from the Pan Handler franchise in 1996. With her new independence, Lorenz began stocking specialty home decor items to appeal specifically to her customer's tastes.

Those who have left the Border City and return for a visit are genuinely surprised at how quickly the retail and service sector is growing. As the city continues to grow, Lloydminster's role as a regional service centre becomes more established. Increased traffic allows both small and large businesses to benefit. As our businesses succeed, Lloydminster draws people from greater distances. We are close to reaching that important goal of being a self-sustaining economy.

One of the keys to reaching our century long goal is going to be the quality of the service our businesses provide. The Chamber of Commerce works hard to encourage better customer service and there are many outstanding examples. However, it is also true that too many businesses take customers for granted and inflict higher prices and poorer service than the population deserves. As well, the high levels of employment have made it difficult to recruit and retain qualified, effective staff members. Recent years have seen erosion in both business loyalty to employees and staff loyalty to a business.

Fortunately, business contains a self-correcting mechanism. As some businesses fall victim to complacency or arrogance, new opportunities will be opened in the marketplace for those who can provide the higher qualities of goods and services which customers are increasingly demanding. The retail and service sector of Lloydminster is truly - bordering on greatness.

Chapter Eleven

Transportation

Research and draft writing by Heather Yuzik

Photo courtesy of BCHCC

Above: Down and out on the trail to Lloydminster. Not only did most Barr Colonists not know how to harness or drive horses and oxen, they did not know how to care for them by providing adequate feed or rest. Driven day after day on short rations, frequently bogged in mud, the result was often as pictured above - one ox collapsed from exhaustion, the other looking for an exit.

Below: Horse-driven sleighs and "cutters" were used in the winter months.

Photo courtesy of BCHCC

There was a time when composite illustrations of the various means of transportation were popular. Usually they featured a happy family in a 1950's convertible waving at a passing train while in the background a great ship loomed and aircraft soared overhead. The Barr Colonists lived their own such tableau. Many travelled by rail to Liverpool, boarded a great ship to cross the Atlantic, then clambered aboard special trains for days of rocks and trees scenery, finally arriving in the village of Saskatoon. Then the final, much storied leg of the journey when "colonists" acquired wagons and oxen or horses for the near 200 mile trek to the settlement. By the time they arrived at the future Lloydminster site, they had had about all the transportation they could stand.

Part of the problem was that the "colonists" were well ahead of the construction of the Canadian Northern Railway. Until rail service began in the fall of 1905, supplies continued to be hauled by wagon or were floated down the North Saskatchewan River on scows to Hewitt's Landing. The scows had a one way trip, being dismantled after being offloaded and the lumber used for building construction after being hauled by horse and ox teams the 20 remaining miles to Lloydminster.

The Horse and the Automobile

When Lloydminster was founded in 1903, it was still very much the era of the horse. Other than walking, horse-drawn wagons, buggies, and sleighs were the common mode of everyday transportation. As it happened, many of the men, women and children did have to walk the many miles to the new colony because their famous Bain wagons were piled high with personal belongings brought to establish their new lives.

The town of Lloydminster grew quickly and traffic increased. By January 1908, a bylaw was passed compelling the use of sleigh bells so that teams could be easily heard at a distance. Offenders were to be fined a sum not exceeding twenty dollars.

However, Lloydminster, along with the rest of North America, was already witnessing the birth of the automobile revolution. Some of the first "motor cars" were bought out of province and shipped to their proud owners via the railway. Perhaps the most common was the Ford Model T, the affordable, mass produced runabout introduced in 1908 by Henry Ford. Fondly nicknamed the "Tin Lizzie", it could reach speeds of 45 miles per hour (70 km/h).

At first, some people were reluctant to get the new "horseless carriage" preferring to travel and work their land with horses. Some people could not afford a vehicle and the gasoline to run it. There were complaints about motorists frightening horses and startling people walking on the street. Initially there were few roads and motorists angered farmers by travelling in their fields. Dust was also a nuisance when vehicles sped by.

In July of 1919 a speed limit of 12 miles per hour was imposed in the town of Lloydminster because some people were travelling at excessive speeds. In 1928 a bylaw was passed stating that "no person shall drive a motor vehicle upon a highway in the Town of Lloydminster, in a race or on a bet or wager." By then, cars had to stop at railway crossings, and drive on the right hand side of the road. Chauffeurs of public service passenger carrying vehicles, or liveries for delivering or doing work had to obtain a license in 1931 within the town of Lloydminster. As of 1928 in Alberta and 1932 in Saskatchewan, all motorists were required to be licensed.

There were some advantages to the new automobile. The early cars went 20-30 miles per hour. A trip that would take a team of horses one week could be completed in one day by an automobile. According to John Willoughby, Dr. G. L. Cooke, who owned a 1929 McLaughlin Buick, was the first person to eat breakfast in Lloydminster and supper in Calgary.

During dry weather the roads were dusty, but when it rained they turned to a muddy, sticky mess trapping many motorists. Chris Benson recalls her father, Ruben Benson, having his 1935 Model A Ford pulled to Highway 17 by a team of horses

Photo courtesy of BCHCC

Eventually, the horse gave way to the automobile, as the dominant mode of transportation. The men in the photo above are identified as Arthur Baker (left) and Mr. Carlson, from 1918.

"No person shall drive a motor vehicle upon a highway in the Town of Lloydminster, in a race or on a bet or wager."
1928 Bylaw

1911 I.H.C. Autowagon, 2 cylinders, air cooled.

Photo courtesy of BCHCC

The Bus Depot has moved several times in the past 100 years. In the 1930's, buses departed from the Texaco Station (left) (present site of the Co-op Parkade), and later from the Royal Cafe beside the old Post Office.

each spring, and then he would drive his car the 24 miles to Lloydminster at 30-40 mph. In later years he would use a tractor to pull his car to the highway. In the early days motorists were very willing to help each other out when they were stuck or had a flat tire.

During the Depression years in the 1930's, fuel was not always available. Therefore, some people hitched a team of horses to their Model T Ford, and called it a "Bennett Buggy", as a jibe at Prime Minister R. B. Bennett for the desperate situation in which the people found themselves.

In the winter, main highways were not regularly ploughed until 1935, which made winter travel difficult. It was impossible to drive on roads covered with snowdrifts. Cars would be put away until the spring and people would travel from their farms, to school, and within the town of Lloydminster by horse and sleigh or "cutter" (a sleigh with a cab-like structure).

While winter was a major challenge, some "motoring" enthusiasts were determined they would run their cars in the freezing weather. They would put chains on their tires or purchase a kit that allowed them to replace their front wheels with skis. The night before a trip they would take the battery out of the car and place it near the kitchen stove. The next day they would put hot coals under the oil pan, hot water in the radiator, put in the warmed battery, and then attempt to start the automobile. Often, even after all of this effort, the vehicle would not go. Some desperate drivers would hitch a team of horses to the car, put it in gear and hope the horses could pull it fast enough to bring the motor to life.

Even if they finally got the car running, their was no pleasant journey ahead. Cars built before the 1920's did not have enclosed bodies, so in cold weather, people needed to use blankets and foot warmers filled with hot coals or heated rocks.

Photo by Don Whiting

Travel by automobile became impossible once the snow fell because there was no snow removal equipment and few graded roads. In the early 1930's, Les Rendell and E. Lehne designed a Larch snowplane, similar to the one photographed above, built from aircraft material and a Model A Ford engine. Dr. G. L. Cooke and local merchants hired Les Rendell to transport them during the winter months.

Students in rural areas were taken to school in horse-drawn "cutters". Covered in blankets and robes, they travelled miles in freezing weather. "After five miles, we'd get so cold we'd start to freeze and fall asleep. We'd have to stop and jump up and down to keep warm," recalls Chris Benson, who grew up on a farm northeast of Lloydminster. Usually by the time they arrived at school their lunches were frozen and they had to be placed on the school's stove to thaw by lunchtime.

Earth was the most common road surface until after World War II when highway construction boomed. Initially horse drawn ploughs and scrapers developed the roads until motorized graders and tractor-pulled scrapers replaced them. In 1949, the town of Lloydminster paved 50th Avenue from 44th Street to 57th Street. During the mid 1960's and 1970's local improvements were made such as curbs, gutters, sidewalks and paved streets.

As Lloydminster's population has increased so has the traffic flow within the city. By 1971 vehicles crossing the railway tracks on 50th Avenue often had long waits while trains passed through. Eventually the crossing on 49th Avenue was opened to relieve some of this congestion. Over the past thirty years traffic counts have increased dramatically along 44th Street, the Yellowhead Highway. In 2000, average daily volumes of almost 24,000 vehicles were recorded in some months. Due to the increase in traffic volumes, there are currently studies being done to determine a route for a highway bypass to the south of the city.

The Yellowhead Highway is being twinned from Marshall to the Battlefords, and it is projected that it will take until the year 2010. With an increase in traffic flow the twinning of the Yellowhead Highway will improve driver safety. Above: Highway and Transportation Minister Maynard Sonntag and officials from the R.M. of Wilton and R.M of Eldon at the ribbon cutting officially opening the 10.6 km Marshall to Lashburn section in August 2000. Grading continues on the additional 16.2 km to just west of Maidstone, and the paving of this will begin in the summer of 2001.

Above left: Road workers build a grade through a slough in Brittania in the 1930's.

Below: This early 1950's photo of the Lloydminster Stockyards shows a range of late 1940's and early 1950's automobiles.

Trucking

Initially grain and supplies were hauled with horse drawn wagons in the summer and sleighs in the winter, but by 1925, trucks were becoming more popular. The trucks were able to haul bigger loads and travel more miles in a day than horse drawn wagons. The last Model T truck was manufactured in 1927, and then the Ford Model A became available in 1928. By 1930 more trucks were taking to the roads with Ford, Chevrolet, International,

Lloydminster Family Invents the RV?

By Geraldine Swank

My family's 1928 Model Ford Pickup has always remained a precious memory. In 1929, my father Frank Wood, assisted by Art Shortell in Lloydminster, adapted it so the truck was roofed over. Roll up curtains could be snapped down for overnight sleeping space. We five kids, Agatha, a teenage helper, and Ma and Pa all drove in this rig from Lloydminster to Sooke, B.C. for a holiday trip.

We rolled two straw-filled mattresses for seating for the drive and pitched a tent each night, brought a lot of our food, and drove all those miles on rough gravel roads.

We did not go on the all-Canadian route, with the dangerous Fraser Canyon. We were advised to go south to Spokane and across to Everett for a ferry to Anacortes. It was heaven to find forty miles of paved highway near Spokane and a few miles near Everett. We crossed a desert and great forested mountain ranges.

At campsites (mostly occupied by Americans), we had many people look us over with more than passing interest. There was nothing like our rig anywhere. It made us wonder if it started a trend, as a few years later camper trucks became the vehicle of choice at campsites.

I have been forever grateful to my father, who hatched up this whole idea and gave us prairie kids a look at mountains and such wonders as Radium Hot Springs. Every one of us has loved travel ever since.

The staunch Model A survived to take us on another trip five years later. This time there was the addition of twins, born late in 1929 and a visiting aunt from England. We went back to our favourite campsite in the Sinclair Canyon: Radium Hot Springs.

We have laughed all these years and aped the voice we heard once when we pulled into a gas station: "How many in the fam-i-ly?" This came from a piping boy's voice in the car next to us.

Since our farm was 12 miles from Lloydminster, the truck was an indispensable piece of equipment. It took us many a dusty mile through the dirty '30s.

Photo courtesy of Chris Wood

Christopher Wood of Lloydminster learned to drive in this Ford truck when he was a young lad. He recalls that when his family went on their holiday he slept in a tent with his parents, his older brother, Harry, slept in the cab, while the girls, Janet, Margaret, and Geraldine bunked out in the back of the truck. The truck belonged to the family until 1949 when it was sold.

Dodge, and GMC being the popular makes. One ton trucks were most common. They could hold 60 - 100 bushels of wheat, with wheat weighing sixty pounds to a bushel. By the late 1930's two-ton trucks came on the scene and then the tractor-trailer truck in the 1940's making it possible to haul heavier loads.

John Willoughby began hauling grain for John Ford of Kitscoty in 1942 using a three-ton truck. John remembers; "the first trucks had mechanical or cable breaks. Mechanical breaks would stop at stop signs, but cable breaks wouldn't stop anywhere. I had to shift down to stop. Going down a hill was something else." Fords didn't have hydraulic brakes until 1939.

From 1942 - 1946 John, and his brothers Harry and Howard, hauled grain and cattle for farmers. In 1947, they came to Lloydminster and hauled lumber, cement blocks, and bricks for Beaver Lumber Co. In 1948, John and Harry Willoughby, and Clarence Weaver unloaded the first load of lumber for Nelson Lumber. In 1949, with Lloydminster's oil industry taking off, the Willoughbys began hauling oil for Husky. They started with two small trucks and eventually "had about 35 - 40 trucks running. We went into semis in the late 1940's. John McKay had the first International K model in the 1940's with heaters to haul perishables. John Remple used the first semis and hauled liquids, such as gasoline and oil."

It was in 1949 that the first pavement from Lloydminster to Kitscoty was applied. Prior to this, the road was difficult at times. John Willoughby remembers in the spring of 1948 when he and his brother saw a Greyhound bus and jeep that were stuck 5 miles west of Lloydminster. Luckily, the brothers were able to go around the bus and jeep in their Model A half-ton truck. "It was a terrible six miles of road to Blackfoot. It was kind of muskegy. Everyone got stuck along there."

In 1950 the Willoughbys hauled the first asphalt out of Lloydminster in a tanker truck from the Kodiak Refinery to Mundare and Jasper, Alberta. The railway went on strike so the brothers moved the asphalt. "This was the beginning of asphalt being moved with trucks and it has continued throughout the years. Jack Moore, the asphalt salesman told me to

Photo courtesy of John Willoughby

Above: The first truck in Lloydminster for hauling drilling mud out of pits and spreading it. Willoughby Bros. had it built by Universal Industries in town, and the plumbing was done by Jack Ross. Don Rammel, field foreman of Husky Oil talked the Willoughby Bros. into building the unit to clean out Husky Oil's storage pits. It was later sold to Jack Ross.

Ways to Leave Lloydminster - 1954

CNR Train - to Edmonton, daily @ 12:45 AM
- to Saskatoon, daily @ 5:15 AM

CPR Train - to Edmonton, daily except
Sunday @ 6:00 AM
- to Wilkie, Tuesday, Thursday,
Saturday @ 9:00 AM
- to Paradise Valley,
Thursday only @ 8:00 AM
- to Hillmond,
Friday only @ 7:30 AM

Bus - to Edmonton, daily
@ 12:50 PM and 11:00 PM
- to Saskatoon, daily
@ 6:30 AM and 6:45 PM

Airplane (Canadian Pacific Airlines)
- to Edmonton, daily except Sunday @
12:20 PM
- to North Battleford and other Sask.
points, daily except Sunday @
4:10 PM

Photo courtesy of John Willoughby

Left: The last of the asphalt trucks which the Willoughby brothers owned were sold in the early 1970's.

insulate the oil tank with insulation, tar paper and chicken wire. Asphalt was loaded at 400 F and we wanted to keep it that temperature while transporting it."

Willoughby Bros. Transportation Ltd. was established in 1951 and was located at the site of the current Tropical Inn. The brothers did not have much luck with the garage on this site. "We had two garages that burned down there. In the second fire we had a truck in the garage. My brother Harry was in the garage and the wind blew, the pump was leaking, and the fumes went in and she ignited. My brother jumped in the truck and backed it out. There must have been enough gas in the truck's carburetor to back it out. Pretty lucky." After two fires in one year, the brothers moved a mile west and in 1952 built a shop at what is now 66 Avenue. That building was sold to Ross Brothers Trucking in 1958, and John and his brothers opened their third and final site 5 miles west of the Meridian where Cam's Trucking is now located . Willoughby Bros. Transportation Ltd. closed in the early 1980's.

Left to right:
Workers laying the last leg of the long awaited railroad into Lloydminster in July 1905.

Engine #2635 pulled the first CPR train to arrive in Lloydminster in 1926.

The Canadian Northern station was built in 1905. It became the Canadian National station in the 1920's.

The Canadian Pacific Railway station was built in the late 1920's.

Photo courtesy of Glenbow Provincial Archives NA 4514-10

Photos above and right, courtesy of BCHCC

The Railway

After the Barr Colonists arrived in Lloydminster, they were isolated until the arrival of the Canadian Northern Railway on July 28, 1905 just before Saskatchewan and Alberta each became a province. The railway was a welcome sight because it provided a rapid means of transporting items such as grain, manufactured goods, and even people in those days. Consequently the price of various goods dropped once the rail came through Lloydminster. Long distance hauling remained the job of the railway until the 1930's when trucking firms began to haul commercial goods and supplies. The Canadian Northern Station, built in 1905, was located just on the Alberta side of the border. In 1917 the Canadian Government gave the name Canadian National Railways to all of the lines that it owned. Eventually, the Canadian Northern went bankrupt and became part of Canadian National. Today the railway system still uses its CN symbol.

Photo by Don Whiting

BORDERING ON GREATNESS

Lloydminster was also served by the Canadian Pacific Railway, which reached here in 1926. It operated between Wilkie and Edmonton with branch lines to Hillmond in the northeast and to Paradise Valley in the southwest. On August 9, 1926, the first CPR passenger train arrived in Lloydminster. It had been promised since 1905, but took twenty-one years to arrive in the town. That same day, the first day of the exhibition in Lloydminster, the Barr Colonists arrived for a reunion.

According to the *Lloydminster Times*, August 12, 1926 issue, it was an exciting sight to behold as thousands of people came out to see the arrival of the long promised train. Many of the Barr Colonists were present and some were passengers on the train. The man at the controls was the Vice-President of the CPR, Mr. D. C. Coleman. The train consisted of twelve coaches, Mr. Coleman's private car, and an engine.

The mayor of the time, Mr. Huxley, summed it up when he said, "You will know, Mr. Coleman, that it is generally accepted that settlement on the prairies follows the railways. While that may be, substantially true, the men and women of the Barr Colony reversed that dictum, for most certainly the

> "It is generally accepted that settlement on the prairies follows the railways. While that may be, substantially true, the men and women of the Barr Colony reversed that dictum, for most certainly the railways followed them."
> Mayor Huxley, 1926

railways followed them. They blazed the way with wagons and teams and the railways followed them from Saskatoon to this border town."

Aviation

The first airport in Lloydminster was situated across from the current industrial area at 62nd Street. Inaugurated in December 1950, it began as a gravel airstrip 3500 ft long x 75 ft wide. According to C. Wetton in *The Promised Land*, the airport was served by Canadian Pacific Airlines and was called Chapman Field after, R. C. Chapman, who was president of the Board of Trade at that time. However, other sources state that the airport was known simply as The Lloydminster Airport.

Herle's Husky: "The Truck Stops Here"

Brothers Wilfred and Gordon Herle took over the Husky gas station from George Reinholt and Helmer Thorsen who owned it from 1958 to 1973. Wilfred Herle

was working at the station when he heard it was for sale. He "put the bug" in his brother Gordon's ear to go into business with him. Gordon had worked for George and Helmer and was then in the Canadian Air Force at Cold Lake, Alberta. On February 1, 1973 Wilfred and Gordon took over the operation and named it Herle's Husky Car/Truck Stop. In 1980 their younger brother Robert joined to help with bookkeeping and overall managerial duties.

In the 1970's there were only a few houses near the station and they had no running water. The people would bring pails to get water from the Husky station at no cost.

There have been many changes. The original service station was just east of the current building. In the late 1970's Husky Oil Ltd. purchased the Herb Robinson farm located at the west end of the lot. Prior to 1980 the service station shared the lot with the Husky Bulk Station operated by Ed King. In 1980 the old building was demolished and the company moved into the current building in May of that year. The back part of the

lot had never been paved and semi-trailers would get stuck. Gordon recalls, "We'd use another semi truck to get them out. Sometimes a winch truck from K & S Oilfield or Border Trucking pulled trucks out for a fee". The lot was fully paved in 1980 when the new building was constructed.

In the beginning, Gordon recalls, "we used to just sell fuel and repair truck tires. We made a decent living at it. Now truck tire repairs are almost nonexistent since tires have gone tubeless."

When the brothers moved into servicing vehicles, they saw how rapidly automo-

Photos courtesy of Gordon Herle

Above left: (l-r) Wilfred and Gordon Herle bought the Husky Gas Station in 1973 and renamed it "Herle's Husky Car/Truck Stop" (above right, Highway 16 in foreground).

biles were changing: "Back then we only needed a crescent wrench, screwdriver, and a pair of pliers. Now you need hundreds of thousands of dollars worth of tools to diagnose and repair vehicles."

Today, The Husky Truck Stop is as busy as ever. Often at night one cannot find a parking spot. Fuel sales, an ever increasing confectionery and convenience store market, a 24 hour restaurant, and a very busy service shop make Herle's Husky a popular stop in Lloydminster.

During the 1950's, there were scheduled flights to and from both Saskatoon and Edmonton. Unfortunately, Lloydminster did not prove to be a big enough market and the flights were later scrapped.

In September of 1971 the original airport saw some necessary improvements. $100,000 was spent for a paved runway and lights. According to the September 8, 1971 issue of the *Lloydminster Times*, funds were available as follows: $85,000 by the federal Department of Transport, $20,000 by the Saskatchewan Government, and a Husky rebate on asphalt was given in the amount of $6000. The difference was made up by the City. Today the Border City Radio Control Club is using this paved airway.

In 1979, new land was purchased for the current airport, which is situated two miles northwest of Lloydminster. In 1980, the pavement for the 5577 ft x 150 ft runway was completed, and the terminal building was finished in 1981. The cost of the project was $6.6 million. In the 1980's, Time Air, a feeder for Air Canada, began operating a daily return flight to Calgary. In the latter '80's Time Air lost the bid to AirBC,

Photo courtesy of BCHCC

First airplane in Lloydminster - landed in 1919 at the B. Circuit fair
L to R: John Blackwell, Noel Noyes, R. J. Rowley Noyes, Cyril Noyes, and Robert J. R. Noyes

Look up in the Sky! It's Ed Jenson!

The first air charter operator in Lloydminster, Ed Jenson, played an important role in the development of air travel to and from the Border City. Ed came to Lloydminster in 1964 to open a flying training and charter service, which he called "Interprovincial Airways". "I did everything in those days," Jenson recollects. "I flew, serviced the planes, swept out the terminal." Jenson's company also performed airplane maintenance, sold fuel, and oversaw the operations of the Lloydminster Airport.

Jenson recalls that Lloydminster quickly outgrew the old airport. The runway was not long enough for larger planes to land, and if they did choose to land or take-off in Lloydminster, they had to lighten their passenger load and limit their fuel. For this reason, air travel in Lloydminster was limited to mostly smaller aircraft.

Photos courtesy of Ed Jenson

The new Lloydminster Airport, for which Ed Jenson (inset) helped to locate an adequate site, was completed in 1981.

Selecting a site for the new airport was not easy. Because of Lloydminster's prevailing northwest winds, the runway had to run East/West in order for planes to land safely. It was difficult to find a site where an East/West runway would be possible with few geographical restrictions.

It was Jenson who spotted a possible site while up in the air with a student one day. City commissioner, Russ Robertson acted quickly to secure the site, and the new airport and terminal were completed in 1981.

Jenson was a member of the Civil Aviation Tribunal for Canada for many years. In addition, he served on many local committees and boards for organizations such as the Bi-Provincial Upgrader, the Lloydminster Theatre Project, Border Credit Union, and Lakeland College.

Mildred Beamish: Queen of the Airways

Mildred Beamish, an enthusiastic flyer who logged a total of 3022 hours flying time, was recognized as the oldest female pilot in Canada. The daughter of Barr Colonist, Robert Holtby and his wife, May; Mildred took to the air first as navigator for her husband, Somerville (Somers) Beamish. The couple married in 1928 and settled on a farm near Marshall, later operated by their son, Eric, and his wife, Leona.

The Beamish family were well known flyers. Somers, his brother, Oswald, and Oswald's wife, May, started flying lessons in California in 1947, and later completed them in Vermilion because Lloydminster had no suitable facilities at that time. The two brothers bought their first aircraft in 1947. Mildred flew as navigator with Somers to Wichita, Kansas to pick up the all-metal, two-seater Luscombe airplane that they would share with Oswald and May.

In 1957, Mildred decided to take flying lessons herself, initially for safety reasons in case Somers, needed help. However, it wasn't long before she grew to love flying. After the death of her husband, she flew solo. In an interview with CTV she stated, "Every trip is a challenge ... which way you're going to take off ... where you're going to land or what landing you're going to make. Every landing is different."

Mildred Beamish with her Cessna Skyhawk.

Mildred qualified for her commercial license which meant she had to have a medical every six months. Considered an older woman, she had to take many tests to prove her abilities. Mildred flew throughout Canada and the United States and was a member of the Lloydminster Flying Club, the Saskatchewan Flying Farmers, of which she was queen in 1966, and "the 99s", a flying club for women established by the famous Amelia Earhart.

Mildred flew her Cessna Skyhawk 172 for the last time in 1993. She was 83.

The Lloydminster Kiwanis Club brought an airshow, featuring the Snowbirds, to Lloydminster in 1995 and 1998.

which has been operating the flights ever since.

In the spring of 1982, the Flight Service Station moved from Vermilion to Lloydminster. Formerly managed by Transport Canada, it is now operated by NAV Canada. The NAV Canada Flight Service Station provides airport advisory service, vehicle control service, flight planning service, alerting service, weather briefing service and complete weather-observation.

A 1500 ft x 75 ft turf addition, was built in the spring of 1984 by the airport staff at little cost to the Government of Alberta. Operated by Alberta Transport and Utilities from 1981 to 1995, the Lloydminster Airport is now owned by the City of Lloydminster which took over the operation on April 1, 1995.

Our modes of transportation have changed dramatically over the past one hundred years. Vehicle shapes have gone through their phases, speeds have increased, and the travelling conditions have improved considerably. Nowadays a family can retrace the route of the Barr Colonists from Saskatoon to Lloydminster in their mini-van in less than three hours. With either the heater or air conditioner running full blast, they are not exposed to the weather. They can listen to the radio or turn on their cassette or CD player and sing along to the music. They can even pop in a video for the children to watch as they take their "long trip".

But are we really better off or has something not been lost as well as gained. The Barr Colonist family had a difficult two-week journey with hardships it is true. But along the way there were the good days when the children would stare in wonder as ducks wheeled through the air and splashed into a nearby slough, or smell the deeply fresh breeze lightly scented with prairie grasses and budding willow, or hear the piercing shriek of the killdeer or the throaty trill of the meadowlark. One hundred years later, our children whiz by in their sealed containers, listening to or watching made-up adventures from foreign cultures. They may know nothing of the history of those who travelled these roads before them, indeed, have no contact with the present reality through which they pass. Can we help but wonder what their destination will be?

Inset: Blaine and Rosemary Almond with son David, and their new 2001 Chevrolet Suburban, while (main photo) the old wagon has reached the end of its trail,.

Background Photo and Inset Photo by Don Whiting

Chapter Twelve

Communications

Research by Alan Griffith, Heather Yuzik, and Ian Goodwillie

Above: George F. Baynton at work (1940's) on the linotype/typewriter keyboard which he invented. Below: The Times office with the press in the foreground in the 1930's.

I solation from family and friends, and from world events, was a major problem for the Barr Colonists. Their diaries are filled with joyful notes about receiving a letter from home or the excitement of a bundle of newspapers, even if they were up to six months old.

One of the first projects undertaken that first winter was building a telegraph line north to Onion Lake to tap into the line there that carried telegrams and "wire stories" to Edmonton. They also thirsted for news of local happenings and took heart from the success stories of their peers.

Rapid advancements in communications technology would bring Lloydminster into contact with the world much more quickly than any of the Colonists could have ever expected.

Newspapers

Less than two years after the Barr Colonists first arrived, Lloydminster's longest serving business and newspaper was established. *The Times*, named after the famous *Times* in London, England, was founded by a company of shareholders who realized the boon that a newspaper would be to a pioneer community.

As none of these shareholders had any experience running a newspaper or print shop, they recruited Joseph George Willard, a colonist who had 30 years of experience in the newspaper business.

The first issue of *The Lloydminster Times* was distributed on April 25th, 1905, and Willard had single-handedly typeset it. From then on, the newspaper was published weekly, keeping residents more closely in touch with community happenings.

The Times' first printing press was a far cry from what is used today. Producing a newspaper with a circulation of 400 proved to be laborious work. The press only printed one page of a four-page sheet at a time. This meant that each sheet had to be fed into the press four times, powered by a foot pedal that had to be pumped eight times to print one page of the four page sheet. To produce enough papers for distribution, 12,800 pumps of the pedal were required.

After J. G. Willard's death in 1938, his son-in-law, George F. Baynton became the publisher, in partnership with his wife Dorothy, one of J. G. and Ellen Willard's daughters. During Baynton's era, *The Lloydminster Times* became a powerful voice, reflecting the desires and concerns of the Lloydminster people.

In the 1960's, George's son, Frederick Willard Baynton, began to manage the newspaper. Printing technology had changed dramatically since that first newspaper in 1905. The new offset printing equipment had rendered letterpress equipment obsolete. The automation allowed *The Times* to publish on a bi-weekly basis.

By 1970, *The Times*, in a new building on 44th Street, went daily. George's health began to fail, and he took a less active role. Frederick, who had worked at *The Times* all of his life, now became its Editor and Publisher. Unfortunately, he too had health problems, and in September 1979, he sold *The Times* to the Sterling Newspapers Syndicate of Vancouver, concluding 74 years of local ownership of the newspaper.

The Lloydminster Times continued to be published until 2000, when it was acquired by owners of *The Meridian Booster* Sadly, it was discontinued, and *The Lloydminster Times*, which had informed local residents for 95 years, ceased to be.

> The invention of the Linotype machine significantly automated typesetting. The operator sat at a keyboard similar to a typewriter keyboard except for the locations of the keys. As the keys were pressed, the appropriate alphanumeric characters in the form of brass matrices dropped onto a conveyor belt and were carried to an assembler where they formed a line of characters. The operator transferred each line of assembled matrices to a vice where the machine squirted a hot molten lead alloy under pressure into the tiny molds of each matrix. This produced a metal "slug" that contained the impressions of all the individual characters in that line.
>
> Producing a newspaper column line by line was much faster than doing so letter by letter. As well, if an assembled page ever fell apart on its way to the press, a chaotic heap of metal slugs was far less daunting to reassemble than a chaotic heap of tiny pieces of type!
>
> - George Baynton, Jr.

In 1959, the Meridian Booster became The Times' major competitor. In 1976, Meridian Printing built a large plant (below) on Highway 16 west.

Photo courtesy of Byron Keebaugh

Joseph George Willard: The Legacy Begins

Joseph George Willard settled, with his wife Louisa, on a farm four miles west of Marshall in the Dulwich district in 1904. George's three eldest sons had journeyed to Lloydminster with the Barr Colony in 1903, and acquired the land for their parents. J. G., as he was later known, had 30 years of experience as a craftsman printer and publisher of the *Kent and Sussex Post* in England. Willard soon realized after his arrival that he was not well suited to farming, and he eagerly accepted the opportunity

Photo courtesy of George Baynton Jr.

Joseph Willard came to Lloydminster in 1904 to take up farming. An experienced printer and publisher, Willard soon realized that farm life was not for him, and he became the first editor and publisher of the Lloydminster Times. Throughout the majority of its 95 years in operation, the Times remained under the ownership of Willard's family.

to become the first editor and publisher of Lloydminster's proposed newspaper.

It wasn't too long before *The Times* changed hands. The shareholders sold the paper to harnessmaker Bert Smith. J.G. Willard continued to print and publish the newspaper, and in 1909, he bought it with partner J. A. Jacobs. Their first action was to replace the Pedal Newspaper Press with a gas-powered Wharfdale Press. For a time though, they could not find a big enough gas engine to run it, and they had to operate it by turning the flywheel by hand.

In the Spring of 1912, J. G. left for Edmonton to work for Esdale Press which published the *Edmonton Bulletin*. *The Times* was sold to R. G. Tuckwell who, along with his son Ron, took over the responsibility of printing and publishing it. In 1915,

they erected a new building for *The Times* located on the Southeast corner of 49th Avenue and 49th Street. J. G. Willard returned to Lloydminster in 1916, and in partnership with R. G. Stewart, he re-acquired *The Times*. A linotype machine was purchased to automate the tedious task of typesetting, and the press was once again replaced – this time with a Babcock press, capable of printing two pages at one time. In 1920, J. G. bought out his partner's interest, and from then until his death in 1938, remained the newspaper's sole owner, editor, and publisher.

As a pioneer newspaper editor, J. G. was involved in all aspects of public life in the community. A respected civic leader, justice of the peace, and a founding member of the First Baptist Church, Willard served his community and church in many different capacities. He supplemented his income by doing watchmaking and gunsmithing, skills which he had acquired in England. He received many honours during his career. One of the most meaningful was a presentation by the Board of Trade that recognized his many contributions to the community, on the occasion of his 60th year in the newspaper business. Willard's hard work was worth it; *The Times* was considered to be one of the best weeklies in the northwest.

George Franklin Baynton: A Voice in Print

George Baynton had no experience in the printing or publishing business. However, he was known around town as an outspoken eccentric and a non-conformist who tirelessly promoted Lloydminster and put his community ahead of his own business interests.

Baynton used his position as owner and editor of *The Times* to fight for better roads, bridges, schools, junior colleges, and other public facilities. He was known well by municipal, federal, and provincial politicians whom he would hound relentlessly to start projects for the benefit of Lloydminster. If they ignored him, they became the subject of a blistering editorial in the next edition of *The Times*.

Left to right: Times' employee Art Gellert, Frederick Baynton, Dorothy Baynton, and George F. Baynton.

Photo courtesy of George Baynton Jr.

George had a keen mechanical aptitude, and designed numerous devices and pieces of equipment for his newspaper business. One was an adapter for the linotype keyboard that electronically converted typewriter keystrokes into linotype keystrokes. This allowed a typist to operate a linotype without first having to learn the confusing linotype keyboard.

In the 1940's, he purchased a newspaper press from the *Edmonton Bulletin*. It was sold to him as salvage because the manufacturer could not get it to work properly. Baynton completely redesigned and rebuilt it, using it successfully for years to print *The Times* each week.

Baynton saw the realization of many of his causes in the form of worthwhile, projects, facilities and infrastructure components that Lloydminster now enjoys. He was always looking for ways to market Lloydminster's heavy crude oil. One way was to convince the railways to substitute refined Lloydminster crude for the coal they then used. He was instrumental in getting them to do so.

His trips, long-distance telephone calls, letters and briefs to the various levels and seats of government were all undertaken and provided at his own expense. On one occasion, a group of northern residents provided him with a purse of money they had collected in appreciation of his efforts in getting the two provincial governments to provide them with an all-weather road from Lloydminster to the North Saskatchewan River. Before the new road was built, Jumbo Hill was a formidable obstacle that became impassable in bad weather and put the communities north of the river at risk in medical emergencies. True to form, George donated the money toward a new cause he had already embarked upon; the construction of a bridge across the river that would serve the northern communities on both sides of the Saskatchewan-Alberta border.

He was eventually successful in brokering a cost sharing agreement between the federal and the two provincial governments for the construction of the bridge. It is fitting that shortly after he died, the bridge was named after him, and in this way, continues to be a memorial and a tribute to him.

Photo courtesy of Byron Keebaugh

Above: Byron Keebaugh (right), the original owner and publisher of the Meridian Booster, with production supervisor Dan Doda. Keebaugh began his newspaper in Lloydminster in 1959 and oversaw the operation through major technological advancements in printing; including the purchase of an offset printing press in 1959, a web offset press in 1968, computer typesetters, and digital production into the 1990's.

A leader in his industry, Byron Keebaugh served as president of the Alberta Weekly Newspaper Association, and later, the Canadian Weekly Newspaper Association.

Always conscious of how he could best get his newspaper out to the public and satisfy his advertising clients, Keebaugh came up with the idea of the Booster Box. Previously, the newspaper had used the post office to deliver the newspaper to readers, but the expense was high and circulation was difficult to predict. The Booster Boxes, placed on street corners around Lloydminster and in nearby communities, allowed the newspaper to track how many copies were being read, and project how many should be printed in the future.

Centrespread: Doug Tait, Mel McKevitt, and Brad Johnson operating presses in the Meridian Booster's job printing shop in 1991.

In 1958, Byron Keebaugh came to town and opened his business, Meridian Printing, in the basement of a building on 50th Avenue across from the Prince Charles hotel. Keebaugh was an experienced compositor printer who had started in the newspaper business in Priestville, Saskatchewan when he was only thirteen years old.

At age fifteen, Byron left the small town of Priestville and headed out on his own and into a series of jobs which took him across Alberta working for weekly newspapers. By 1955, he was running the *Cutknife Grinder* in Cutknife, Saskatchewan.

Keebaugh left Cutknife in 1958 to open Meridian Printing. He quickly established his operation, which printed a variety of materials such as wedding invitations, receipt books, and legal forms. An astute businessman and knowledgeable tradesperson, Byron Keebaugh took notice of a technological advancement in printing which was sure to change the industry. The innovation was offset printing. The offset method was less time consuming and saved a considerable amount of physical space compared to the old linotype presses. Cameras were used to photograph individual pages. The negatives were then used to transfer the content to metal plates, which were put on the press. It was expensive at the time, but Keebaugh could see that it was a valuable investment. The printer had little in assets, yet the Industrial Development Bank in Winnipeg had enough faith in his plan to grant him a $15,000 loan to purchase the offset equipment.

The press came in the spring of 1959 and Keebaugh became a pioneer in the use of offset printing equipment in Western Canada. He soon realized, though, that there were not enough printing jobs in Lloydminster for him to pay back his hefty loan, and he decided to re-visit the newspaper business. The first issue of the *Meridian Booster*, an advertiser news-

Photo courtesy of Byron Keebaugh

paper which would carry a front page of local news, was handed out to 5000 people in attendance at the parade for the 1959 Lloydminster Exhibition. The newspaper's advertising sales grew rapidly at an increase of 25% for years to follow, and Keebaugh's assertive approach to doing business and selling advertising allowed for the great success of his company.

Technological advancements followed which led to lucrative deals. With the increased speed of their new equipment, the printing company was awarded a long-standing contract to print flyers for the OK Economy in Saskatoon in 1968.

In 1995, Byron Keebaugh retired and Meridian Printing was sold to Bowes Publishing. The days of the locally owned newspaper in Lloydminster had come to an end. A large western Canadian publisher, Bowes continued to push ahead with further technological advancements. Computers were put to use to produce a negative of each newspaper page. In turn, plates would be made from the negatives. The newspaper also began to use high end digital cameras for the majority of its photographs.

From its beginnings, the *Booster* established itself as a leading weekly newspaper in its market size. Awards and accolades from the Alberta Weekly Newspaper Association and the Canadian Weekly Newspaper Association were presented to the newspaper over the years, including "Best Front Page".

The Telephone

Telephone service came to Lloydminster in 1906, organized by J. T. Hill, W. W. Amos, W. R. Ridington, J. Reg Bell, and J. McCarthy. The main engineer was Dr. Robertson, the dentist. The switchboard and several telephone extensions were located in the Curtis' book store, and the wires were hung outside on 2 x 4's.

In September of 1906 the Alberta Government started vigorously constructing long distance telephone lines in the province, and in 1907, the 208 miles of line from Edmonton to Lloydminster was completed. In the spring of 1907, there were demands to make a decision about the telephone situation in Lloydminster.

AGT, Alberta Government Telephones, asked to acquire the exchange across the border

The Telephone Girl

The telephone girl sits in a chair
And listens to voices from everywhere.

She hears all the gossip
She knows all the news.
She knows who is happy
And who has the blues.
She knows all our sorrows
She knows all our joys.
She knows every girl who is chasing the boys.

She knows all our troubles
She knows all our strife.
She knows every man who is mean to his wife.
She knows every time we are out with the boys
She hears the excuses every fellow employs.

She knows every woman who has a dark past.
She knows every man that's inclined to be fast.
In fact there is a secret in each saucy curl
Of that quiet demur looking telephone girl.

If the telephone girl told all that she knows
It would turn half our friends to bitterest foes.
She could sow a small wind that would reap a big gale
Engulf us in trouble and land us in jail.

She could let go a story which gaining in force
Would cause half our wives to sue for divorce,
Get all our churches mixed up in a flight
And turn all our days into sorrowing nights.

In fact she could keep all the town in a stew
If she'd tell the tenth part of the things that she knew.
Oh really now, doesn't it make your head swirl
When you think what you owe to the telephone girl?

- contributed by Larraine Davidson,
a former telephone girl

Photo by Foster Learning Inc.

Barb McKeand, Director of the Barr Colony Heritage Cultural Centre, takes a call on a wooden wall phone, common into the 1940's.

The first telephone building in Lloydminster in 1909.

Below: The opening of the Alberta Government Telephone Building in 1928. In the same year, the first long-distance call between Alberta and overseas took place when commercial long distance radio-telephone service was introduced. From Lloydminster, the operator had to go through three different switchboard operators to make an appointment to talk to someone overseas, such as in England. These appointments were set up almost two weeks in advance.
Seated (l to r): Mr. Jackson, Evelyne Proctor, Joyce Tomlinson, Dorothy Jones, Amy Spence, Ena Hollands, Ada Noyes, Mr. Lansey.
Manager W. H. Mitchell is standing top right.

in the Saskatchewan town. The Saskatchewan Government made no objections, and AGT bought the local system for $1200, operating both sides of the border until 1989.

During the 1930's Depression, AGT was unable to maintain service to the rural lines. Local farmers formed mutual companies to purchase the lines and operate them themselves. A monthly fee was paid to AGT, which maintained the central station.

The New Deal Mutual Telephone Company, for example, was formed in 1934 with farmers Ed Martin, Sam Clark, and Fred Whitfield in charge. To pay AGT for the lines and telephone the company sold shares to subscribers at a cost of $24.00 to be paid over a three-year period in $8.00 instalments.

Unless a full time lineman was hired, the local farmers were responsible for the repair and maintenance of the telephone lines themselves - a large task as storms wreaked havoc on the lines across the prairies frequently. The rural mutual companies continued to operate until the late 1960's and early 1970's when AGT once again took over the responsibility of providing telephone service to the rural residents of Alberta. Next, AGT buried cable along the roads and the telephone poles disappeared.

Initially, connections between telephones were made manually; early switchboard operators had a challenging, yet rewarding job. In 1946, Lloydminster had a total of 219 commercial and residential telephones with their numbers starting at 1 and ending with 219. Each time a person made a call, the operator would answer, "Number, please." She would then connect the cable to the proper number and ring it manually. If the line was busy, the operator would often take a message, and later call the person to deliver it. In Lloydminster, the operator often knew where a person was and would transfer the call to the building where they were at

that time. As Larraine Davidson, an AGT operator from 1946-1947, remembers, "Since there were only 219 telephones in Lloydminster, sometimes the lines would be busy. We would often go pick up workers for a long distance call. We'd slip across to the Alberta Hotel and get a person to come to the phone."

Photo courtesy of BCHCC

The switchboard operator was responsible for making the General Ring, one long ring, which everyone would answer, to inform people of community events, health concerns, school closures, and emergencies. A General Ring, for instance, was made in 1929 to warn people of the "Great Fire" which was raging through downtown Lloydminster.

In rural areas, multi-line party telephones were in use until the 1970's and 1980's. Two to twenty subscribers shared one line, with a different ring for each subscriber.

In the 1950's, a series of mechanical and electronic devices were introduced that allowed switching to be done automatically. The switchboard operators in Lloydminster were no longer needed since this allowed direct dialing to the party required.

The early settlers would certainly find the advances in telephone technology astounding: from telephone wires constructed on 2 x 4's to underground lines, from crank style phones to cell phones, and from party lines to multiple lines in one residence. Making a quick call to a friend or family member on the other side of the world is now routine. (Just remember to check the time zone before calling!)

Above: Inside the Lloydminster Telegraph office in 1908. Prior to the introduction of long distance telephone service, messages were often relayed through telegraph..

Advances in telephone technology have made countless options available, such as call forwarding, call waiting, call display, voice mail, busy call return, three-way calling, video-conferencing, and relay service for the hearing impaired.

One of the greatest advancements, though, has been the introduction of the cellular phone, which first came to Canada in 1982. In its early years, the device primarily served resource industries, but by 1986 competitive cellular phone service was launched. By the beginning of the 21st century, small hand-held phones were a familiar sight on the streets of Lloydminster. Below: Jason Whiting receives a call.

Television and Radio

In 1957, it was questionable whether Lloydminster, with a population of approximately 5000 people, provided a large enough market for a radio station. Yet, Arthur Shortell forged ahead with his plan. He established Sask-Alta Broadcasters Limited, and CKSA Radio was born at 1150 on the radio dial.

In 1960, CKSA expanded into the television arena offering the residents of the Border City their access to a medium that had swept to international popularity, forever changing our lifestyle.

In 1963, CHSA TV (as it was called briefly) and CKSA Radio adopted the same call letters. CKSA Television was broadcast on channel 2 and CKSA radio's frequency changed to 1080. CBC colour programs began airing in 1966, and the station spent considerable money in 1968 to provide local colour programming. CKSA's staff was excited by the many technological advances which were improving their service to the surrounding communities.

Photo by Don Whiting

Photos courtesy of Wes Saunders

Arthur Shortell had the vision to establish a radio and television station in Lloydminster, a small community of 5000 people in 1957. Above left: Arthur poses with CKSA's radio transmitter in the late '50's. Shortell's technical know-how was an asset to the station. There were very few owners who could fix their own transmitters when they broke down, but Shortell could. Arthur Shortell understood the technical aspects of his business inside out, which helped to catapult the station to success. Prior to establishing the station, Art was a Ham radio operator, and this gave him the inspiration to establish a radio and television station in Lloydminster.
Above right: At the C.P.R. station, Wes Saunders (right) interviews Shortell (centre), President of the Chamber of Commerce at the time. Arthur Shortell was an active community member who served many local organizations including Town Council and the Lloydminster Fire Department. "He had a deep interest in doing what was best for Lloydminster," recalls broadcaster Wes Saunders. CKSA has continued Shortell's legacy through involvement in many community projects over the years, such as the Lloydminster Exhibition Grandstand, Lloydminster Regional Hospital Foundation, Lloydminster Leisure Centre, Tournament of Champions, Gift of Christmas, Alberta Winter Games, Alberta Summer Games, and the Vic Juba Community Theatre.

Broadcast Centre's operation has grown over the years as re-broadcasting stations were added at Bonnyville, Provost and Meadow Lake in the 1970's. A second television station, CITL, began broadcasting in 1978, and the radio station increased its power from 10,000 to 50,000 watts in 1989. Top inset: In the studio for Election '82. Residents have greatly appreciated CKSA's local election coverage over the years. Bottom inset: Wes Saunders (right) with colleague and CTV national news anchor Lloyd Robertson.

The next major boon to the station came in 1976 when a second channel, CTV affiliate, CITL was added. The CRTC had been looking for an operator interested in offering the CTV affiliate in the Lloydminster area, but there were no bites. CKSA President Arthur Shortell had been looking into the matter for several years, and he finally convinced the CRTC that he could make it viable. The CTV affiliate was granted to CKSA, and Shortell became one of few broadcasters to operate a "twin stick" station.

Unfortunately, in the same year, Arthur Shortell died. His wife Mary assumed operation, and the station forged ahead. The station continued to expand its broadcast area and rebroadcasting stations were added in Bonnyville and Provost.

Over the years, the station continued to maintain a technological edge. In 1993, CKSA radio purchased a computer system which allowed them to bypass tape and broadcast songs and commercials from computer hard drives. In 1995, a similar system for video was purchased. As one of the first stations to use the system for the scheduling of commercials, CKSA was a pioneer. Prior to the introduction of the digital system, commercials had been broadcast from tape, which occupied valuable space and eventually deteriorated.

It is uncertain how the station will adapt as the communications industry continues to evolve.

broadcast center

Photos courtesy of Wes Saunders

Wes Saunders - "The People's Voice"

When Wes Saunders was 12 years old, he became ill with pneumonia. Confined to his bed with only a radio to keep him company, Wes tuned into radio shows such as "The Lone Ranger", and he realized his future career path. Saunders' father was a radio/television technician and a ham radio hobbyist. "When I was fifteen years old," Saunders recalls, "I had my dad build a mock radio control

Wes Saunders (above) anchored the evening news in Lloydminster for years in addition to hosting other local programs such as "Response", a local political program.

room in the basement of our Hamilton home. Together with my brother, we broadcast music and news reports to our upstairs living room for our neighbourhood pals."

In 1944, Wes and his brother, Al Saunders, auditioned for the job of hosting a teen radio show, sponsored by Kellogg's. The station realized Wes' potential, and he was hired, at the age of seventeen, as a control room operator and weekend anchor (the youngest the station had ever hired) doing weather, time, and station breaks.

Saunders eventually went on to CHML AM where he took a job as program operator and worked with the famous Gordie Tapp, who later starred as cousin Clem on Country Hoedown, Tommy Hunter, and Hee Haw. Saunders did production work on the radio star's show "What's on Tapp"; it was a fast-paced demanding job and Saunders valued the experience greatly.

After a short stint in Brantford, Ontario, Wes moved to Edmonton in 1954 to be closer to his future wife Vera. In no time at all, Saunders was the morning newsman for CFRN Radio, eventually becoming a disc jockey for the station. In 1960, Saunders moved to CHED, the top radio station in Edmonton. taking the only available shift, the night shift in order to work there.

Two years later, he ran into former CFRN director Jim Findlay, who had become the general manager for CKSA radio in Lloydminster. Tired of his night shift, Saunders asked Jim for a job, and he was offered the position of Program Director of Radio at the Lloydminster station. Saunders was involved in all aspects of CKSA radio, hosting a three-hour mid-morning show, and supervising production in the afternoons.

In 1963, he began double duty as Program Director of both Radio and Television. Saunders was responsible for everything that aired. In the fast paced world of television, it was a seven-day a week job. Eventually it proved to be more than one person could handle, and Saunders' was scaled down to news director for television and radio, which he continued for many years.

One of the biggest local stories came to Saunders in March of 1977 when the Alberta Hotel caught fire. Saunders received the call at 3:00 in the morning. Videotape was not yet a reality, and the newsman raced to the scene with his 35 mm black and white camera. The story was put together for the evening broadcast using the fourteen photographs, which Saunders had taken to show the sequence of events as the fire raged from the main floor office to the third floor.

Before the advent of video tape all local programs were live and in-studio. In the 1960's, CKSA television only had one black and white camera (above) which was used for all local programming. Above: Wes Saunders cautiously offers a treat to a hungry cheetah while guest Al Oeming looks on.

In 1993, Saunders retired, receiving honours from across Canada, including membership in the "Half Century Club" for broadcasters who had been in the profession for more than fifty years. CTV anchor Lloyd Robertson sent his well wishes at the end of his evening broadcast, and Deputy Prime Minister Don Mazankowski awarded Saunders a commemorative plaque which hailed him as "the people's voice".

Communications - Bill Till Style

Bill Till has made his life in the communications industry. In the mid 1950's, Till built his first HAM radio, and since he did not have a tower handy, he used the closest telephone pole. This worked well until the telephone company informed him of their displeasure and cut him off.

Although there were many Lloydminster HAM radio enthusiasts, such as Rowley Noyes and Basil King, for years, a club was not formed until 1975. A VHF Repeater was installed on a tower located on Mount Joy Ski Hill, where it has remained ever since. Most who have been part of the Lloydminster club, such as Ron Gillies and Len Pryor, credit Bill with keeping the club alive almost purely through his enthusiasm for the medium.

The first radio system in town was a remote control radio base station on the old water tower, owned by Husky Oil. In 1964, Husky built its own tower at the top of Mount Joy with a repeater on it to increase mobile capacity. As time passed, more contractors hooked into the system for their own uses increasing strain on the system.

Photo courtesy of Bill Till

When the oil patch started to boom in 1970, Bill decided to start his own business, Till Communications Ltd. The business was devoted to sales, repairs and leasing of towers, but the repeater service was one of their biggest fields. They equipped, licensed and maintained repeater channels for rent on radio common carriers, until Motorola bought them out in 1985.

The future of communications is in the internet and the wireless web according to Bill Till. Soon satellites will provide rural areas with better connections and greater options. Maintenance of web related services will become even more important, but service shops will become less common, as parts in cellular phones and other portable communications devices become smaller, increasing the difficulty and expense for private shops to repair them. On the other hand, prices of such devices continue to drop, making it increasingly common to purchase new rather than having a faulty device repaired. Many stores have adapted to the trend, moving out of repair services and into sales.

One of the most colourful characters to ever reach radio listeners and television viewers in the Midwest was Ernie Ford. Born on September 13, 1924, Ford served in the Navy and participated in the D-Day invasion in World War II. After the war, Ford decided on a career in radio, which began in Shelby, Montana. Ford had his demons; he was dealing with alcoholism, and over several years he worked for more than thirty radio stations in the United States, landing in and out of hospitals and jails on a regular basis. By 1967, he had sobered up and landed in Lloydminster to broadcast for CKSA Radio. Later on in his career, Ford became known as "Mr. Rodeo". Despite having an artificial leg, he travelled over a million miles during his lifetime promoting the sport..

Photo courtesy of Wes Saunders

Digital satellite service, for example, posed a threat to local television stations such as CKSA in the 1990's. Local channels were not available to customers lured by satellite service provider's numerous channels and options. Now, with the launch of larger satellites with greater storage capacity, it may be possible to offer local programming options to the satellite service subscriber in the not too distant future.

Radio listeners had more alternatives near the end of the century. Alberta public radio station CKUA added a re-broadcasting station on the roof of Lakeland College in 1992. Later, in May of 2001, CKSA radio faced a new local competitor. CKLM "The Goat", began broadcasting Top 40 and Classic Rock at 100,000 watts at 106.1 on the FM dial.

Midwest Broadcasting has avoided the lure and the offers of larger companies to merge or take control of its operation. As of 2001, the station remains a family owned business with Mary Shortell, Arthur's wife as president, and her sons-in-law, Ken Ruptash, vice-president and general manager, and Graham Brown, vice-president of sales.

The communications industry has evolved rapidly over the past century. Local residents have always been keen adopters of the latest technology to stay in touch with local and world happenings. Today, no matter where one is, news from home is only a telephone call or an e-mail away. The danger is that all of the global communication options available may draw us away from our local community and into the generic national and global media. Recently, many Lloydminsterites have opted for satellite television service which does not offer a local channel. In the past, whether it was George Baynton's hectoring editorials pushing for development in Lloydminster, or the reassuring voice of Wes Saunders providing us with a locally flavoured summary of the days events, we had a sense of locality which may now be lost.

Above: Ernie Ford, as "Grandpa Sneezby", endeared himself to the children of the Lloydminster area with his afternoon television program. Avalanches of fan mail poured in to the station weekly.

Ernie has become a part of Lloydminster mythology with stories that grow larger through the years. During a break on one live episode of Grandpa Sneezby, Ford made some off-colour remarks to the cameraman on the set. Unfortunately, Ford's microphone had not been turned off and the remark was broadcast to the entire viewing audience.

After eighteen consecutive years of broadcasting for CKSA Radio and TV, Ernie passed away in 1984. He secured a place forever in Lloydminster folklore, and it is unlikely that he will ever be forgotten.

Michael Higgins (below) began working for CKSA in the radio news department in 1990. After a stint in television reporting, Higgins became the News Director in the Summer of 1992. Michael most enjoys the managerial aspect of his job which allows him to "shape a lot of young careers"; Higgins is also seen every evening as the anchor of News Hour.

Chapter Thirteen

Community Service

Research by Linda Nykolaychuk, Ian Goodwillie, Penny Manners, and Denise Ramsay Mackenzie

Decoration Day, 1954: The Royal Canadian Legion, Branch # 39

By 1992, the Foresters had given a combined 633 years of service to Lloydminster. Members from left to right: (Back) Ken Moncrief, Ralph Conlon, Bill Conlon, Elmer Enzenauer, Pete Dribnenky, Jon Wich, Roy Hawkins. (Middle) Bill Lomas, Lawrence Davidson, Art Bexson, Jack Handel, Ed Kobsar, Joe Rooks. (Front) Lloyd Holmes, Lloyd Andrews, Tony Patton, Hugh Hilts, Pete Heide, Lawrence Tripp

If not for the millions of hours, literally, that the people of Lloydminster have volunteered in the service of our community over the past 100 years, where would we be? The spirit of lending a helping hand to a neighbour, which allowed many a Colonist to survive, is still alive today, enriching and enhancing our community life. Every single resident has benefited from the efforts of the scores of volunteers who contributed to our parks, swimming pools, arenas, and recreational facilities. They have provided educational opportunities for children, they have fed and clothed the disadvantaged, and they have encouraged us to live as one, in a community where all are welcome. If it were possible, all should be honoured, but space constraints allow us only to highlight a few of the many special people who have given of themselves greatly.

The Canadian Foresters

The Canadian Foresters established in Lloydminster on November 30, 1906, with fourteen charter members including school caretaker Martin Browne, and druggist "Pop" Ellis, who had been a member of the organization in P.E.I. before coming west. The Foresters re-established themselves in June of 1952 as Court Rising Sun # 1173. The first ladies court, Court Border Star, began shortly after. Cancer research support has been one of the major focuses of the Foresters. In 1994, efforts to combat family stress and child abuse, especially at a national level, were highlighted.

The organization has also contributed to many important local organizations including the United Way, W.A. Thorpe Recovery Centre, and the Lloydminster Hospital. As well, the Foresters have granted scholarships to junior high students and bought a bus for the Boy Scouts to name only a few of their many worthy deeds.

The Royal Canadian Legion – Branch # 39

At the conclusion of World War I, Lloydminster's returned veterans formed a branch of the Great War Veteran's Association. The year was 1919, and Col. B. Laws became the first president with Harry Pick as secretary. They held their meetings in a variety of places: Immigration Hall, the Drill Hall, Hall's Store, and even a booth in one of the local cafes.

In 1926, the Branch took on a new name: the Canadian Legion British Empire Service League. "B.E.S.L." was dropped from the name in 1958, and in 1961, the organization made one final name change to "The Royal Canadian Legion".

The end of World War II brought an influx of new veterans into the Legion. They soon became involved and assumed the responsibilities of the Great War Veterans. The first World War II veteran to be president of Branch # 39 was Wardy Clifford, in 1947. Clifford held office again in 1972, in his silver anniversary with the Legion.

In Clifford's first term as president, the Legion brought Model "T" Ford Races to Lloydminster, a spectacle that was well received by the community. In 1948, the Branch began to sponsor baseball tournaments with teams from places such as Delisle, Swift Current, and Kamloops competing for $5,500 in prize money. In addition, members donated their time to build bleachers to accommodate the growing numbers of people who were watching the games.

Through the hard work of Ted Mitchell, Slim Thorpe and others, a semi-pro baseball team was established in 1953. The Legion was able to secure land to the east of town for a ball diamond. Today it is known as the Legion Ball Park. Unfortunately, semi-pro ball came to an end six years later.

As happened across Canada, the Legion in Lloydminster experienced declining memberships as veterans aged. Today, the Legion is

Photo courtesy of Wardy Clifford

The Legion has long organized and taken part in parades and Remembrance Day services which honour their fallen comrades and honour the service which all veterans gave to their country in times of war.

Photo courtesy of Wardy Clifford

Construction of the first Legion Hall began in 1948, but due to a lack of funds, it was not fully completed for several years and functions were held in the basement. The Legion Hall hosted many well-attended events and performers such as Johnny Horton. The hall was also rented for anniversaries, weddings, and meetings. Most importantly, the Legion now had a home for the annual "Remembrance Day Service".

In 1957, the Legion held a "Burning of the Mortgage" of the Hall (shown in picture - left). Mayor Miner and other guests attended. The membership chose to sell the Hall to the Lloydminster and District Cooperative Ltd. in 1984, and a new facility was built on 49th Avenue. After moving into the new building, the Branch took on new projects including winter cribbage tournaments with large payouts.

open to anyone who wishes to join, but only servicemen or descendants of servicemen have voting power. The Royal Canadian Legion has been an active part of Lloydminster for over eighty years, and it is well recognized for its efforts within the community.

The Benevolent and Protective Order of the Elks # 171 and the Royal Purple

Inaugurated in the Fall of 1927, the Lloydminster Elks Club originally met upstairs in the old Town Hall. Unfortunately, the original charter was lost in a fire, and the current replacement charter dates back to 1938.

As a service club, the Elks supported many important projects. In the 1930's, they sponsored Christmas Matinees for children. During World War II, they raised money to send milk to Britain and were recognized in 1943 as being the top fundraiser in the "Save the Children" campaign.

The Elks have continued their efforts on behalf of children, both locally and nationally. In recent years, they raised money to help produce a series of videos on the issue of bullying in school. The videos were made available to all interested schools. Today, the club continues to contribute to local charities, bursaries, and scholarships.

In 1947, the Secretary of the Lloydminster Elks, Mrs. Alfred Studds, led the organizing of a female chapter of the service club, the Royal Purple. For many years, the Royal Purple raised the majority of its funds by catering local community events. The first banquet they catered was on Dec. 20, 1947 - the Husky Refinery Christmas Party. In 1957, the Elks' Hall was built on the Meridian on the north end of town. The ladies became very busy with catering jobs at the new location, and the money raised was put directly back into the community. As Lloydminster has grown, the Royal Purple has shifted their focus away from the catering as the Elk's Hall is no longer capable of holding the growing crowds.

The original charter members of the Royal Purple, 1947. Left to right: Rita Bailey, Claire (Coward) Ellis, Doris Clutterbuck, Marg Philpotts, Erma Avery, Marj Hoskins, ?, Mary Ross, Mardy Gallagher, Lil Scogland, Ann Kinney. Seated officers: ?, Bessie Noyes, ?

One of the best known Kinsmen events in Saskatchewan is the TeleMiracle and the Lloydminster Club is always active in its support. Below: Kinsmen and Kinettes take part in "Sitting in a Hot Tub" in 1996, a pledge fundraiser for Telemiracle.

The Kinsmen and Kinettes of Lloydminster

The Lloydminster Kinsmen Club was organized in 1929. Initially, the Kinsmen was a service club for young men between the ages of 19 to 44. In recent years, the upper age limit has been lifted.

The Kinettes were organized some years later in 1952. Although the club originally only accepted the wives of Kinsmen, today the Kinettes Club is open to any female over the age of 19. One of the first Kinette projects was a "piKINic Booth" at Sandy Beach. Cold plates, hot dogs, lemonade, pop, pie, and ice cream were all sold to raise money for the many Kin projects.

In Saskatchewan, the most visible Kinsmen project has been "Telemiracle", which started in 1977. The Kinsmen Foundation manages request of funds raised through Telemiracle; local families and organizations have benefited tremendously. The Bea Fisher Centre, Lloydminster Sexual Assault Centre, Interval Home, and the Handivan have all received funding. Dr. Fred Murray, Delores Funk, and Alex Robertson, all of Lloydminster, were instrumental in establishing the Kinsmen Foundation and Telemiracle in 1977.

Of the many men and women who have been Lloydminster Kinsmen and Kinettes, the Swift family is well recognized for their involvement. Three generations of Swifts served as president of the club. Jack Swift followed in the footsteps of his father Earle and his grandfather Jack. Jack's mother, Gwen, and his wife, Sharon, joined the three men in being awarded life memberships.

Rotary Club of Lloydminster

The world's oldest service club, Rotary International, extended to Lloydminster with the chartering of a club here on February 13, 1929. Rotary encourages fellowship across the community by basing membership on vocational classifications.

The early weekly meetings were held in the Britannia Hotel until that burned down in the Great Fire of August 1929. The Club remained active though and took on the Great Depression in stride. Local members travelled extensively to Rotary functions in the United States and Canada.

They were also active in serving the community at home. During the 1930's the Public Library was an entirely volunteer effort. Rotary assisted with numerous fund-raising activities on the library's behalf. One of the more popular of these was the screening of motion picture shows which during the late 1930's generated almost $40.00 per year, more than 70% of the funds necessary to operate the library. During World War II Rotarians raised funds to buy blankets for refugees from the war and shipped magazines to the soldiers.

Support of students has always been a high priority of Rotary. The Lloydminster Club has been sending a delegate to the Rotary hosted Adventure in Citizenship program in Ottawa since 1952. Over the years, other Adventures have been added until in recent years over 20 students annually experience everything from weekend vocational tours to one-year exchange visits to far away countries, the latter involving Lloydminster students since 1984.

The Rotary Club of Lloydminster sponsored the formation of new clubs in Vegreville in 1951, in Vermilion in 1955, and on June 3, 1999, a second local club – the Rotary Club of Lloydminster – Border City was chartered.

Thus, Rotary remains an active and growing force in Lloydminster. A fund raising venture such as

Charter Members of the Rotary Club of Lloydminster	
February 13, 1929	
Tom Barber	Baker
Lionel M. Bourns	Garage
James W. Bowyer	Cartage
William L. Cameron	Merchant
Herman L. Coles	Insurance
Rev. Canon A. Cross	Clergy
Charles G. Davidson	Manager
John F. Davidson	Hotel
Rene Delalande	Gunsmith
Rev. Father Dobson	Priest
Charles H. Elger	Railway Agent
E. W. H. Howell	Auto Dealer
Harold Huxley	Auctioneer
Charles H. Moxley	Druggist
A. J. Nichols	Butcher
A. F. Pals	Creamery
J. H. Stevenson	Real Estate
Thomas Westcombe	Oil
Joseph G. Willard	Publisher
O. C. Yates	Agent

Rotary support of the Public Library continues as 1993-1994 Club President, Dr. Vic Stelmaschuk, assists Dorothy Baynton unveil a microfilm reader to assist readers of the collection of Lloydminster Times newspapers Mrs. Baynton had helped secure.

Photo courtesy Rotary Club of Lloydminster

Photo by Charles Lamb Photography

Back row l-r: John Acton, Jeff Spencer, Frank Tuplin, Les Harper, Gordon Herle, Amador Lopez, Ross Ulmer, Bob Christie, Stan Bugiera, Ron Harris, Jr., John Vinek, Ron Mailman, Randy Aston, Tracy Ball. Fourth row l-r: Dwight Mushtaler, Lloyd Manning, Bob Jack, Sr., Barry Stevens, Gordon Harris, Ray McIlwrick, Scott Musgrave, David McCaw, Emil Lychak, Daniel Moskal, Doug Aston, Bob Steeg, Darrell Howell, John Harvey, Bob Noyes, Ken Burke, Bob Little. Third row l-r: Betty Christensen, Mike Sydoryk, Trevor Coulombe, Ron Harris, Sr., Mel Lowe, Dean Sauer, Wayde Blythe, Vern Belsheim, Kevin Kromery, John Skene, Jack Allen, Rod Sellers, Ed Andersen, Bill Musgrave, Arne Baron, Pat Skinner, Ron Walsh. Second row l-r: Glenda Elkow, Leona Beamish, Mimi McMaster, Merv Loewen, Doug Gray, Pat Gulak, Franklin Foster, Don Whiting, Bill Till, Elmer Nykiforuk, Brian McCook, Raffath Sayeed, Bob Myers, Ron Gillies, Charles Lamb. Front Row l-r: Celene Polischuk, Joanne Berry, Kelly Russell, Robin Acton, Terri Selin, Glenys Coleman, Ken Coleman, Gerald Gagnon, Dwaine Bexson, Bernal Ulsifer.

Rotary emphasizes building international good will and friendship. Below left: Jakob Eliasen of Sweden was hosted for the 1999-2000 year and learned about Western Canada.

the annual LobsterFest attracts a crowd of over 700 and some years has raised over $12,000.00. Such community support allows Rotary to provide a variety of student and community services. Rotary seems well positioned to continue to provide community service well into our second century.

Photos by Don Whiting

Centre: Since 1934, the Rotary Club has held Rural Urban meetings to foster area goodwill. Shown here is the 1992 committee: (l-r) John Skinner, Don Whiting, Dr. Vic Stelmaschuk, Barry Stevens, Henry Wilson, guest speaker, Dan Moskal, Dr. Glenn Weir, Dr. Richard Starke, and Bob Jack, Sr.
Above right: Kevin Kromrey of Evergreen Greenhouses has for several years donated a number of poinsettias which are auctioned at a Rotary meeting and the proceeds donated to various Christmas charities.

The Boy Scouts and Girl Guides of Canada

Scouting came to Canada in 1914. It is estimated that the First Lloydminster Scouts was organized in the late teens or early 1920's.

In the beginning, Scouting was for boys ages 11 and older, but as time went on, younger boys were introduced to the organization via Beavers and Cubs (ages 5 to 10). In 1995, co-ed Scouting began.

In 1954, an agreement was made with the Lloydminster Public School District for the use of a portion of their land beside the Meridian School. A Girl Guide/Scout Hall was built on the location, and it remained there until the Guides and Scouts moved to 37th Street on the Saskatchewan side of the border in 1995.

The 1st Lloydminster Pack (Brownie unit) was registered on August 27, 1936. The program quickly grew in popularity and the 1st Lloydminster Guide Company was formed three years later. Word spread, and a 2nd Guide Company was registered in April 1939. By 1943, there were five registered Guiding Companies and five Packs. As the Guides got older they progressed

into a Ranger Company (established in 1944) and a Pathfinder Unit (established in 1979). In the 1990's, a younger unit for five and six year olds, the Sparks, was added.

The groups first held meetings at the

Town Hall. Eventually, they moved to the United Church, Legion Hall, and the Scout/Guide Hall in 1954.

The Boy Scouts and Girl Guides march past McLeod's Store in the 1930's.
Girl Guides preparing camp at Dilberry Lake.
Cubs winter camping. January 2001.

Helene Geier (below) was a noteworthy volunteer who gave more than twenty-two years of service to the Lloydminster Exhibition Association, including 19 years as a director. Dedicated to keeping our pioneer heritage alive, Helene devoted endless hours to making Home Arts an interesting and educational part of the fair; Throughout the years she was an active volunteer always there to lend a hand, be it painting the grandstand with a toilet bowl brush, or moving great piles of rock for landscaping. In 1992, Helene passed away. She will always be remembered, though, for her enthusiasm, thoughtfulness, and valuable service to the community.

Community Service is an important aspect of the Scouting and Guiding movement. In 1947, the Ranger's main service project was making and collecting clothing for European relief, while the Girl Guides were the first volunteers at the Lloydminster Public Library. In the year of Canada's Centennial, 1967, Brownie Packs collected pennies for a special Centennial Tree, donating the money raised to the hospital for the purchase of two infant recliners. Today, Guides are just as involved in the community with visits to senior citizen centres, craft projects, coat checks, and babysitting.

With a membership growth of 20% since 1999, the Scouts and Guides movement continues to thrive in the Border City.

Photo courtesy of Florence Harris

Ronald C. Harris served in the R.C.A.F. during World War II as Senior Flight Engineer with the Eastern Command Air Crew. In 1948, Ron moved his wife Florence and their children to Lloydminster where he founded Harris Electric. An active member of the community, Ron held positions with the Rotary Club, St. Anthony's Pastoral Council, Lloydminster Chamber of Commerce, Knights of Columbus, and was Captain and Commanding Officer of Squadron #186 RCACS. Harris was awarded the Canadian Forces Decoration Medal in 1966, the Centennial Medal in 1967, and the Lion's Club Citizen of the Year in 1987.

The Lloydminster Royal Canadian Air Cadet Squadron

On September 25, 1942 a group met with Flight Lieutenant Dall of the R.C.A.F. to consider starting an Air Cadet Squadron in Lloydminster. He suggested that the work could be integrated with local High School courses with instructors from Lloydminster and North Battleford. On October 1, 1942, an organizing committee, chaired by Dr. G. L. Cooke and made up of D. McKenna, J. D. Hamilton, G. F. Baynton, and S. S. Hall, began the work.

Boys who completed the requirements of the Air Cadet course while attending school would be given full credit for it. A large amount of equipment for training purposes was sent to the squadron by the R.C.A.F. The major cost to the local committee was providing uniforms for the boys.

The immediate objective was to raise $300 as part payment for the first 50 uniforms. This objective was met mainly through donations from service clubs such as Rotary and Elks, along with business contributions, and dollar donations from private citizens. It being wartime, support was encouraged from ladies of the town and district who had husbands, sons, brothers and boyfriends in the RCAF.

By November 26, 1942, there were 33 Lloydminster High School students enrolled in the newly formed Air Cadet Flight, commanded by Flying Officer E. S. Laird, principal of the local High School. Mr. Laird felt that Air Cadet training was a valuable asset for civilian life,

Photo courtesy of Gwen Rempel

The Lloydminster Squadron in 1943. **Back Row:** *Ken McCurdy, George Phillips, Tom Wilson, Bob Freyman, Sandy Hill, Bob Anderson, Jim Hill, Headley Manners, Barry Packman* **Second Row:** *Jay Burns, Emmitt Holmes, Percy Marshall, Ian Campbell, Don Alward, George Larviere, Bill Warmington, Art Strautman, Dick George, Wayne Oliver, Antony Bourne* **Third Row:** *Bob Oliver, Bill Till, Harry Byrt, Alan Walker, Alan Miller, Mr. E.S. Laird O/C, Mr. M.L. Hydes AOJ, Dennis McGale, Bill Laird, Bob Howell, Gerald Wright* **Front Row:** *John Ellis, Harvey Westcombe, Art Morgan, Morley Falkingham*

A "United Way"

Left: United Way Directors, 2000. Centre: Ray Kizinger and Mayor Pat Gulak raise the United Way flag, 1988. Right: Raising funds for the United Way, the Annual Corporate Bed Race, 1988. Photos courtesy of Ken Gillis

There can be no doubt that the service clubs of Lloydminster have contributed enormously to the community over the years. One organization, the Lloydminster Community Chest, which had been known as the Council of Service Clubs, was established in 1953 to better organize and unite the various community organizations to meet common fundraising objectives. Initially, the Chest organized canvasses and drives for funds to be shared within the community. By 1955, eleven clubs were involved with the fundraising efforts. The organization had difficulties in these years meeting their objectives, and the chest was re-organized in 1961 into the "United Appeal", which changed its name to the "United Way" in 1974.

Until the 1990's, many members of the Board of the Lloydminster and District United Way were also affiliated with the charitable agencies in the community. Under the guidance of president Ken Gillis (front right in left photo above) in 1992, the United Way freed up Agency personnel allowing greater involvement of local community-minded citizens. In 2000, there were 19 United Way Agencies, and the campaign goal was $150,000. They achieved this target, marking the most successful United Way year to date.

---

instilling the values of discipline, esprit de corps, and positive mental and moral attitudes.

Air Cadets consisted of boys aged 12 – 15 and 15 – 18. They were under adult officers and instructors appointed by a civilian committee responsible for the work. The course of studies required 288 hours of work over a two year period, and included such subjects as: aircraft recognition, airmanship, hygiene and sanitation, knots and splices, mathematics, meteorology, air navigation, physical training, signals, and drill.

Courses were added over the years, including: civil defense, leadership, radio, engines, electricity, electronics, photography, aero-engines, safe driving, band, first aid, and marksmanship. Lloydminster's youth have benefitted from a program which encourages discipline, strength, and wisdom.

The Lloydminster Lions Club

The Lloydminster Lions Club dates back to September 1949, when the Unity Lions Club sponsored the Lloydminster branch. Charter Night was held on February 13, 1950 with 62 members installed.

The first large club project was undertaken in 1951 when the Lions began publishing a Business and Residential Telephone Directory. The only other directory available at the time was the rather large and somewhat cumbersome Edmonton and District Directory.

Photo by Don Whiting

One of the major goals of the Centennial Association was to establish a local archives. With community support a space was secured in the basement of the Atrium Centre. Shown above (standing: l-r) are long time archives volunteers Donna Arie and Kay Hauer, accepting a donation regarding the Kenilworth Lake Goose Project.

Below: Art Gellert, a long serving member of the Lloydminster Lions Club.

Photo courtesy of Sandy Hill

A female chapter, the Lloydminster Lion'ls, was organized in 1962. This club operated for many years before the rules were eventually changed by Lions international. Today, both men and women enjoy membership in the Lions Club. Above: Bea Summersgill on a parade float in 1982, holding one of the large print books which the Lion'L's donated to the library, seniors' homes, and the hospital.

Above: A kiosk and cemetery gate was sponsored by the Lions.

The first Lloydminster chapter of Beta Sigma Phi existed from 1951 - 1959. A new chapter (below) was chartered in 1971. The chapter has given many hours of service and financial contributions to the community over the years. Back row (l-r): Darlene Jacques, Joyce Hamilton, Phyllis Stephens, Marg Cline, Wendy Bodnar, Colleen Brauer, Doris Brooks, Georgia McConnell, Pat Kwasnica, Vivian Knisley, Marilyn Plant. Front row (l-r) Geri Hill, Florence Malmgren, Jean Baker, Linda Webb, Joan Steeg, Grace Falasca.

The Lions continued to publish their directory for seven years until the Alberta Attorney General wrote the club a letter informing them that they were infringing copyright. The club discontinued publication, but all was not in vain. The government saw the need for the directory and began to publish it themselves.

In 1953, the Club built and raffled off a house on 50th Street west. The venture raised several thousand dollars, and the money was used to build the Lions Club Children's Playground on Highway 16. The Club continued its enhancement of the city by providing three additional parks: Glendale Park in 1970, Colonial Park in 1974, and Anniversary Park in 1979, the Club's 30th year.

Working with the blind is a target for Lions' clubs throughout the world. The local club has supported many projects to assist people with sight impairments. Local projects have included blind bowling, an annual supper for the blind, and annual contributions to the CNIB. The Lions also became involved in delivering donated corneas to the Saskatchewan Eye Bank. In 1998, the club was honoured for delivering more corneas to Saskatoon than any other club or agency.

Since 1986, the Club's greatest on-going project has been Lions Quest, a positive youth development program which teaches important life skills such as solving problems without violence, communicating effectively, taking responsibility, and learning to appreciate differences. The combined efforts of the Lloydminster Lions and the Border City Lions Club has funded the training of over 300 teachers in Lloydminster and area. Today, the program is being used in classrooms, public and separate, from kindergarten to grade eight.

The Border City Lions Club was formed in 1982 to accommodate the growing number of people who wished to become a part of the Lions organization. Known as the Lloydminster Breakfast Lions Club in its early years, the Border City Lions' most noteworthy project was the Annual Lions Telethon. First broadcast in 1993, the Telethon was well received by the community. The Lloyminster Lions Club was asked to assist in 1998, and as of 2001, the Telethon continues to be broadcast every year with proceeds used to help cover the annual Lions Quest budget, and donations made to many organizations including The Twin Rivers Health Foundation, The Bea Fisher Foundation, L.A.B.I.S., and the Lloydminster Regional Health Foundation.

A number of local members have served at district level. Lion Peter Sleight served a term as District Governor, while Lions Vic Juba, Reg Summers-Gill, and Sandy Hill have all been Deputy District Governors.

In July of 1999, the Border City Lions Club's five remaining members transferred to the Lloydminster Lions Club. The spirit of the Lions Club continues to live and grow within the organization. Members hold socials, toboggan parties, fishing outings, golf tournaments, and whist parties. "Couple this with fellowship and the joy of achievement," says a club member, "and you have a winning combination of why club membership in the Lloydminster Lions Club has been so satisfying for the last fifty years!"

Lloydminster Association for Community Living

An advocacy organization committed to ensuring true community living for all people, the organization which would later be known as the Lloydminster Association for Community Living (LACL) was founded in 1957. Early members such as Bea Fisher, Evelyn Nelson, Ray Brown, and Clayton Reeves came together to advocate the right to education for all children. The organization has a longstanding history of supporting individuals with disabilities, their families, and the community.

> "Community living is about neighborhoods where all people live, learn, and work together. Everyone deserves a good life in the community."
>
> The Lloydminster Association for Community Living

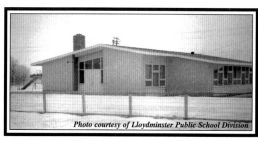

Photo courtesy of Lloydminster Public School Division

The L.A.C.L. played a key role in the establishment of a school for children with developmental disabilities. After several years of shifting from location to location, Parkland School was built in 1966.

Today, the school is no longer in operation as advocacy efforts are enabling students to attend regular classrooms with appropriate supports.

The LACL was involved in the establishment of initiatives such as the Bea Fisher Centre, the Lloydminster Early Intervention Program, the Volunteer Telephone Device for the Deaf, and the Respite program.

In 1969, the LACL pushed for a "Sheltered Workshop" in

Zuhy Sayeed - Building an Inclusive Community

In 1981, Zuhy Sayeed and her husband Dr. Raffath Sayeed, who was serving as the chairman of the Bea Fisher Centre, attended the Canadian National Conference on Disabilities in Quebec. "I had never been brought up with people with disabilities," she said in an interview printed in the March 29, 1995 issue of the *Lloydminster Times*. "I knew there were facilities but I had not thought any further." For Sayeed, it was an awakening.

Shortly after, the Sayeed's second son Rashaad was born with a disability; the couple committed themselves to providing a quality of life for their son and all people with disabilities.

Zuhy joined the Lloydminster Association for Community Living in 1984, and since then, she has been involved on the front lines of local, provincial, national, and international associations which promote the inclusion of persons with disabilities into the community. In 1987, she and her husband were appointed to a provincial task force on inclu-

Zuhy Sayeed, a former schoolteacher in Bombay, India, moved to Lloydminster in 1978. Zuhy has always maintained a commitment to children as a pre-school teacher at Happy Days Nursery School (above) and through her advocacy efforts including serving as a representative for Inclusion International on a United Nations Panel of Experts (inset).

Photos courtesy of Zuhy Sayeed

sive education to review the services available to students with developmental disabilities. Zuhy served on the Saskatchewan Board and Executive until 1995, and as President of the Alberta Association for Community Living from 1995 to 1999.

Zuhy has been well recognized for her efforts, receiving a Governor General's Commemorative medal in 1992, the 1995 Immigration Award for Contributions to Social Issues, and the Lloydminster Lion's Club Citizen of the Year Award in 1998.

Internationally, Sayeed has made great contributions as well. In 1995, Inclusion International appointed the local volunteer to a United Nations Working Group on the Rights of Children with Disabilities.

The City of Lloydminster has been built upon volunteers, and Zuhy Sayeed will always be remembered as one of the border city's great social contributors. Her commitment to building an equal, inclusive community remains strong today.

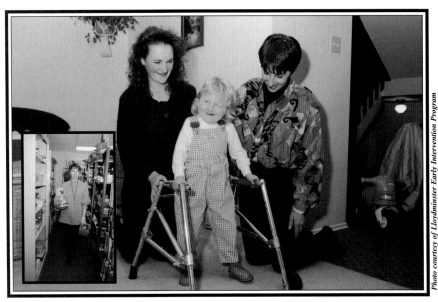

Photo courtesy of Lloydminster Early Intervention Program

The LACL established the Lloydminster Early Intervention Program in 1982 to provide children with developmental disabilities and their parents access to supports in the community as early as possible. In the early 1980's, parent-run Early Intervention Programs were springing up across Saskatchewan with the support of Saskatchewan Social Services. Although this made it possible to fund the program for children on the Saskatchewan side of the border, the province of Alberta had no equivalent program from which to draw funding. After significant lobbying, Alberta provincial funding was obtained, creating the only parent-driven, Social Services Funded Early Intervention Program in Alberta.

Above: A home visit by an interventionist. Inset: The Lloydminster Early Intervention Program offers a toy lending library to assist parents in providing stimulation for their children.

Below: Howard Barnsley leads the Shriners' Mini Car Oil Patrol at the Lloydminster parade. The Shriners' major purpose over its years of existence in Lloydminster has been to "make sure that all chilren have access to hospital care, regardless of race, colour or creed." - Sandy Hill

Lloydminster to employ people with developmental disabilities. As usual, one of the major difficulties in receiving government funding was Lloydminster's bi-provincial status. However, at a joint meeting of the provinces in May of 1971, both governments gave a verbal agreement to share in the capital cost of a building at 25% each; the remaining 50% was to be raised by the committee in the community.

Anticipating a positive resolution, Hardy Salt donated one acre of land on the eastern edge of the city for the use of a workshop or residence. It was decided that an Alberta location would be more advantageous, and the City agreed to exchange the donated land for 4 lots at 3514-51st Ave.

The community and its organizations provided incredible support from the beginning, and the LACL was able to obtain generous donations and fundraising dollars allotted for the centre. The Lloydminster Sheltered Workshop and Training Centre Society opened on August 21, 1972 with ten trainees registered. Within less than a year, the Centre had grown to include 27 trainees, and three additional staff had to be hired. Once the Sheltered Workshop board was incorporated and finances were in place, the Lloydminster Association for Community Living turned its attention to building a residence. Financial support was secured from both provincial governments and directed through the Alberta Housing Corporation. Nelson Lumber Company was awarded the contract to construct the building which would house sixteen trainees, eight from each province. The building was completed in 1973, and a married couple were hired to act as house supervisors.

As the LACL moved more towards advocacy, they assisted the Sheltered Workshop in assuming responsibility for residential services, which soon branched out to apartment settings outside of the main residence. The LACL recreation and leisure program was shifted over to the workshop in the 1980's; trainees participated in many different community events and took vacations to places such as Vancouver, Nashville and Disneyland.

With its growing emphasis on service delivery, the Sheltered Workshop recognized the importance of communicating its new-found role to the community. The Society changed its name on June 21, 1989 to "The Bea Fisher Centre Inc.".

On the business side, the Centre's contracts continued to grow. In addition to the highly successful bottle depot, the Bea Fisher Centre took on the Blue Box Recycling Program, the Meals on Wheels contract, and the addition of a tree farm in the 1990's. With its successes in business, a separate board, the

Photo courtesy of Sandy Hill

Una Faber

As a successful businesswoman for over 30 years, Una Faber always stressed the importance of "staying vitally interested in your community and surroundings."

Una began her career in the beauty salon business in the lower floor of the Prince Charles Hotel in 1960. Una's Beauty Salon offered a complete beauty service, cutting and styling hair, fitting and selling wigs, toupees and hair pieces, hair colouring, facials, makeup, eyebrow arching, and manicuring. Faber started with one assistant, but after 25 years, she had grown to nine employees, open six days a week and two weeknights.

Faber played an active role in the community. In 1961, she sponsored a little league baseball team, the "Acadians". She was a founding member of the Allied Arts Council,

Above left: Una Faber was recognized nationally as a pioneer and role model for women in business. Above right: as President of the Chamber of Commerce, she spoke at the opening of the Alberta Provincial Building, flanked by Mayor Kay Matheson (left) and MLA Bud Miller (right).

the first woman director of the Lloydminster Credit Union, and the first woman president of the Lloydminster Chamber of Commerce in 1981. She also took special interest in downtown projects and successfully advocated securing the old post office as a heritage site. An active Liberal, Una was an elected delegate to policy conventions in Ottawa when Pierre Trudeau was Prime Minister.

Managing a business, raising three children, and handling her many volunteer activities after the death of her husband, Walter, in 1970, is proof of the strength of her principles of life. She believed in being ready for the next step. In 1976, she began designing and building a cabin at Turtle Lake. This served as a lovely spot for the family to relax and have fun. Since 1990, the uniquely crafted structure has served as her retirement home.

Bill Rekrutiak

Bill Rekrutiak has been a life-long volunteer. "That's the way of my life," says Bill. Rekrutiak's father was an immigrant who encouraged his children to give back to the country which had adopted him. Bill remembers his father saying, "Make sure you always pay the rent."

During Bill's farming career he was a Councillor of the R.M. of Wilton for five years and Reeve for two. Three Municipalities, Wilton Rural, R.M. Brittania and the City of Lloydminster joined together to form the Sandy Beach Regional Park Board with Bill as one of the founding members.

Bill and his wife, Julia, raised two daughters, Connie and Donna. In supporting his girls' interests, he worked with the 4H Junior Club for 11 years, receiving a 10 year Leadership Award; he was also a Director and Chairman of the Figure Skating Club for fourteen years.

Rekrutiak always has the community at heart, and he has served on many committees and organizations, health being his biggest priority. The years spent in this area are as follows: Trustee on the Lloydminster Hospital Board (14); Chairman (7); Director of Northwest Regional Health

District (6); Director of Saskatchewan Health Care Association (5); Director of Twin Rivers Home Care (9); Director of Twin Rivers Foundation (9); Director of the Lloydminster Regional Health Board (6), a founding member of the W.A. Thorpe Recovery Centre, and President of the Lloydminster Cancer Unit. During these years, several programs came into being: Meals on Wheels, Home Care, Life Call, the Wellness Clinics and Foot Care. Bill cites obtaining approval for a new hospital as a major achievement in his dedication to community health services.

The Lloydminster Co-op recruited Rekrutiak as Director in 1985, and chairman from1984-1986 and 1992-1993. As well, he served as a Director with the Federated Co-op Ltd. for six years.

This remarkable service to our community goes on to include a 40 year life membership in the Benevolent Protective Order of Elks, and Director and Chairman of the Lloydminster Housing Authority.

Bill Rekrutiak exemplifies what a great self giving volunteer is! Rekrutiak has taken on many challenges in providing leadership as a local volunteer, and he recognizes that nothing is gained without effort and persistence.

Photos courtesy of Herb Duczek

Photo courtesy of Gwen Kempel

The Catholic Men's Club was organized and encouraged by Father Gorman, the parish priest in the 1940's. The men helped with chores and jobs in the parish including the building of the church in 1949.

Ed Lavoie, the first Grand Knight in Lloydminster, was instrumental in the formation of the Knights of Columbus Council in 1951. Several years later, the name was changed to Father Thomas Dobson Council to honor the retired priest who served the parish for almost forty years.

Aside from their service to the church, the organization gave generously to the community participating in the annual United Way drive and Sno-Fest activities. In the 1970's, the Knights acquired property on the Meridian and developed "Columbus Park". They also supported various minor sports associations, a Marriage Encounter Movement, a Pro-life League, and the Lloydminster Catholic School System.

Above: The K of C hosted the Alberta State Convention in 1994 at Lakeland College. Inset: The Knights of Colubus Hall was completed in 1981.

The Lloydminster Unit of the Canadian Cancer Society has held many fundraisers over the years including "The Longest Day of Golf" (top right) since 1990. A community-based organization of volunteers, the organization's mission is "the eradication of cancer and the enhancement of the quality of life of people living with cancer.".

The Lloydminster Unit was formed in 1983, and the decision was made to become a part of the Saskatchewan Division as North Battleford was closer than Edmonton.

Shirley Aston (bottom right) was involved from the beginning with the first office of the Cancer Society located in the basement of her home. The Unit started small and steadily grew as individuals and businesses began donating space and furniture.

Aston received the Governor General's Award od Distinction in 1998 in recognition of her service and dedication to the Canadian Cancer Society. Photo, bottom right: Shirley Aston thanks George Baynton in 1990 for his outstanding service to the Cancer Society.

Bea Fisher Enterprises Inc., was established to manage the business operational affairs of the Centre's various enterprises.

The eighties saw the beginning of a tremendous movement towards community living. In its early stages, it allowed trainees simple benefits such as grocery shopping or casual outings in the community. In the 21st century, the movement has grown significantly, where people with disabilities now own businesses, attend college, and live in their own homes, which they have mortgaged or bought. The dedication of the LACL and Bea Fisher Centre has led to these great advancements in community living.

Photo courtesy of Doug Aston

Big Brothers and Big Sisters of Lloydminster

The family changed markedly in the twentieth century, and many children found themselves outside traditional models such as a two-parent family or aunts, uncles, or grandparents who lived in the same community. Throughout its history, the Big Brothers organization's focus has been to provide a one-to-one child/adult friendship for each child in the program.

In the Border City, Big Brothers first established itself in 1971. Big Sisters followed in 1979. Both organizations maintained a strong presence in the community over the years, and in 1994, the two amalgamated to become the Big Brothers and Big Sister Association of Lloydminster, incorporated in both Alberta and Saskatchewan as a registered charity.

There was an overwhelming demand for the program. "Kids and Kops" a mentorship program between local R.C.M.P. officers and groups of children, and "Big Bunch", a group mentoring program, were developed to accommodate children who were on the waiting list for a big brother or big sister.

Photo courtesy of BCHCC

The Kiwanis Club of Lloydminster

The Kiwanis Club has six permanent objectives: "To give primacy to the human spirit, to promote higher social business and professional standards, to encourage living by the golden rule, to develop citizenship, to provide a means to promote friendship, and to increase patriotism and good will." Locally, the club received its charter in March of 1984. Staff Sergeant Roy Beaton of the Lloydminster R.C.M.P. detachment was the first president.

Locally and nationally, the organization's emphasis has been on children. The program has sponsored projects such as B.U.G.S. (Bring Up Grades) and "Terrific Kids" which inspire and honour students to improve their grades and behaviour. The Lloydminster and District Kiwanis Music Festival is one of the service club's most noteworthy events. The Kiwanis Club first became the major sponsor of the event, which had its start in the 1930's, in 1997.

Several other projects have been undertaken in recent years, including Lloydminster's only air shows with the Canadian Forces Snow Birds in 1995 and 1998, the Family Day picnic at Bud Miller Park, Arrest by Request on April Fool's Day, and an on-going community 50-50 draw with all funds raised put back into the community and Kiwanis sponsored projects.

Above: The John Deere Slow Races, organized by the Classic Green Two-Cylinder Club, have become a popular part of the Canada Day celebrations in Lloydminster. The Heritage Society, a group promoting the preservation and restoration of our historical artifacts, sponsors the Canada Day festivities annually at Weaver Park.

Below: Kiwanis Club members are shown on December 17, 1993 facilitating a visit by Santa to a Grade 1 class at Rendell Park School. (Standing, l-r): Dick Conley, Jim Coleman, Harvey Bodnard, Eric Bloch-Hansen, Rick McMahon, Jim Wilde and Ken Ebert. (Seated, l-r): Santa Claus and John Oatway.

The Spirit of Volunteerism

Lloydminster residents have long been inspired by the spirit of volunteerism as countless volunteers have stepped forward to offer their contributions to the community. Vic Juba, whose volunteer contributions began almost from the time he first arrived in Lloydminster in 1953, reflects this spirit. Over the years, he served on many committees and in service clubs (see sidebar to left). People most remember Juba for several large scale projects which he was

Photo courtesy of Dick Conley

instrumental in moving from dream to reality.

In 1982, Juba chaired the Alberta Winter Games, held in Lloydminster for the first time. Although a massive undertaking, the games were a success. As a result, the Minister of Recreation asked Juba, along with 13 other Albertans, to become char-

Above: 1982 Alberta Winter Games Executive: (Back row l-r) Ron Lane, Dave Dmytryshyn, Fred Mabey, Stuke Wilson, Myron Strilchuk, Lyle Shortt. (Seated l-r) Hamish Garland, Dr. Fred Murray, Vic Juba, Shirley Willis, Harvey Willett.

ter members of the Alberta Sport Council. Vic accepted, and chaired the Games and Competition Committee for six years. He also travelled to the Soviet Union representing the Council.

One of the largest projects Juba chaired was the Indoor Swimming Pool. It took five years from discussion to completion. Originally slated to open in 1987, a massive drop in crude oil prices in March, 1986 spurred a large number of lay-offs in Lloydminster, and forced the committee to delay the project for a year. When completed, the $5,000000 cost was funded through corporate and private donations.

When it was announced that Lloydminster would host the 1997 Alberta Summer Games, Juba attempted to step back but, with the urging of the mayor, he once again took on heading the games and a major fund-raising campaign which collected over $1,200,000. Culture became an increasingly important component of the games. Vic appointed Linda Nykolaychuk as cultural coordinator. Art displays, musical performances, and theatre sports took their place beside the games, and the community and volunteers were applauded for their efforts.

Another project of interest to Vic was the preservation of the history of the local oil industry. Vic was on the museum board which decided to collect artifacts for a small display at the museum, however, soon the dream was for much more than that. The Heavy Oil Visitors' Centre Committee was established with Juba as the chair. Major funding was provided by the Oilfield Technical Society with a goal to create a world class interpretive centre to promote Lloydminster's heavy oil expertise. Westwind Design of Calgary designed and built the displays and Foster Learning Inc. of Lloydminster did the research and writing. Some $850,000 was collected from the industry and the OTS Heavy Oil Science Centre opened August 5, 1999.

With his wealth of experience in fundraising and community project development, Juba next became involved with the Lloydminster Theatre Project, acting as chair of the fund-raising committee. Originally, the idea was to build the theatre at Lakeland College, but when the College faced cutbacks, they were uncertain about their role in the large project.

Above: 1987 Alberta Summer Games Executive: (Back l-r) Randy Aston, Randy Taves, Mike Sidoryk, Lloyd Mack, Greg Hnatuk, Bob Kinasewich. (Middle l-r) Stuke Wilson, Linda Nykolaychuk, Vic Juba, Greg Switenkey, Wendy Plandowski, Ken Gillis. (Seated l-r) Roy Clark, Elmer Nykiforuk, Pat Gulak and Todd Leibel.

The public school division expressed interest and a feasibility study was done to examine the possibility of adding the theatre to the Lloydminster Comprehensive High School. Eventually, though, Lakeland College felt that they were able to get behind the project. The Separate and Public school divisions soon agreed that the College was the best place for the facility.

Considering Vic Juba's lifetime of contribution to the Lloydminster community, and the thousands who will continue to benefit from the facilities he helped bring into reality, it was announced at the sod turning ceremony for the new theatre on April 6, 2001, that it would be officially named the Vic Juba Community Theatre.

Whenever applause fills that theatre, at least a part of it will be saying, "Bravo, Vic!"

> "I get great satisfaction in achievement, I like challenges, and I enjoy the camaraderie which develops from taking on these projects. People used to ask me where my wife and I were going to move when we retired. Lloydminster is a tremendously friendly community. We wouldn't even consider leaving."
>
> - Vic Juba

Below: Dr. Don Duncan, Lloydminster Public School Division Director and MC Elmer Nykiforuk look on from the platform while the official sod turners do their work.
(l-r) Ross Ulmer, Theatre Planning Committee; Lloyd Snelgrove, MLA; Ken Baker, Mayor of Lloydminster; Dr. Mark Lee, President of Lakeland College; and the theatre's new namesake - Vic Juba.

Chapter Fourteen

Sports and Recreation

Research by Penny Manners and Alan Griffith

S ports and Recreation in Lloydminster is as old as the community itself. In between the many chores of establishing a settlement, early residents enthusiastically took part in spontaneous soccer and cricket matches. The long, cold winters gave rise to popular ice sports, such as: hockey, curling, and broom ball. Eager participants were cheered on by enthusiastic fans - then as now. Over the years, sport has leavened our lives and recreation has renewed our spirit.

It is a daunting task to cover this aspect of Lloydminster's history, especially in light of this being the one area where previous work has been done. In 1979, *75 Years of Sport and Culture,* was published by the Lloydminster Senior Citizen's Society and we acknowledge our debt to this valuable source of personal reflections.

In this chapter we strive not to be comprehensive, but rather we try to provide a sampling of the unbridled enthusiasm for sport which Lloydminsterites have demonstrated over the past 100 years.

Below: This Lloydminster side was one of several which won league championships in both Saskatchewan and Alberta in the days before World War I. Football (now known as soccer) was the most popular sport among the Barr Colonists who brought high skill levels with them. Some had even played in the equivalent of today's British professional leagues.

Soccer

Football, or Soccer as it later came to be known in North America, was often played in the colony's early days as a diversion. Groups of workers formed teams such as the Telegraph Gang and the Village Well Diggers who played a memorable game on Boxing Day 1903.

Teams became more formally organized later and travelling matches were held against Onion Lake, Tangleflags, Southminster, and other surrounding communities. A local team was formed in 1904, and played several matches with Battleford. In the years between 1907 and 1915, Lloydminster teams won several league titles and the Alberta Championship twice.

Soccer was taken seriously in town. Large crowds attended games, players became local celebrities, businesses and individuals donated money to support the team's travel expenses. When a skilled player was discovered, such as English League veteran Frank Booth, on his homestead near Onion Lake, a livery team was sent out to bring him to town and all his expenses were paid.

Virtually all the soccer team volunteered to serve in World War I and many died overseas. Soccer was an indirect casualty of the lost players and changing times. By the 1930's, adult soccer was non-existent. Though it was sometimes played at school, enthusiasts had difficulty reviving an organized league. In the 1950's and 1960's, the game experienced a brief renewal with organized games being held against Cold Lake, North Battleford, and Vermilion.

While interest in Soccer may have faded in North America for a time, world-wide interest in the game was only growing. When Chilean immigrant Ricardo Guerrero came to Lloydminster in 1975, he organized a local Chilean team, some of whom had professional experience playing in European countries.

Not long after, the Lloydminster Soccer Association was formed under president George Van Der Loos. Youth leagues grew rapidly in popularity, until, by the 1990's more fields were demanded, and an in-door soccer facility at the proposed Sports-Multiplex was suggested.

Cricket

Cricket was one of the most popular sports in Britain at the turn of the century. In April of 1905, the Britannia Cricket Club was formed. Officers of the Club were: H. R. Miles, A. F. Fugl, W. H. Holland, H. Sutton, J. J. Slater, W. Rendell, J. F. Bird and C. A. Samm. By Empire Day (May 24) the team was ready for competition and took on a team from the Gully. Despite a heavy wind and a "pitch in terrible condition" according to the *Lloydminster Times*, a large and enthusiastic crowd gathered to watch the Lloydminster team best the rural side 58 to 37. During the following summer, games were played against teams from Marshall, Lashburn and Battleford. Cricket continued as a popular sport until World War I when many of its practitioners were called away. Like many of them, cricket was never the same again and can be counted as another casualty of war.

Sandy Beach became a popular recreational area soon after the colonists arrived. Top: "Taking the air" at Sandy Beach in 1916. Many families set up tents (middle) and women and children camped there for the summer while fathers travelled into town to work. Others were more inventive, such as the Skinner family (bottom), who arrived in a homemade recreational vehicle made from an old wagon.

Above left:: The Brittania Rifle Association as photographed in 1913

Above right:: Brian Sheppard, a member of the Lloydminster Gun Club and avid trap shooter, won numerous provincial and national trophies, including the Canadian doubles title in Hamilton (1987) and Brandon (1988)

One strand of the Lloydminster Gun Club evolved into the Lloydminster Fish and Game Association. The organization's main efforts centred around perpetuating adequate stocks of fish and wildlife and shooting species such as coyotes and ducks which were said to damage crops and livestock. The focus shifted more to conservation over the years, and members contributed to a number of worthwhile projects in the area.

Below: The Habitat Trust Program was established to assist landowners, such as Bill Luchinski (right), who wish to donate land to remain as wildlife habitat in perpetuity. Left: Bill Armstrong; Centre: Larry Chambers.

Shooting

The Barr Colonists came heavily armed; with rifles, shot guns, and revolvers. They were prepared to defend themselves against dangers, real and imagined, and many looked forward to shooting wild game. There is a much told story of some Colonists shooting gophers from the train windows as they made their way toward Saskatoon. Certainly, shooting ducks and partridges supplemented the diet along the trail and in the early days on the homesteads.

An active, 100 member strong, Brittania Rifle Association, was formed in 1903 with H. B. Hall and William Rendell as lieutenants. Rendell was a particularly adept shooter who apparently outshot the Dominion Representative in an early competition. The sport was popular with local women as well. A Ladies Rifle Club was formed in 1916 with fourteen members including some familiar names such as Cooke, Crossley, Aston, and Philpott.

By 1922, interest in trap shooting was growing and many locals such as Dr. Lindley, Archie Miller, H. B. Hall, and F. Ivan Crossley became involved in the sport. The Lloydminster Gun Club began with a focus on trap and skeet shooting. Shells became scarce during the World War II, and the sport was discontinued for a time. In 1957, the club was formally revived with the support of the Lloydminster Fish and Game League. A six acre gun club field and club house was established six miles south of town.

Baseball, Fastball, and Softball

While Cricket and Football were distinctly British sports, Baseball was an "American game" invented in New York state in 1839. Made popular here by Ontario and American settlers, a baseball club was formed in 1906 with the first tournament held on July 17th. Three teams, Marshall, Rat Creek, and Lloydminster, competed for a first place prize of $50.00 and a second place prize of $25.00.

A Baseball team at the 1934 Exhibition featured the Lampitt brothers who later went on to play for the first Meridians team in 1938. L to R. Back: F.T. Lampitt, Tom Lampitt, Charlie Mitchell, Art Lampitt, Lawrence Wells, Reg Lampitt, Alf Lampitt. Front: Ken Wright, Jack MacMillan, John Harrison, Jack Lampitt, Bob Lampitt.

Interest in the sport grew rapidly. In 1907, the first league was formed. Tournaments were good for business in the town. With teams from Mannville, Marshall, Maidstone, and Lashburn competing, an estimated 300 to 400 fans would arrive in town by rail at midnight from the east and 4:30 AM from the west. Available accommodations were stretched to the limit, and on more than one occasion, the local Drill Hall was converted into a dormitory.

In 1938, the Meridians were formed. The Lampitt brothers (Tom, Art, Robert, John, and Alfred) were all members of the team along with Charlie Mitchell, Paul Brown, Alex Barstow, Harris McRae, Richard Pick, and Roger Pick. The team was followed closely until they disbanded during the World War II.

When the War was over, a new team was formed. The Oilers began playing in 1946 and many talented ball players were given jobs in the oil industry to allow them to play in town. "The fact that shift workers were not always available to play ball created many a nightmare," Alf Lampitt recalled in *75 Years of Sport and Culture*.

A highlight for many ball fans in the Lloydminster area was the formation of a semi-pro team in 1954. The team adopted a familiar name - The Lloydminster Meridians. The Meridians played in the Saskatchewan Baseball League and the Western Canada Baseball League against teams such as Edmonton, North Battleford, Regina, Moose Jaw, and Saskatoon. Slim Thorpe was on the club executive, and Bob Linck was the coach. Russ Robertson, Joe McLean, and Frank Hamilton were also key in making the team a reality.

The Meridians consisted of young American college players and pro-baseball veterans who had encountered racial barriers in the major leagues. Many, such as Roberto Zayas and Curly Williams (see feature on the next page) expressed their gratitude to the people of Lloydminster for the warm welcome they received.

The 1956 Lloydminster Meridians. Left to right. Back: John Karpinski, Ben Lott, Gary Ball, Bill Bailey, Jim Hansen, Keith Gustin, Ed Kalski, Curly Williams, Stan Karpinski.
Front: Dick Satalich, Jim Valentine, Eddie Morris, Roberto Zayas, Harvey (Jay-Dell) Mah (batboy), Barney Brown.
* Special thanks to Jay-Dell Mah for preserving the history of the Lloydminster Meridians and the Western Canada Baseball League at www.attheplate.com.

Edmonton Eskimos playing at Lloydminster Legion Sportsman Park against the Meridians on Wednesday, August 24, 1955.

Curly Williams

In the near decade of semi-professional baseball in Lloydminster (1954-1961), one of the league's best players was Willy "Curly" Williams. Before arriving in Lloydminster, Williams had a career in the "Negro League", and a stint with the Chicago White Sox organization. But racial barriers made it impossible for the talented Dominican to rise to the top, and Curly made his way to Canada and the Western Canada Baseball League where he was drafted by the Lloydminster Meridians in 1955.

"I cried so much when I was in professional baseball," Williams remarked in an interview years later. "[In Canada] we were treated so well. That's why I stayed up there so long. Everybody was accepted, you know, didn't have any problems going any place we wanted to eat. Just wonderful people. May not have made a whole lot of money, but people were excited and they enjoyed you and would invite you to their homes."

In his first year with the Meridians, Williams hit .280, and as a third baseman, he led the league in fielding. In the following year he hit .314 and again led the league

Curly Williams (left) clowns with teammate, Collins Jones on July 1, 1955.

Photo courtesy of Leona Brost

in fielding, this time as a short stop. In 1961, Williams took a turn as team manager leading the team to 25 wins in 32 games.

The Western Canada League came to an abrupt halt in 1961, but Williams returned to the city and ended his baseball career with the Greencaps, Lloydminster's entry in the Northern Saskatchewan League. In his final year, he went out with a whopping .391 batting average.

Williams retired to Sarasota County, Florida where he took a job with the coroner's office, from which he retired in 1990. In 1997, he and other members of the former Negro League were honoured for their contributions to the sport of baseball at a Florida Marlins game. In the same year, Sarasota Council declared a "Curly Williams Day" to recognize the athlete's efforts to raise funds to provide college scholarships for needy students.

In Lloydminster, Curly left his mark. Those who were there will always fondly remember the days when semi-pro ball was played in Lloydminster and Curly Williams was our superstar.

Below: Jim Mah (right), owner of the National Cafe, and later the Elite Cafe, was the National's Sponsor. Mah's cafe also became a local hangout for the Lloydminster Meridians. 1955 Meridian first baseman Bob Bayless poses on the left.

Photo courtesy of Jay-Dell Mah

The Meridians were runners up in the Saskatoon Exhibition Event that year, and they won tournaments in Rosetown and at home in a final 4-3 match against Saskatoon.

Unfortunately, the team faced a dismal financial situation. Slim Thorpe commented on the difficulties in *75 Years of Sport and Culture*: "[We] tried to work with the big leagues - saying 'For God's sake, put a little money in this thing. We don't need a lot of money and you are coming up here and stealing our ball players, giving them forty, fifty thousand dollars to go south.'... It was just too hard to finance it." Like many of the other teams in the league, Lloydminster continued to have trouble making their team float.

In 1960, the Meridians won the right to represent Canada at the World Tournament. Unfortunately, the league folded in 1961, and the team never went.

Since the Meridians, other high calibre ball teams have existed in Lloydminster. The Greencaps played for several years in the Northern Saskatchewan League. The North Saskatchewan River Baseball League, was formed in 1977, and the Lloydminster Meridian Twins were born, winning the championship for the first time in 2000.

Women also took an interest in the game, and in 1935, a talented ladies' softball team called the Nationals was formed.

Photos: above: courtesy of Una Faber; right: courtesy of Doreen Plant

Minor Baseball in Lloydminster is worthy of a book of its own. Countless children have taken part over the years. Above: Una Faber sponsored the "Acadians" in 1961.

In the late Thirties and early Forties, the Nationals, under coach George McIvor won the Estey Trophy five years in a row. Crowds of over 1000 people attended some games played at Sandy Beach. By 1941, the team was beginning to disintegrate with several key players, Penny Cooke, Eileen Buchanan, Tillie Lampitt, Muriel Wade, and Lucella MacLean drafted to the Saskatoon Pats.

Catcher Lucella Maclean went on to gain fame as a ball player outside of Canada. After several years with the Saskatoon Pats, McLean signed a contract in 1943 with the "All American Girls Softball League" based out of Chicago, Illinois. With professional men's ball at a standstill due to World War II, professional women's leagues were catching on across the United States. MacLean played with the Southbend Blue Sox, Chicago Chicks, and Music Maids. Lucella MacLean (later Lucella Ross) ended her professional career in 1952.

It is impossible within the space provided to adequately do justice to the many ball teams of men, women, and minors who have participated in baseball, softball, fastball, and slow-pitch in the Lloydminster area. One thing is certain; the sport has remained highly popular in the area throughout our first century.

L to R. Back: Alf Graham, Alice Anthony, Tillie Fisher, M. Wade, E. Harrison, Dorothy MacLean, George McIvor. Middle: Amy Graham, Penny Martin, Eileen MacLean, Lucella MacLean. Front: Marie Turtle, L. Henry.

"Large Crowd is Thrilled with Donkey Baseball"

In 1941, the Lloydminster Kinsmen Club played the Nationals in a game of "Donkey Baseball". If the hitter struck out, they were allowed to round the bases ... except, they had to do so on the back of a donkey. If the rider fell from the mount twice before reaching first base, he or she was automatically out. The **Lloydminster Times** *chronicled the event:*

Photo courtesy of the Lloydminster Lions

The sport evolved over the years to include donkey mounted fielders. Some claim it may just become Lloydminsterites' single favourite pass-time.

"That the donkey is the most stubborn animal on four legs was proved much to the discomfort of some players. The antics of the animals and the efforts of the riders kept the crowd in roars of laughter from the time the first ball was pitched. From start to finish, the game was filled with comical and absurd situations which could only be realized and appreciated by actual observation."

Photo courtesy of Ron Gerhardt

In 1988, the Cardinals (above) participated in the Canadian Senior Championship Tournament in St. Hyacinthe, Quebec.

Photo courtesy of Jeanne Holt

Gail Holt, only eleven years old in 1963, became the Juvenile Ladies Champion in the Prairie Sections Championships in Weyburn, Saskatchewan (the above photo was taken after her victory). Holt continued to excel; she was the first in Lloydminster to get her gold medal in figures and free skating, later adding gold medals in dance and free dance to her accomplishments.

Below: The 1986 Border Bladettes Precision Skating Team. Back row (l-r): Carrie Pinske, Carmen Ellis, Tanya Russell, Michelle Emslie, Keri Wright.
Middle row: Jan Wilson, Cindy McInnes, Lori-Lynn Leach, Sharlene Wilson, Deborah Flexhaug, Carolyn Hines (Coach)
Front row: Lana Russell, Brenda Sheppard, Laura Keichinger, Jennifer Metherall, Terina Stern.

Photo courtesy of Lana Lane

Figure Skating

Winter carnival skating events were held as early as 1906, and anyone with skating prowess was encouraged to demonstrate his or her abilities. The events, more of a costume affair than anything else, were well attended and enjoyed by all. With no professional skater in Lloydminster, club members had to help each other to improve. Archie Miller was an impressive skater, who performed in many of the carnivals of the 1920's. He also organized a group who wished to be taught by him.

Until 1928, Lloydminster skaters rehearsed and performed on open ice arenas, often in harsh winter temperatures. When the covered arena was built, the Elks Club sponsored the first of many Carnivals. They were popular events in which local skaters performed in addition to stunt skating exhibitions, races, and professional figure skating performances.

Julius Beer and Bertha (Dilling) Dubyk were two of the founders of the Lloydminster Figure Skating Club, formally organized in 1949. In addition to the carnivals, club members skated between hockey periods as entertainment for the local crowds.

By 1958, the club was large enough to entice two professional skaters from North Battleford to come to Lloydminster once a week to instruct the skaters. Fortunately for the club, professional skater Noelle Asleson moved to Lloydminster in 1960. Under her direction, the club began to improve remarkably. As Noelle lived in town, she was able to offer private lessons to skaters, and their skills quickly improved. Bonnie Phoenix of Edmonton took over when Asleson moved to Edmonton in 1963.

After the closure of Stettler's summer figure skating school in 1965, local parents decided to take it upon themselves to organize a six-week figure skating school in Lloydminster. With the newly built Centennial Civic Centre, the club now had a facility which could make it possible. The program began in 1967 with eighty students from all over Alberta and Saskatchewan in attendance. The Summer School continued to grow over the years, and by the mid 1970's, students from across Canada were in attendance.

For many years, the Lloydminster Figure Skating Club has also been involved in teaching young people to skate. With several programs, including Can-Skate, Can-Power, Can-Precision, and Kid-Skate, the club has introduced many border city youngsters to the joy of ice skating and contributed to the sport of figure skating and hockey.

Photos courtesy of Provincial Archives of Alberta - PA4300, PA4567

The Archie Miller Arena (inset) was a great improvement over colder outdoor rinks. However, local figure skaters could not have been more pleased with the added warmth and quality of the artificial ice in the Centennial Civic Centre (opened in 1965). Skaters had become accustomed to having to avoid large cracks prior to the introduction of the artificial ice surface.

Curling

The sport of curling also dates back to Lloydminster's early years. In *75 Years of Sports and Culture*, Dorothy Hill estimates that people began playing the sport in 1907 when the first curling rink was built. Bonspiels were big and the prizes were small, with community spirit and togetherness emphasized over prizes. In good humour, curlers often made excuses for poor shots including "blaming the train for shifting due to its rumbling."

The early natural ice arenas usually saw their first Bonspiels around Christmas time. According to Ron Nattress, when the wind blew, strips of snow were blown through the cracks in the walls across the ice. Warm February Chinooks also meant that some games had to be played after midnight when the thin layer of water on the ice was re-frozen by the cooler night air.

In the late forties, there was plenty of curling action in the city and bonspiels were getting between 30 and 40 teams to play. Over the years, the club switched back and forth between provincial associations. In the 40's the club was associated with the Saskatchewan Curling Association; currently the Lloydminster Curling Club is affiliated with the Northern Alberta Curling Association.

The 1950's saw a change in the sport. Curling became much more technical and competitive. Lloydminster rinks went to Bonspiels in larger centres including Edmonton and Saskatoon, competing for larger prizes, such as automobiles. In December of 1952, a Lloydminster rink skipped by Frank Nundahl and including, Jim

Above left: Local curlers (l to r) James Dale, Stan Warmington, Mac MacLeod, and Harold Aston won the Lloydminster Bonspiel in 1956.

Above right: A Legion women's curling bonspiel from 1955.

By November 1955, the 4-sheet "Colosseum" was under construction at the Exhibition Grounds and bonds and shares were being sold to fund the project. The construction of the new rink paved the way for the city to host a national championship. In July of 1955, it was announced that the Legion Dominion Curling championships would be held in Lloydminster in 1956.

Left: Ladies afternoon League Curling in the "Colosseum"

Centre: (l-r) Ted Collins, Bob Manners, Keith Collinge, and Doug Manners were the Northern Alberta Curling Champions in 1988, 1990, and 1991.

Right: (l-r) Viv Backer, Sylvia Moir, Jean Ostertag, and Joanne Cross, winners of the Alberta Ladies' Northerns.

Many local athletes have risen to the highest levels of competition making Border City residents proud of the pool of talent which exists in the city. We also know how to have fun: From swimming in the outdoor pool and leisurely walks in Bud Miller Park on hot summer days to cutting fresh snow with our cross country skis in the cool crispness of a prairie winter, people still take the time to enjoy our natural environment.

A. *Krisy Myers started speed skating in 1991. In 1995, she was honoured as Lloydminster Athlete of the year. In 1999, she made the Canadian Senior Sprint Team. Krisy finished 3rd at the Canadian Sprint Championships in 2001 qualifying her to compete in the First World Sprint Championships.* Photo courtesy of Krisy Myers

B. *Kristy Reiber (nee Foote) began show jumping and equestrian in 1982. By the 1990's she was named to the Canadian National Team Talent Squad for potential Olympic hopefuls and competed at the North American Young Riders Championships in Chicago. Reiber credits Dorothy and Jim Hill for getting the sport going in Lloydminster.* Photo courtesy of Kristy Reiber

C. *A team from the 1997 Alberta Summer Games poses in front of one of the border markers. The 1982 Alberta Winter Games were also hosted in Lloydminster.* Photo by Don Whiting

D. *Chuckwagon racing has become a popular event and major attraction of the Lloydminster Colonial Days.* Photo by Don Whiting

E. *Lawn bowling got its start in Lloydminster after Bud Miller Park All Seasons Park opened. The Lloydminster Lawn Bowls Club was formed, and the new green was opened on June 14, 1987.* Photo courtesy of Betty Hengelhaupt

F. *The Tai Chi Club began meeting in the Lloydminster Heritage Co-op in the early '90's. Tai Chi is an ancient martial art, which many have found to be a useful form of exercise and relaxation.* Photo courtesy of Yvonne Jensen

G. *Three Mile Lake and Sandy Beach were popular swimming holes in early years. In 1957, it was announced that the Lloydminster Kinsmen would contribute to the construction of a new outdoor swimming pool. The cost was estimated at $65,000. The Lloydminster Leisure Centre became a reality in 1998.* Photo by Don Whiting

H. *An entry in the Lloydminster Parade held on the first day of the Exhibition every year.* Photo courtesy of Lloydminster Regional Archives

I. *The Lloydminster Exhibition has featured a midway since the 1930's. In the '90's, the annual event, which also featured entertainment, grandstands, and agricultural displays, became known as Colonial Days.* Photo by Don Whiting

J. *Bud Miller All Seasons Park came into existence in 1986. Residents have made great use of the park for tennis, jogging, swimming, cross country skiing, skating, and annual events such as Fathers' Day.* Photo by Don Whiting

K. *A women's indoor soccer team.* Photo courtesy of Shannon Holman

L. *David Gislason was one of eight Saskatchewan participants to attend the International Special Olympics at Mount Pleasant, Michigan in 1975. The athlete came home with the Bronze medal in the 50 yard dash.* Photo courtesy of Pauline Minish

M. *The Lloydminster Cross Country Ski Club has existed since 1974. By 1982, the club had received permission to use the old Landrose School, east of Lloydminster, as a clubhouse. The site was used in 1982 for the cross country skiing events for the Alberta Winter Games.* Photo courtesy of Chris Wood

Don Christie, Headley Manners, Ron Hardy, and Ron Nattress (in the blue sweaters l. to r) competed in the Canadian Senior Men's Nationals in St. John, New Brunswick in 1980.

With plans to build an office building in Lloydminster in 1967, Husky Oil donated $10,000 for improvements to the Lloydminster golf course. They stated that they would be re-locating many of their people from other centres, and they wanted to contribute to making Lloydminster an attractive place to live. The club decided to use the money to install grass greens, as opposed to expanding the course to 18 holes. An additional $24,000 was put into the project, and the new and improved course was officially opened on August 24, 1969.

The clubhouse was relocated to the new Communiplex in 1975, and plans were under way to add another nine holes to the course. However, the expansion did not become a reality until 1983 after a fund-raising committee spearheaded by Bill Kondro and Bill Foster was able to raise $630,000. Finally Lloydminster had its "champion calibre course". In 2000, the course (below) was rated as the third best public golf course in Saskatchewan.

Top inset: Jim Born Sr. accepts the 1977 Men's open trophy from Gary Loney. As of 2000, Loney held the most titles of any player in the history of the club.

Bottom inset: Tom Wyse takes a swing at the local course in 1994.

Top inset courtesy of Don and Rose Patton; bottom inset courtesy of Rusty Russell

Sellers, Rusty Graham, and Jim Mah, came in third at the Granite Bonspiel in Edmonton, and in 1954 the rink of Lloyd Madnus, Art Hanson, Jim Sellers and Harold Fossey won the opening round of Brier Playoffs in Lashburn. Lloydminster curlers were becoming more competitive and proving their might in larger curling centres.

Ron Harris organized the first Lloydminster Farmers' Bonspiel in 1962. Fifty two rinks entered, and the Grand Challenge Winner was Bob Manners, who was the Grand Challenge winner 6 more times in his curling career. At one time with 80 rinks, it was the largest Farmers' Bonspiel in Western Canada.

Viv and Walter Backer opened the door to youth in the winter of 1966 when they started the Junior curling program. In its first year, thirty children took part, but by 2001, more than 150 students were involved, and the Backers were still a driving force. For her efforts, Viv was recognized by the Lloydminster Kinsmen as the first ever female Sportsman of the Year.

In 1978, the Communiplex was opened, and curlers had a brand new state of the art facility to replace the deteriorating Colosseum. Eight sheets of ice became available to curlers in the border city.

The first Lloydminster Curling Classic was held in 1987. At an annual curling club meeting, Cliff Rose suggested hosting the event. A committee was formed in the spring of 1986 to determine the feasibility of the project. Since its inception, the Classic has raised over $100,000 for the Lloydminster Curling Club and the Communiplex. The main intention of the Classic was to provide a community forum to see Brier champions curling in our own rinks. The Classic developed a positive image and a greater awareness of curling in the community.

Golf

In the late 1920's, golf came to Lloydminster with a course situated in close proximity to the present day course. The sport did not catch on as some avid golfers had hoped, in part due to the fact that the greens were not maintained. To attract more interest in the game, the club focused on building a course at Sandy Beach, a popular recreational spot, in 1934. Sandboxes, rakes, and other equipment were transported from the old course out to Sandy Beach by wagon, and a new course was constructed on the east side of the lake. A new course, consisting of nine holes (although the ninth hole was a repeat of the first hole) was built at the exhibition grounds in 1938.

Many local golfers have excelled over the years. In 1966, Tom Wyse had a tremendous year, winning the Lloydminster, Loon Lake, Meadow Lake, Wainwright, and Saskatchewan Legion opens. Another noteworthy golfer was Bob MacDermott, who lost his left leg, left arm, and right thumb in an unfortunate farm accident in 1988. Bob rebounded after the incident, and improved upon his game. By 1996, MacDermott won the Double Amputee British Open, the Alberta Amputee Open (five times), and the double amputee division of the Canadian open

The first golf cart on the course was actually a 1959 Volkswagon Beetle with the top and doors removed and bald tires. When Roland Lawson retired, he decided to take up golf. Due to his difficulty in walking the course, he modified the vehicle and soon became a familiar sight "beetling" around the course with his buddies.

Photo courtesy of Alex Sokalofsky

Basketball

Prior to World War I, Basketball was played in the Drill Hall as a part of the soldiers' military training. Casual games were played outdoors through the 1930's and 1940's. The sport really got its boost after the gymnasium was added to the Lloydminster Composite High

Hugh Morrell was known to generations of Lloydminster students as "Coach". An intense competitor, he built active programs in a number of sports. His contribution to basketball is recognized through the aptly named annual tournament - the Hugh Morrell Classic.

Photos courtesy of Larry and Chris Leach

With a father like Larry Leach, who possesses an immense enthusiasm for the game of hockey and sports in general, it is no wonder that his family has continued in his footsteps. Larry Leach (2nd from left) played eighteen years of professional hockey with the WHL, American League, and the NHL Boston Bruins (1954-1960). Larry's wife Chris (bottom right photo, second from left) played basketball, softball, and golf. Chris played on the Borderettes fastball team in the 1960's when the team won the Intermediate Provincial Championship against Calgary.

Renn Leach (far left) played for the Victoria Cougars during his hockey career. Jay Leach (3rd from left) was active in many sports including handball. Garry Leach (far right) was coached by his father before he went on to play Senior AAA and Canadian College Hockey. He also played with the Border Kings. Lori-Lynn Leach (bottom left) was involved in swimming, track and field, and cross country running before turning to the Ironman Triathlon event in which she has placed in numerous competitions, including 1998 Triathlon Canadian Nationals (winner), 1999 Ironman Canada (2nd), 2000 (3rd), and 2000 Ironman Austria (3rd)

The Lloydminster Tigers were the champions of the Western Saskatchewan Hockey League in 1923, its first year. Left to right, back: W.Spence, R. Leonard, L. G. Lindsay, J.B. Boyd; Middle: E.A. Rendell, W.D. Price, G.K. Ross, W.L. Rendell, Archie Miller; Front: J.A. Fretwell, J. Spence.

School in 1951. The Physical Education teacher at the school was Hugh Morrell who put together consistently strong teams, including a girls team which won the Northwest Championship of Saskatchewan.

In all, Morrell was active in the sport of basketball for seven decades. In the early '90's the Lloydminster Comprehensive High School's annual basketball tournament became the "Hugh Morrell Classic" in recognition of all that Hugh had done for the sport. The Kinsmen elected the former teacher to their hall of fame in 1995.

Hockey

Over its estimated 200 year history, no sport has become a greater part of the Canadian identity than that of Ice Hockey. Hockey gained popularity rapidly, and by the end of the nineteenth century had surpassed Lacrosse as Canada's most popular sport. In 1893, Canadian

Above: Left: When the Lloydminster Jets travelled to Brandon, Manitoba for the Western Canadian Finals in 1954, a local entourage followed the team. (l-r) Back row: Archie Miller, John Williams; Third row: George K. Ross, Bill Forbes, Russ Robertson, Roy Johns, George Baynton; Second row: Eddie Myers, John Salt, Margaret Salt, Blanche Mills, Art Shortell, O.C. Yates; Front: Vern Miner and grandchild, Mrs. E. Myers, Mrs.Tommy Gregg, Mary Shortell, Mary Ross, Joe McLean, Sadie Miner, Edna Miller, Mrs. Bill Forbes.
Above Right: The Lloydminster Jets in Brandon, 1954. (l-r) Back: "Pop" Summers (trainer), Art Knutson, Mo Price, George Parker (coach), Harvey Cottrell, "Jeep" George, Ernie Behm, Scotty Fleming (manager), Jim Hill, Don Stewart, Tommy Gregg, Dan Baunl, Al Dornstauder, Wilf Masterman; Front: Vince Weller, Isadore Strubey, Jimmy Stewart, Rollie Hobbs, Wally Laubman, Grant King, Blair Jeffrey, Jerry Mills, W. Zier.

Governor General, Lord Stanley of Preston, donated a three foot high silver cup, to be given annually to the top Canadian team. It became known as the Stanley Cup, and, over the years, many a Lloydminster boy dreamed of holding that trophy high over his head.

Two short years after the Barr Colonists arrived, a hockey club was organized with Mr. G. M. Phillips as the club manager. Townspeople were encouraged to support the new sport. An advertisement in a December 1905 issue of the *Lloydminster Times* announced the first hockey game: "As this is the initiation of Canada's national game into our town, it is hoped that everybody will render as much assistance as possible to help the boys along."

The team played on outdoor rinks until the first covered rink was built in 1907. Unfortunately, the rink burned down in early 1908. In the same year, the Eastern Alberta Hockey League was formed with teams from Lloydminster, Kitscoty, Vermilion, and Islay.

Hockey in Lloydminster continued to grow over the next few years, but World War I left teams with few players as young men voyaged overseas. During this time, exhibition games were played. However, there were no organized leagues again until 1923 when the

Western Saskatchewan Hockey League was formed with teams from Lloydminster, Lashburn, and Maidstone competing against each other. In the inception year, Lloydminster emerged as league champion.

In January of 1928, the next covered rink was opened, bringing teams away from the elements and into better playing conditions. The Lloydminster Elks Hockey Team won 1929-1930 Alberta Intermediate A Championships. In 1934, the team disbanded, and the "Prolites", a name chosen because all members wore Prolite CCM skates, was formed. Fire seemed to be attracted to Lloydminster arenas as the second covered rink burned to the ground in 1934. Within two months, a new arena was built but that did not help the Prolites who had lost all of their equipment in the fire. They had to finish their season "…with begged, borrowed, or stolen equipment." (The *Lloydminster Times*). Remarkably, the Prolites overcame their great loss to win the Craig Cup against Vegreville in triple overtime. Over the next several

Before Minor Hockey was organized in the late 1960's, the sport was an extra-curricular activity in local schools. Teacher Elmo Price was especially instrumental in organizing the school teams in the '40's and '50's. Since its inception, thousands of young people (such as the team below left) have taken part in the sport of hockey in Lloydminster.

A new outlook on sport which emphasized participation over skill led to the formation of a hockey league for players who "dusted off their skates and equipment to once again pursue the game they loved."
In 1974, the Lloydminster Neversweats Oldimers Hockey team, named after the Lloydminster High School team of the 1940's, was formed, and it is still going strong today.

Photo courtesy of Lloydminster Regional Archives

Photo courtesy of Bill Armstrong

years, the team won such titles as Saskatchewan Intermediate "A" Champions, Craig Cup – Second Place in Alberta, and second place in the Saskatchewan Intermediate "A" Provincials.

Hockey continued to become more popular than ever. Adding to it's popularity were some changes in 1936 to the rules of the game: "The new rules to be enforced this season in hockey, permitting body checking anywhere on the ice, will add greatly to the thrills associated with the sport." (The *Lloydminster Times*: November 26, 1936)

As the sport caught on, teams were organized at lower age levels. In the 1940's, Public School District teachers organized Bantam and Atom teams. Once a student was in grade three, he could begin to take part. Teachers such as Walter Peterson, Al Dornstauder, Mo Price and Alf Lampitt all gave generously of their time. There was a certain expectation though. "One of the questions asked of teachers at their job interviews was whether or not they could skate!" remembers former teacher Lou Crockett. Teachers were responsible for refereeing, time keeping, recording stats, goal judging, organizing games and finding sponsors. As equipment was expensive and difficult to come by, teachers were also constantly on the look out for used equipment to give to the players. Famous teams such as the Canadians, Rangers, Maple Leafs and Maroons

Another established oldtimer team, the Shuddahadems, has operated for many years.
Both teams have participated in local, national, and international tournaments with the Neversweats having competed in Japan, Australia, Scotland, Spain, Hawaii, and Phoenix, Arizona. In March 2000, the Lloydminster Neversweats played in a World Tournament in Vancouver involving 133 teams from various countries around the world. The tournament involved several age divisions, a number of players over 80 years of age played in the 70 and over division. "This would have been absolutely unheard of 40 years ago," remarks Bill Armstrong, a member. The Neversweats emerged as World Champions in the 50 and over division.
Left to right; Back row: Elvin Miller, Roger Brekko, Morris Smith, Desmond MacMillan, Ross Perkins, Jack Kaluski, Bob Dunham, Les Armstrong.
Front Row left to right: Bill Armstrong, George Smith, Tony Kossey, Wayne Moore, Don Sagriff, Ken Kile

Photo courtesy of B & R Photography

Above: Two Junior A Blazers carry the hopes and dreams of Lloydminster Hockey fans over the blue line. The Blazers were formed in 1988 and compete in the Alberta Amateur Junior Hockey League. Previously, the Lloydminster Lancers had played in the Saskatchewan Amateur Junior Hockey League. When the new team was formed, Bill Kondro was Team President and General Manager and Willard Kondro was Team Manager. Over the years, the Blazers organization has assisted players to pursue an education as well as develop and showcase their hockey talent. Several players were scouted and went on to University and professional leagues. Former Blazer, Cory Cross, started his NHL career in 1993 with the Tampa Bay Lightning.

Below: One of the highlights in the 1940's and 1950's was the Board of Trade Hockey Tournament played every March. Teams and fans would come by special trains from the surrounding area. Many of the teams were essentially pick-up teams bearing such colourful names as Stampeders, River Rats, and the Deer Creek Ferries. Here Ben Gulak presents the trophy to the 1955? winners.

became the namesakes for the local teams. Principal Chester Avery and caretaker Martin Browne contributed by making the league trophy, fittingly called the "Stanley Cup" by its players. For the students and parents, it was as respected and sought after as the real thing! There were no coaches at the time, and not many parents attended games, though they did provide transportation for 'away' games. High school level teams were Midget and Juvenile at the time and were sponsored by many of the local service clubs. Ed Garrish was one of the driving forces behind the high school leagues.

In 1967, the Lloydminster Minor Hockey Association was formed. Hockey had grown so significantly that it now needed its own organization, and moved out of the public school system. Parents became more involved; coaching, refereeing and taking part in the organization. One of the key founders, organizers, administrators and operators of both the minor and senior organizations was Al Dornstauder.

The future of hockey in Lloydminster looks very bright, with a sound organizational structure at all levels. Today, many men and women are volunteering countless hours to fill the positions required to run an effective organization. From executive members of the Lloydminster Minor Hockey Association, who organize and operate the various age-group categories, to the coaches, referees, parent fund raising committees, and the boys and girls who participate as players, this co-operative structure bodes well for the future.

The 1950's was the era of the Jets, the team that had replaced the Prolites. For three consecutive years, from 1953-1956, the Lloydminster Jets won the Saskatchewan Intermediate "A" title and became Western Canadian Finalists. Many of the Jets players left in the Spring of 1955, and so with a mix of new and some old players, the team joined the Eastern Alberta Hockey League. The 'Jets' name was dropped, and the team, sponsored by the R.J.R. Noyes Chevrolet Dealership, became the "Chevies". The Chevies had a few bad years from 1960-1963, and fan support dwindled. In order to muster community support the team name changed again. After much discussion and input from the community, the "Chevies" became the "Border Kings"

The Border Kings managed to re-capture the glory days of former hockey teams. Former Border King captain Bill Armstrong remembers the team's success. "During the late 1960's and early 1970's the Lloydminster Border Kings were playing in perhaps the most significant era in their history – in a seven year span – six provincial championships, four inter-provincial championships, three Western Canadian Championships, and one Canadian Championship."

Photo courtesy of Lloydminster Regional Archives

Once again, in 1981, the Saskatchewan Senior A championship came back to Lloydminster. The Border Kings played in the Wild Goose Hockey League, capturing the Saskatchewan AA Championship in 1986. In the next ten or so years the team had trouble getting players, and a sponsor, a similar problem faced by teams earlier in the century. The team played in the Big Four League for 3 or 4 years, but was later able to re-join the Wild Goose League. In 1996, 1998 and 1999 the Border Kings won the Saskatchewan AAA Championship. In the year 2000 the Allan Cup came to Lloydminster - another major sporting event held in the Border City.

They had come ever so close in 2000, but in 2001, the dream of capturing the Allan Cup was realized in Sarnia, Ontario. The Kings beat the Petrolia Squires 7-2 in the final game earning the 93 year old national senior AAA title.

From hot summer diamonds to icy winter rinks, from spontaneous pick-up games to tightly scheduled leagues, from the tentative beginning efforts of tiny tots to the huffs and puffs of seniors determined not to let it end, for 100 years Lloydminsterites have demonstrated their love of their games - whether or not they were bordering on greatness.

Above: Border Kings captain Merv Mann holds the Allan Cup proudly over his head in March 2001.

Below: The Border Kings at Sarnia, 2001. Back row: Elmer Franks (team president), Bill Thon (head coach) Willie Ewert (trainer) Robert Quist, Todd Murphy, Dustin Fallsheer, Steve Zinger, Jeff Noble, Trevor Bygrove, Owen Noble (assistant coach)
Middle row: Tyler Scott, Barkley Swenson, Clint Chocan, Jason Jutte, Brad Bensmiller, Jason Ross, Ray Nielsen, Mark Odut, Greg Buchanan (general manager)
Front row: Morgan Mann, Jeff Rosner, Dave Morrell, Mervin Mann, Cory Dallyn, Scott Hood, Greg Brown, Jason Clague, Trevor Rapchalk, Chad Emigh, Ian Munro, Michelle Chourchesne (stats)

Chapter Fifteen

Arts and Culture

Research and draft writing by Linda Nykolaychuk

Photo courtesy of BCHCC

Right: A self portrait of Berthold Imhoff, the famous artist whose work is currently housed in the Barr Colony Heritage Cultural Centre.

When the Barr Colonists made their epic trek, almost one-third way round the globe, they brought with them more than just the "bare necessities". Among the mountains of valises and steamer trunks came the "cultural baggage" of violins, accordions, trumpets, drums, harps, and even pianos.

The daily rigours of life in a pioneer settlement in the Canadian Northwest, it might be assumed, would leave little enough time for "arts and culture". Nothing could be further from the truth. On their first Christmas, the "Colonists" assembled an art gallery of Currier and Ives illustrations, had choral singing, dramatic skits, and topped it off with some energetic round dancing which didn't conclude until 4:00 AM.

Over the years since, Lloydminster has maintained a rich tradition of artistic activity. True, the arts were often relegated to makeshift facilities while business, industry and sports took the limelight, but thanks to motivated individuals, the arts were sustained. As our first century came to a close, finally the facilities began to match the talent and dedication of the artists. The opening of the Barr Colony Heritage Cultural Centre (BCHCC) in 1989 was a giant step and now we eagerly anticipate the curtain rising in the Vic Juba Community Theatre to be completed in 2002. The pioneers celebrated their true arrival when they moved from their shacks and soddies into substantial residences. It has taken a century, but Arts and Culture in Lloydminster has finally found a home.

Visual Arts

Many accomplished artists are part of Lloydminster's story. The most famous, perhaps, is Berthold Imhoff. Deeply religious, Imhoff ignored the Impressionist movement of the 1890's, in favour of painting more traditional religious scenes inspired by the Italian

Photo courtesy of BCHCC and the Imhoff family.

Renaissance. Much of his work, including many unique murals, portray religious and historic scenes in truly arresting grandeur.

After his death in 1939, his family opened the Imhoff studio to the public and a constant stream of people came to see the work of the great artist. After more than forty years of caring for the collection, the family reached an agreement with the City of Lloydminster and now almost the entirety of the remarkable Imhoff collection is housed in the Barr Colony Heritage Cultural Centre.

Our art scene became more formally organized in 1946. The Lloydminster Art Club was formed with local artist, Lindsay Evans, the first president. The group offered support and training for aspiring and established border city artists.

Photo courtesy of BCHCC

Evans, adept with charcoal and pencil, specialized in sketching the human figure. He spent World War II in London as a war artist, commissioned to do several paintings, portraits, and murals.

Olinda Tindall, an early member, recalls one of the Club highlights was when A. Y. Jackson, a friend of Lindsay Evans, and the last living member of the "Group of Seven", visited the Lloydminster Art Club in 1967. She recalls the unique experience of sitting on the hillside at Lea Park and painting alongside a true Canadian legend.

Although the Art Club dissolved into the Lloydminster Allied Arts, they held a special anniversary showing in 1987. Opened by Hon. Don Mazankowski, Deputy Prime Minister, it was a retrospective of almost 50 years of Lloydminster art.

In more recent years, artists such as Allen Wallington and Jerry Didur have undertaken community projects. Wallington was commissioned in 1985 to paint a mural commemorating the Barr Colonists. The almost two-story high mural beside the Heritage Building has become a familiar feature of downtown Lloydminster.

As artist-in-residence at the BCHCC, Jerry Didur worked with local schools; his murals remain in the Barr Colony School today. He also gave demonstrations to the community, taught classes in pottery and painting techniques, and completed a major ceramic tile project, which frames the entrance of the BCHCC.

Photo courtesy of BCHCC

Above: Jerry Didur's residency was sponsored by various provincial and local organizations including the Organization of Saskatchewan Arts Councils (OSAC), Lloydminster Allied Arts Council, and the Lloydminster local of the Saskatchewan Society for Education Through Art. He is pictured above with the ceramic tile project which he created for the Barr Colony Heritage Cultural Centre.

Photos by Don Whiting

Allen Wallington (inset) was commissioned in 1985 to paint a mural (above) commemorating the Barr Colonists. It features both G. E. Lloyd and I. M. Barr.

Lindsay Evans

The story of the Lloydminster Art Club is really part of the Lindsay Evans story. After his return from World War II, Lindsay turned to organizing the local art and craft people. He called a meeting in 1946 in the Meridian School and was chosen the first president. Lindsay was the key person in the Club. He opened and closed the school, arranged for speakers and instructors, and was the person to whom all turned for encouragement, inspiration and advice about their paintings and drawings.

In the 1950's, Saskatchewan instituted the 'Lighted School" program, by which grants were offered for visual arts night classes held in schools. Lindsay applied for the grant and an instructor from the University of Alberta Exten-

Photos courtesy of BCHCC

Left: Lindsay Evans in later years. Right: One of the artist's many paintings, this one depicting a local winter scene.

sion Department was hired. Lindsay also established a connection with Alberta's Culture Coordinator, Blake McKenzie, who frequently visited Lloydminster to speak to the Art Club. McKenzie was instrumental in the organization of the Lloydminster Allied Arts Council.

Lindsay Evan's vast array of art works depicts his life experiences: western life and homesteading, the oilfields and prairie landscape, and the people with whom he lived. His pieces hang in the Saskatchewan Provincial Archives, the National Portrait Gallery, the Canadian Military Headquarters in Ontario, and the Barr Colony Heritage Cultural Centre.

Organizations, Clubs, and Guilds

By September 1974, both plumbing and wiring had been completed in the revamped basement of the old post office (bottom centre); a kiln and potter's wheels were moved in, chairs, work tables, and cupboards were ordered; and in late September, pottery classes began. At the annual meeting in October, the centre was named the "Lloydminster Allied Arts Centre". By December the centre had hosted art and pottery sales and the first one woman show – that of Solveig Jeffery. The members functioned as administrators, voluntary janitors, painters, carpenters, instructors, bankers, and curators.

The dedicated membership of the Lloydminster Art Club was a driving force behind the unification of the various arts and cultural strands of Lloydminster under the Lloydminster Allied Arts Council in 1974. A bylaw dated December 2, 1974, states "... the purpose of establishing the Lloydminster Allied Arts Council ... [is] to provide and promote cultural and artistic activities for the residents of the City of Lloydminster". Membership of the Council consisted of representatives of the City Council and the Recreation Board, each of the School Boards, members elected from the annual meetings, and members at large, ranging from teenagers to senior citizens from other performing and visual arts clubs.

The official opening ceremony, in the basement of the old Post Office, took place in May 1975 when a "Spring Festival of the Arts" featured local craftspeople, artists, musicians, and dancers.

The Lloydminster Allied Arts won wide acclaim for bringing the performing arts to Lloydminster in the

Photo by Professional Touch Photography

form of "Overture Concerts" held in both the High School and Neville Goss Auditoriums. The council also hosted the "Stars for Saskatchewan" Series as well as "Concerts for Kids". Over the years it hosted Operas by the Canadian Opera Company, well-known artists such as pianists Frank Mills, and John Kimura Parker, classical guitarist Leona Boyd and many others.

The cultural community was growing but was still bereft of suitable facilities. When the Communiplex was to be built, the Allied Arts Council was asked to partner in order to secure cultural grants. However, after the building opened, only the dance program could sustain itself given the added rental costs. Pottery classes and other arts-related activities continued in more affordable spaces around Lloydminster including the basement of the old post office and in the Meridian School.

Education was important to maintaining art awareness. The Lloydminster local of the Saskatchewan Society for Education through Art was formed in 1984. Its goal was to encourage and support art opportunities for the youth in Lloydminster. One method was a series of exhibits, beginning at the Lloyd Mall in 1984, which has become the yearly "May is Student Art Month" in Lloydminster.

The BCHCC provided an additional facility for the promotion of arts

Photo courtesy of BCHCC

and culture in the border city. One of the early driving forces behind the idea that became the Centre was Richard Larsen. A quiet, gentle man, he remained fiercely determined to mobilize the community in the 1960's to build what is now the north wing of the Richard Larsen Museum. Despite his pronounced Danish ac-

Photo courtesy of BCHCC

"May is Student Art Month" moved from the Lloyd Mall to eventually locate at the Barr Colony Heritage Cultural Centre where, as above, student art work is still proudly displayed.

cent, he would persuade and cajole individuals to donate either artifacts or funding and would accept any artifact to preserve it for posterity. Through public donations and bequests, the Barr Colony Antique Museum was built and officially opened in 1968.

On April 7, 1969, City Council established a Barr Colony Museum committee comprised of five members, "to manage and develop the Barr Colony Museum, its facilities and exhibits." The original members were Richard Larsen, Colin Wright, Gordon Hudson, Russ Robertson, and O. C. Yates. Begun with volunteers, until City funding became available, the next thirty years saw a tremendous improvement in the Barr Colony Facilities.

In 1989, significant construction took place. The new building incorporated a viewing hall to exhibit borrowed collections and

With more requests for funding and provincial grants, Allied Arts members served not only on the local board but travelled to provincial meetings as well. Olinda Tindall (above), for example, served on the Alberta Art Foundation for four years, from 1974 – 78.

Below: The Log Cabin Quilter's Guild was one of the many organizations to benefit from the support of the Lloydminster Allied Arts Council. Left to right: Helen Skoretz, Janet Gillis, Thelma Price, Janet Kerr, Kate Van Dusen. Inset: Mrs. Gertrude Hillis, 80 years old, was one of 350 people in Lloydminster who contributed to "A Quilt for Canada" in 1992. Unable to come out to quilt; the quilt was taken to her in Padua Place Seniors Home so that she could add her stitches.

Photos courtesy of Janet Gillis

Photo courtesy of Marg Gilby

Photo courtesy of Eleanor Robertson

Photo courtesy of Janet Gillis

A range of arts organizations has always existed in Lloydminster. With the formation of the Lloydminster Allied Arts Council in the mid 1970's, the groups benefited from a new support system. Left: Members of the Lloydminster Weaving guild practicing their craft; Centre: the Sask/Alta Visual Arts Guild (SAVAG) held many painting workshops, such as the one above; Right: Gen Atkinson and Janet Kerr of the Log Cabin Quilter's Guild decorating a "quilting tree" for the annual Festival of Trees

Photo courtesy of BCHCC

Above: Sharon Mills (left) and Wendy Ellis examine a young Bald Headed Eagle in this 1964 photo at Fuchs' Wildlife Exhibit. Nicholas Fuchs began taxidermy in his home. As the collection grew, it moved first to the Exhibition Grounds in Lloydminster in 1956, then to its present location at the Barr Colony Heritage Cultural Centre, in 1965. Today, the collection is joined to the Centre by an updated corridor, allowing for public viewing throughout the year. It is believed to be the largest one person taxidermy exhibit in North America.

Right: The Barr Colony Antique Museum was officially opened in 1968. Three wings were added, named after the three men who were supporters of the museum and left generous bequests for further expansion. The three wings were the O. C. Yates Wing, W. J. Saunders Wing, and Eric Dunstan Wing.

independent exhibits of professional artists. There was also a community gallery for exhibits of local and regional artists and craftspeople, as well as emerging professional artists. With the construction of the Imhoff Theatre, community events, conferences, seminars and speakers had a welcome new venue.

In 1995 the Barr Colony Heritage Cultural Centre Board was established, and it incorporated the Allied Arts Council. The new board made bold new steps to further enhance the arts in Lloydminster. Projects were undertaken to integrate the many aspects of life in Lloydminster with the arts. One example was the creation of the Oilfield Technical Society (OTS) Heavy Oil Science Centre in the Barr Colony Cultural Heritage Centre. The OTS Heavy Oil Science Centre offered "an interactive adventure into the geology, drilling, refining and uses of the region's heavy oil reserves." Opened on August 5, 1999, the Centre provides a self guided tour through the petroleum industry, its history, and its role in society.

Organizations such as the Lloydminster Allied Arts Council, Barr Colony Heritage Cultural Centre Board, and the Saskatchewan Society

Photo courtesy of BCHCC

for Education through Art worked diligently over the years to increase the profile of the arts in the community. Now artists and art supporters have realized that in unity there is strength. In doing so, arts and culture has found a new base of support.

Performing Arts

Records of the performing arts, musicals and dramas abound in personal scrapbooks, and newspaper accounts from as early as 1905. An article printed in 1907 mentions "a travelling show, a cakewalk, and a street parade, preceded the play 'Uncle Tom's Cabin'."

As time went by, motion pictures began to play a large part in the entertainment of the community. "Up until the advent of talking pictures, music was added to the silent pictures to create the atmosphere and the mood for the scenes being shown on the screen. The pianist had to be an accomplished musician to improvise the right music even though a cue sheet was provided to indicate the type of music needed. Sometimes an orchestra was used, then the admission price was increased," writes George Ross. "Talking pictures" made their debut in Lloydminster in the early 1930's.

Regardless of the fascination with film and screen presentations, groups such as the Lloydminster Little Theatre continued to surface throughout the years. Formed in 1951 by a number of high school graduates who had enjoyed high school drama,

Photo courtesy of Jean Hemstock

Above: A dramatic presentation in the Alberta Hall, c. 1920's. Back row (l. to r.): Jack Farley, Tom Rogers, Fred Mayberry, Tom Barber, Myra Rogers, Mr. Beale (minister), Tom Westcombe. Centre row: ?, Mrs. Ed Davis, Emma Stevenson, Gertrude Miller, ?, Florence Cooke, Margaret Fairey, ?, Ruby Boyd. Front row: Alice Rendell, Alma Westcombe, Ruby Cook

Below: Behind the scenes (left) of Anne of Green Gables, a successful collaboration between Lakeland College Performing Arts Department and the Lloydminster Musical Theatre Group in 1996.
Right: The Chain 'n Circle Square Dance Club of Lloydminster

"Our three act plays were usually comedies, as this seemed to be what the general public enjoyed," wrote Nan Lampitt, a member.

As the years went by, groups reorganized to perform a wide variety of stage productions. In the early 1980's, another group of enthusiastic local actors revived the Lloydminster Little Theatre (LTL) concept with a production of "Leaving Home" in the Neville Goss Auditorium in May 1980. The LTL players had been rehearsing since February, and succeeded not only in reviving interest in live theatre, but ambitiously undertook writing, producing and staging a new play to celebrate Alberta and Saskatchewan's 75th anniversary celebrations. Funded by the City of Lloydminster and Alberta Culture, the play was "greeted enthusiastically" according to reports in the local Meridian Booster.

Lloydminster audiences have demonstrated a preference for wholesome drama and comedy as in such stagings as *Nunsense* and *Steel Magnolias*, while the sometimes controversial fare of the Lloydminster Fringe Festival had difficulty attracting audiences.

The Fringe Festival began in 1996 in the downtown core as a three day event, later moving to the campus of Lakeland College. In 1999, the College opted to keep the space for other events, and The Fringe made yet another move to Weaver Park and the Imhoff Theatre in the BCHCC. Ticket sales at the 2000 Fringe were especially disappointing for the out-of-town performers. Festival organizers were forced to re-evaluate the event and a new organization, the Lloydminster Arts Festival Society hopes to develop a smaller scale festival to highlight local talent, in conjunction with Weaver Park's annual Canada Day celebrations.

While theatre had its ups and downs, dance clubs and studios only grew in popularity. Ukrainian dance classes were first held in the home of Lilian Chomik in 1974, as part of a Ukrainian Educational and Cultural

Photo courtesy of Pat Hankey

Photo courtesy of Edith Cunningham

Photo courtesy of C

Association. The Association's goal was to teach Canadian children an appreciation of their roots and heritage. The group became active in the Allied Arts Council in Lloydminster and helped other groups such as the Highland Dancers.

The Highland Dancers also started with small classes, the first being held in the Knox Presbyterian Church taught by Christina Leach. Chris taught for about seven years. Then there was a term of four to five years without an instructor, before Diane Sutherland (Laidler) resumed instructing.

Alison Lamont was hired by the Allied Arts Council in 1979 to teach at the Lloydminster Dance Academy, which then held classes in the basement of the Communiplex. The program became so popular that it soon outgrew its space and Lamont established her own studio in 1987 (see side-bar).

The arts received a major boost when the Lakeland College Department of Performing Arts was added to the cultural make-up of Lloydminster when the new campus opened in 1990. At that time, there were two separate program areas; Drama and Music.

The first Director of Drama was Andrew Willmer, followed by Vern Thiessen, and Andy Houston. Productions were held in the Lakeland College Blackbox Theatre, presented both by Lakeland College Drama Students and guest performers.

The Conservatory of Music, under the direction of Dr. Rudy Rozanski and later Marg Daly, grew to include instruction in voice, piano, strings and percussion, flute, winds, brass, and guitar, as well as advanced harmony and history.

In the year 2000, the drama and music departments were combined to form a new Department of Performing Arts under Marg Daly.

Photo courtesy of Dolores Ewen

Above: In the early 1980's, another group of enthusiastic local actors revived the Lloydminster Little Theatre concept with an opening production of "Leaving Home" in the Neville Goss Auditorium in May 1980." Left to right: Vernon Sweet, Dolores Ewen, Philip Sharman, Cledwyn Haydn Jones

Bottom left: By 1977 – 78 the dance club, the "Malanka Dancers", was large and advanced enough to be divided into three levels. The club also entered annual dance festivals and won numerous awards and scholarships. In the fall of 1980, the club began to hold classes and workshops in a dance studio in the lower level of the Communiplex.

Bottom right: After several years of operating out of various basements, Diane Laidler opened Studio Encore in 1991. She continued to expand her program in Studio Encore to include a wide range of dance programs. In 1994 she added a new gymnastics program. The Highland Dancers flourished with the aid and support of the Lloydminster Allied Arts Council.

Photo courtesy of Studio Encore

Alison Lamont School of Dance

Alison Lamont was hired by the Lloydminster Dance Academy, under the umbrella of the Lloydminster Allied Arts Council, in 1979. She had graduated from the Canadian College of Dance, in Toronto, in 1978.

The Dance Academy had begun in the basement of the old Post Office, moving to the lower level of the Lloydminster Communiplex in 1979. Alison started teaching with approximately 60 students. The theme of her first Lloydminster recital was "Homecoming", which tied in with the 75th anniversary celebrations of the provinces of Alberta and Saskatchewan. In 1980, her student enrolment doubled to 120 students, and over the next year doubled once again. By this time, she was growing out of the space available in the Lloydminster Communiplex and realized it was time to build her own studio.

In 1987, Alison Lamont built her first studio on 42nd Street. The Alison Lamont School of Dance remained in this location for the next ten years. In 1997, the studio moved to its 44th Street location.

Photo courtesy of Alison Lamont

Alison Lamont instructing a dance class in the basement of the Communiplex in 1980.

This new location allowed for three studios, with sprung hardwood floors, barres and mirrors, three dressing rooms, a large waiting area, eating area, and improved quality sound systems.

Over the years she saw dancers go on to become qualified dance instructors and to perform, not only in prominent national dance productions, but internationally as well. Lloydminster dancers are now in the Alberta Ballet, the Royal Winnipeg Ballet, and a multitude of theatres across Canada and the United States.

Every year students from the Alison Lamont School of Dance participate in many community oriented activities. Some of the many local venues include Senior Citizens' homes, the malls, local festivals and an annual recital. Her dance groups have also travelled to perform on cruise ships, in Disneyland and in Disneyworld.

Alison Lamont has provided quality dance education in Lloydminster for more than twenty years. Lamont's dedication to the art of dance is admirable.

Below: One successful off-shoot of Little Theatre was the Lloydminster Musical Theatre Group which produced several well received musicals in the 1990's including "Two by Two". The musicals featured local talent such as Ron Long and Brad Hougham, who both went on to professional music careers. Norm White (standing, far left) maintained an active involvement in community theatre after moving to Lloydminster in 1975, acting in numerous productions and serving as president of Little Theatre Lloydminster. Left to right:: Kneeling - Marla Stewart, Jeanine Judson; Standing - Norm White, Brenda Ellison, Brad Hougham, Mike Telenga, and Ron Long.

Photo courtesy of Pat Hankey

Music

Joseph Fairbrother formed one of the earliest bands in Lloydminster in 1908. Joe farmed southwest of Lloydminster, and held his practices in the same area, at the home of the Ormiston brothers. In 1911, he formed the Lloydminster Citizen's Band. Until Joe moved into Lloydminster, in 1913, the town supplied him with a horse, buggy and cutter to be used in his twelve-mile journey to band practice. In Lloydminster, the town also provided a suitable band hall.

The band grew and changed over the years, but Joe Fairbrother remained a key member, both in his ability to lead the band and in his ability to perform. Joe was always available when music was required. One account by Libbie Young tells of how the band played "just about everywhere", and describes their mode of travel. "The band would arrive in a wagon pulled by four beautiful horses. Their arrival at a country picnic was a scene to behold". Mrs. Young witnessed them entering a picnic ground, a wagon full of musicians playing to the rhythm of the prancing horses, a scene that would now stop traffic and win loud and long applause.

The Lloydminster Citizen's Band remained a force in the community until 1953 when the Lion's Club produced financing for a new band. Bob Bourassa led the new band, and over the next ten years it performed in concerts, parades and community events, and travelled to parades both in the local area and as far as Edmonton. Many of those who played in his band tell of the patience and effort put forth by their bandleader over those years.

The first music festival in Lloydminster was in 1931. It had 44 entries, including piano, instrumental, vocal and band. Vocal classes were held at the Empress Theatre and the piano and instrumental entries at Grace United Church. The festival continued until 1935. When it was revived in 1963, the forward of the festival book, written by E. W. H. Howell, explained why it had been discontinued: "the former committee worked hard for years to bring us a series of wonderful festivals which had to be dropped for lack of interest and funds during the Depression".

In 1997, the name was changed to the Kiwanis Lloydminster and District Music Festival, when the Kiwanis Club assumed major sponsorship. As Lloydminster welcomed the year 2000, the Lloydminster Music Festival had over 900 entries in a variety of classes.

Photo courtesy of BCHCC

Above: Herb Tebo, Stan Fallows, Scotty Hislop, Lyal McDermid, and Harold Aston of the Harmony 5 take the bandstand so Lloydminsterites can dance in the New Year - 1924.

Below: The Lakeland College Conservatory of Music began with some outstanding talents. Shown here in a 1992 concert are: (l-r) long-time Edmonton Symphony member and recording artist, Harlan Green; internationally renowned concert pianist Dr. Rudy Rozanski, the first Director of the Conservatory; and Kathleen Schoen who along with her husband Thomas went on to a performing career with innovative chamber ensembles. In recent years, under Director Marg Daly, the Conservatory has grown to a dozen instructors and is likely the best known Lakeland College program in the Lloydminster community.

Below: The Lloydminster Community Band, under Director Bob Bourassa, was such a well known institution it was featured in a 1955 CBC documentary about Lloydminster. The band was just one of many evidences of the tremendous musical talent which has characterized Lloydminster over its first century.

Photo courtesy of Sandy Hill (back left with tuba)

Photo courtesy of Janet Rozanski

The beat goes on in Lloydminster. Marching bands, dance bands, trios, quartets; formal concerts to jammin' sessions, the musicians in Lloydminster today follow a long line of musical heritage. Top: The Lloydminster Citizens' Band preparing for a parade in 1920. Below: The Lakelanders entertain visitors at Canada Day.

Cultural Events

Besides the obvious sporting events, the 1982 Alberta Winter Games, hosted by Lloydminster, boasted seven different cultural events: Poetry and Folk writing, The Disabled and the Art Experience, Draw Me Fit, Interfolk '82 - Dance, Song and Costume classes, Musicfest Guitar Competition – classical and folk classes, Theatresports – competitions of amateur actors in improvisation - and presentations by Dance Alberta.

The Lloydminster Culture and Coffeehouse took place at the Wildrose Pavilion and housed live music, ethnic food and artifacts. The coffeehouse incorporated the Interfolk '82 event, featuring ethnic dance groups from across the province of Alberta.

Arts groups in Lloydminster have learned over the years, that they strengthen their role by allying themselves with other strands of the community such as industry or sports. During the 1997 Alberta Summer Games in Lloydminster, Bud Miller Park was transformed into a "Festival In the Park". Once again, Lloydminsterites rose to the occasion to play host to thousands of athletes and visitors to our city. The Festival featured over 100 entertainers, numerous ethnic food booths, and a memorable "taste of the border". Linda Nykolaychuk, worked together with enthusiastic volunteers for two years prior to the games to bring everything together for the weekend event.

The Future

It had long been clear that Lloydminster needed a performing arts theatre. As early as 1985, plans for a 600 – 700 seat theatre were drawn up and the City Parks, Recreation and Culture Master Plan identified a theatre as a priority. In 1987, land for the Lloydminster Campus of Lakeland College was acquired through the purchase of 35 acres by the College and the donation of 30 acres by the City. In 1988, a steering committee was appointed by the City and the College Board of Governors to explore the development, financing and operations of a joint-use theatre facility, to be built in 1997. Major fund-raising of the community portion of funds started.

In 1994, government funds were put on hold and the following year the City reserved funding for the up-coming Alberta Summer Games.

When the college underwent major cutbacks, it appeared that they would no longer be involved in the

Left: "Swing into Summer with Live Jazz" by Kirby and the Groove. Right: Mardi Gras participant Karen Ast.

Mardi Gras evolved from Jazz on the Border, a series of musical performances organized by local businessman and musician, Kirby Hayes. With the help of musicians such as Rudy Rozanski, Harlan Green, the Schoen Duo, Mel Risling, Murray Forbes, Murray McDonnell, Linda Sawtell, Bernie Gantefoer, Jeanine Judson, Ross Ulmer, and teacher Patrick Hoenmans and his school bands, Jazz on the Border played to enthusiastic audiences looking for musical variety. Each year became bigger and better. "It just seemed natural to take the next step," says Kirby, " and in 1997 the first official Lloydminster Mardi Gras was born." Mardi Gras has since moved to the Stockade Convention Centre and each year has entertained sold out audiences of over 500 jazz enthusiasts.

The Treasured Brew Piano

Mary Ann Brew, Avice (Brew) Jensen's Grand-mother, left England with her son, Gordon and daughter, Marie to join her son, Lewis, in Canada in 1904. She brought her household furniture and china along with her - and her piano. When she reached Toronto she was told that her English piano wouldn't survive the cold Canadian weather. She sold it, and purchased a new Heinzman-Wormwith piano that had been made in 1897. It had a beautiful rosewood case and a lovely tone.

The piano was crated and came by train to North Battleford, the end of the rail line. To get to the homestead in the Golden Valley district, the family and their valuable possessions, including the piano, had to travel over the bumpy terrain in a wagon drawn by a team of oxen.

Avice Jensen (Photo taken in 2000) taught many a student on the treasured Brew Piano.

Photo by Don Whiting

The brothers, Gordon and Lewis dug a shelter in the bank of the lake on the homestead, eight miles south of what is now Blackfoot. It was a year and a half before a log shack was built and the piano was out of its crate. There was no other piano for miles around, so the Brew piano was hauled to every concert and musical event. Music was the main source of entertainment and socializing for the new Canadians. Gordon, Avice's father, and Lewis, her uncle, while in England received excellent training in piano, violin, coronet and voice. Their love of playing music took them all over the country accompanying other musicians.

Before the Holy Trinity Golden Valley Church was built on the north-east corner of Gordon's property, services were held in the Brew home for five years. The Brew family provided the music for the services with up to fifty people in attendance. In a few years Gordon's children, Clifford, Avice and Norah learned to play on Granny Brew's piano.

In 1946, Avice Brew, who was married to Nels Jensen, and living in Maidstone, inherited the Brew piano. In those days, money was scarce and Avice taught music to a few neighbourhood children for 25¢ a lesson.

Nels, a keen musician, loved to teach and play instrumental music. He played the violin, and Avice provided the accompaniment on the piano. They were invited to participate in many functions. Many the evening was spent with family and friends singing around the piano.

Avice gave up teaching while her children were small. Her children, who inherited her musical talent, played the piano, violin and coronet. After ten years, the family moved into Lloydminster, and again the piano made the trip.

The Brew piano survived its many moves showing its scars, but it always stayed in tune, even through the many changing atmospheres around it. Avice commented, "In the early times there was no tuning done to the piano. It dropped its tone, but did so evenly."

Unfortunately, Nels became terminally ill and died in 1963, leaving Avice to earn a living for her family. She took on a large number of piano students, teaching them to play on the Brew piano at a charge of 50 cents per one hour lesson. As the economy got stronger, the price per lesson slowly increased until it reached $20 at the turn of the century.

In early 2001, Avice passed away. For almost our entire century, Avice, the Brew family, and their treasured piano, brought joy and music to many lives, children and adults alike.

project, and the committee searched for an alternative site. Lakeland College was able eventually to re-commit to the project and the future site returned to the College.

It was agreed that the project should be modified to a more affordable 500-seat community theatre featuring local performers, as well as visiting artists. On June 15, 2000, the city was presented with the one million dollar cheque. The committee went on to raise $1.9 million. The official sod-turning ceremony for the new facility took place on April 6, 2001. At that time, the announcement was made that the theatre would officially be named the Vic Juba Community Theatre.

"Peter Pan" one of the many performances presented at the "Festival in the Park" during the 1997 Alberta Summer Games. Inset: Summer Games Chair Vic Juba (left) with Border Buddy and Culture Director Linda Nykolaychuk.

Lloydminster Authors

Christine Michels moved to Lloydminster when she was five and completed her schooling here. Initially published under the pen name Sharice Kendyl, she has written, *To Share a Sunset*, (1990), *Ascent to the Stars* and *Danger's Kiss*, (both 1994). All are novels published by Leisure Books in New York. Romance Writers of America, region 4, named *Danger's Kiss* "best single contemporary title". In 1998, Christine released her first Historical Romance, *Beyond Betrayal*.

Violet Copeland, a former member of the Sask-Alta Scribes is listed in the Alberta Poetry Yearbook, won prizes for her poetry, including the Georgia May Cook Sonnet Award.

Edna Alford, a former resident of Lloydminster, listed in the Saskatoon Public Library as a prize-winning author, published *2000% Cracked Wheat*, as well as a wide variety of short stories and poems.

Retired teacher, **Dolores Ewen**, has written short stories, poetry and plays. The Language Experience Program, level 4, published by Gage, uses her short stories. The Globe Theatre presented one of Ewen's plays in Regina in 2001.

Craig George, born in Lloydminster and raised near Marwayne,, shifted from political cartooning to his own comic strip, *Rural Rootz*, published in several newspapers. Craig has published four books in the Rural Rootz collection: *Rural Rootz, Udder Nonsense, Rural Rootz 3*, and his latest, *Farm Aid*.

Franklin Foster's, *John E. Brownlee, A Biography*, (1996), is the life story of John Brownlee, Premier of Alberta from 1925 to 1934. The work reflects Dr. Foster's long time interest in Western Canadian history especially the Reform Movements of the early 20th Century. He also wrote the textual material that appears in the OTS Heavy Oil Science Centre.

The arts in Lloydminster began with the diversity of talents which the first settlers brought with them. The establishment of the Lloydminster Allied Arts Council, Barr Colony Heritage Cultural Centre, and Lakeland College Performing Arts program, along with the dedication of driven individuals has allowed the arts scene in Lloydminster to continue through our first century. With the construction of the Vic Juba Community Theatre, artists, performing artists, and arts enthusiasts are looking forward to arts and culture finally being fully recognized for their significant role in the life of our community.

Photo courtesy of Lakeland College

Theatre enthusiasts kick off the community portion of the fundraising for what would later be named the Vic Juba Community Theatre.

Photo by Don Whiting

Chapter Sixteen

Lloydminster in Canada and the World

Research by Sheila Bennett and Franklin Foster

T oo often in history, especially local history, we overlook the larger context and focus entirely on the goings-on immediately around us. This chapter attempts to remedy this slightly by mentioning a few provincial, national and international issues which impacted Lloydminster during the century past. As well, we note briefly a few of those Lloydminsterites known on the larger stage.

Clearly the Barr Colonists had a world-wide outlook. Their pride in the British Empire was not simply the glorification of England, as many today assume, but rather an excitement about being citizens of an Empire which circled the globe and consituted a major influence in every continent. Barr Colonists were part of a generation which saw India, Australia, New

Right: George Frederick Ives (November 17, 1881 - April 12, 1993) is shown laying a wreath at the cenotaph in London, England on November 11, 1992. He is wearing the South African Service Medal and the Queen Victoria South Africa Medal with Bar. He was honoured by thousands, including members of the Royal Family, as the documented last survivor of the South African War (1899-1902) in which he served in 1st Company, 1st Battalion, 1st Imperial Yeomanry. Following his return from South Africa, Ives saw a letter by Rev. George Lloyd in a British newspaper advocating young men going to Canada for the opportunities there. He later signed on as a Barr Colonist. During the winter of 1903-04, he worked on a crew building a telegraph line from the new Lloydminster to the existing line through Onion Lake. He dismissed such hardships as being lost in a blizzard and living in a pole shack lined with newspapers as "the foolishness of youth". Ives volunteered for service in World War I but was rejected due to concerns about his age and a heart murmur. In 1919, George and his wife Kitty (to whom he was married for 76 years) settled their young family in British Columbia. However, George returned frequently to visit relatives and became one of the best known Barr Colonists. He planned on attending the July 1993 celebrations marking the 90th anniversary of the founding of Lloydminster but he passed away on April 12th, 90 years to the day of his first setting foot on Canadian soil with the Barr Colonists.

Photo courtesy of Jesse Moore

Zealand, South Africa, Rhodesia, and Canada as vital parts of their "country". It is this that helps explain the otherwise odd assumption they had that they were at home in Western Canada and that other recent immigrants were "foreigners".

One of these Barr Colonists was George Ives. As had several of his shipmates on the S.S. Lake Manitoba, he had seen active service in what his generation called the Boer War, in South Africa. Although he would spend little more than ten per cent of his life in Lloydminster, he became one of the better known Barr Colonists through his frequent visits here and through his longevity. In the end he was honoured as the last survivor in the world of the Boer War he had campaigned in in his youth.

The first decade of the 20th Century was a time of heady optimism, fueled by the rapid advances in technology and, locally, the obvious transformation of the countryside. Settlers continued to stream in although Lloydminster retained its reputation as a British settlement. Newspapers were eagerly awaited from Winnipeg and "the old country".

During that first winter in the Colony, news of a successful flight of a heavier than air craft by two American brothers named Wright was pushed to the back pages by headlines of the threat of war between Russia and Japan. Such a war might drag Britain in to support its ally Japan and enforce its policy of checking Russian expansion.

Above: Rev. Lloyd (left) welcomes the Governor General, the Earl of Minto, (centre, in riding breeches) to Lloydminster in the fall of 1904.

As it would happen, Japan easily defeated the Russian navy in two major sea battles in 1904 and 1905. By that time, Britain was keeping a watchful eye on the growing ambition of Germany and called on Canada for assistance in keeping pace in the escalating arms race. The question of the support Canada should provide for Britain's navy divided Canadians and was a major issue in the 1911 election. Lloydminsterites placed themselves firmly on the side of the Empire.

So it was that when word spread rapidly in August of 1914 that Britain had declared war on Germany in protest over the invasion of Belgium by German armies on their way to attack France, Lloydminster responded with a mixture of excitement and resolve. Many thought the war would be an exciting adventure and young men surged forward to volunteer for service, anxious lest the war be over before they could get to Europe to participate.

On Sunday, August 23, 1914, less than three weeks after the declaration of war, a trainload of "Border Boys" left for the war. As the *Lloydminster Times* described it, "a community banquet was held on Friday night with numerous speeches and a presentation of songs to honour the officers and men of the local militia regiment." Captain Carl Ross was in command and "thirty of our bravest and best have gone with the first contingent and if further calls should come, they will be responded to just as heartily whilst there is a man amongst us left."

The *Times* writer was doubtless striving for dramatic effect but his words were prophetic. Canada would make the very ambitious commitment of five divisions for the war effort. Almost 10 per cent of the population would be under arms. And, given the horrific nature of the slaughter,

Roll of Honour
1914 - 1918

C. Addison	H. V. Kift
C. Batty	A. Laws
W. Bates	A. S. K. Lloyd
A. H. Bibby	C. Lynch
A. Bourne	J. W. Mather
S. Brant	H. F. Masterman
A. Bramley-Moore	G. R. Mersereau
E. Brown	H. R. Miles
Ewart Brown	L. S. Moffett
F. Bullock-Webster	W. H. Murray
R. A. Burchnall	G. McAdam
D. Cherry	A. H. McKay
F. Creech	A. McGillivary
D. Crompton	J. H. Noble
F. Daly	H. H. Noyes
J. E. Dalley	A. E. Osborn
W. Dargie	H. Pape
W. Davey	A. S. Patmore
G. Davison	R. F. Power
T. Dent	F. Pritchard
C. B. Despard	F. Reid
F. Everett	T. J. Relf
M. Eustace	E. Robinson
A. Fraser	B. H. Rowles
J. Ford	W. H. Rowley
V. W. Fouracre	H. J. Seels
W. Gayford	W. F. Sloman
C. J. George	C. H. Smith
C. Gilchrist	J. F. Smith
A. Greenshaw	W. F. G. Smith
F. W. Hainsby	G. P. Stephenson
A. F. Hames	B. Still
A. V. Harding	C. Still
H. Hathaway	A. Sturgeon
H. H. Hathaway	J. E. Swindell
C. Henderson	W. Thomson
R. Hill	L. E. R. Thompson
C. Hudson	L. H. Truscott
H. Iremonger	W. McA. Vokins
J. Jeffery	F. Wall
J. Jeffery	F. Webber
W. A. Johnson	W. Weeks
M. Jones	W. Whitehead
H. Judd	R. Wood

Sergeant Charles A. Spencer, served in the Transportation Corps during much of World War I. He is shown here with his wife while home on leave in 1917. Photographers were kept busy during the war providing photos, always potentially final photos, of loved ones.

and the almost continual involvement of Canadians in high risk campaigns, one in ten would be killed.

The enthusiasm and excitement were beginning to wane by the time the second contingent left Lloydminster in November. Then, on Christmas Day, came the first of a long line of dreaded telegrams. Lord Kitchener expressing his sympathy to the parents of Jack Dalley on the death of their son in action with the Royal Welsh Fusiliers. Jack was a quiet spoken young man who had attracted notice around town for his skills on the football team. Now he had died on another field, one of over five million killed in the first year alone. Yet the same newspaper that carried the news of Jack's death also announced a push to recruit 550 more from Lloydminster and District.

Below: Lloydminster's home regiment, the 22nd Saskatchewan Light Horse, pose in front of the Drill Hall in November 1914. They represent the second contingent to leave Lloydminster for the front, 163 officers and men under the command of Lt. Col. Hodson. Part of their training was barrack life in the Drill Hall which proved to be "no fit place during the nights of November for empire defenders to be sleeping without ample covering." A call went out to Lloydminsterites to donate extra blankets. The response was overwhelming.

Photos courtesy of Janet Salt

Above: Lloydminster's Janet Salt spent over two years in the Women's Royal Canadian Naval Service, mostly working in naval hospitals in Nova Scotia. Top left: Janet Salt, 1944. Top right: Janet gets ship board experience, here beside a depth charge. Background: Janet and friend pose on the observation deck of the Empire State Building during a visit to New York City.

In 1939, when Canada entered World War II, there was far less excitement and much more a spirit of grim resolve to do our duty. Lloydminsterites were active in all branches of the service and saw action in campaigns from Dieppe, through North Africa and Italy, to D-Day and the invasion of Normandy, and the gratefully received liberation of the Netherlands.

Again, space does not permit a detailed accounting but one soldier's story can perhaps suggest the experience of many. Bert Lafoy volunteered to serve in 1939. He was 20 years old. He had come to Lloydminster in 1930 after growing up in southern Saskatchewan.

Private Lafoy's first combat action didn't happen until June 6, 1944 - D-Day. At 4 o'clock that morning Lafoy's company of 180 men was ordered over the side of their landing barge into chest deep water. It took 20 minutes of wading to get to the beach under intense artillery and machinegun fire with dead and wounded comrades in the water around him. "It was hell, it was hell. What more can you say?" he asks wistfully 55 years later. There was still a mile of barren beach to cross to reach shelter.

Many Canadian soldiers spent years in Britain. One result was a number of "war brides". Left: Jack and Kathleen Spencer celebrate their August 1943 wedding in England. In May 1946, Kathleen would see Lloydminster for the first time.

Photo courtesy of Spencer family

Roll of Honour
1939 - 1945

A. Barrett	F. S. Lomas
R. Barrett	H. C. Knight
E. S. Blake	C. Meeker
E. W. R. Bolton	S. E. Messum
L. G. Boyd	W. G. Miller
W. L. Brown	C. Mitchell
K. Burleigh	P. Mitchell
W. Cameron	A. B. Morlidge
R. E. Chambers	D. McDonald
E. W. Chapman	H. E. Oddan
H. Cook	D. B. Olson
A. J. Davies	P. Paul
F. Fife	R. Piercy
E. Fines	O. J. Peterson
R. Fox	J. E. Potter
J. Fretwell	T. F. Priest
J. Frost	L. O. Rogers
C. Gerow	T. M. Seabrook
L. Gipes	W. M. Studds
J. K. Greenway	C. B. Sutton
C. Hawkins	M. Taylor
S. L. Haynes	F. W. Turvey
J. T. Hill	C. R. Watts
J. Hofflin	A. Wilkinson
R. Holtby	J. Winthers
W. C. Juggins	

"They shall grow not old,
as we that are left grow old;
Age shall not weary them,
nor the years condemn.
At the going down of the sun
and in the morning
We will remember them."

Lieutenant Jack Kemp

In the Spring of 1931, Jack Kemp came to Lloydminster from his home in England to work for his mother's step-brother, J. G. Willard, the publisher of the Lloydminster Times.

He was eighteen years old, and he had no prior experience in the newspaper business. Jack worked hard and came to know every facet of the newspaper business. In exchange, his uncle allowed him to board with him.

By June of 1940, those newspapers were filled with the shocking headlines of Germany's rapid conquest of Norway, Denmark, Holland, Belgium and then France. Britain and the Commonwealth stood alone as the only world power opposing Nazi aggression. Jack put his newspaper career on hold and joined Lloydmin-

Photos courtesy of Jack Kemp

Above: One of the proudest moments in Jack's military career occurred when he accepted the King's Colours and Regimental Colours from King George VI, July 16, 1943. As a former Englishman and proud Canadian, it was an honour for him to kneel before his king. Queen Elizabeth (now the Queen Mother) looks on from far right. (Inset) Lieutenant John K. Kemp, October 1941.

Photo courtesy of Jack Kemp

(Above) Lt. Kemp answers questions from the Queen regarding Battle Honours on the Regimental Colours of the South Saskatchewan Regiment.

ster's home regiment, now styled the 16/22 Saskatchewan Light Horse. (There were no horses, it was a tank brigade.) Kemp did basic training at Camp Dundurn and then was flagged for officer training school in Winnipeg. Kemp completed his courses and was commissioned as a Lieutenant in September 1940. He was asked to stay on to train new recruits until the following spring.

With the situation increasingly grim in Europe, Kemp knew he would soon be going overseas. On February 12, 1941, Jack married his long-time sweetheart Joyce White, who had come to Lloydminster with her family in the 1920's.

On April 3, 1941, he was sent to a reinforcement camp in Southern England where he joined the South Saskatchewan Regiment to defend the southern coast of England from an anticipated para-trooper attack by the Germans. The attack never happened and the regiment eventually moved to the Isle of Wight where they began intensive training for the Dieppe Offensive.

The offensive was apparently cancelled in the spring, and Kemp was transferred to another assignment. So it was that he missed the disastrous raid on Dieppe on August 19, 1942. Assigned to a virtually suicidal assault on the heavily defended port town, over 1,000 Canadians were killed, 84 from the South Saskatchewan Regiment alone. When Jack eventually returned to his regiment, it was still mourning its losses and it took some time for it to rebuild, a process in which Kemp played a leading part as a company commander.

The regiment was not part of the famous D-Day invasion but it did see extensive action in France beginning on July 8. One of the most difficult assignments was to take the French city of Falaise, still occupied by the Germans. When his regiment arrived on August 16, 1944, the city was covered in a layer of rubble, due to an air raid two nights earlier. Jack's company's objective was to re-take a castle, but the structure's high walls made this task difficult, especially considering his company's numbers had been ravaged from 126 to 53. Lt. Kemp ran ahead of the company to do reconnaissance but was suddenly shot down by a German sniper perched high up in the castle. The bullet entered near the bottom of his nose and exited at the base of his skull.

Amazingly, he survived the incident, and was rushed back to a military hospital in England. Back in Lloydminster, his wife Joyce first received news of her husband's injury through a vague telegram which only stated that he had received a head injury. She waited with their three and a half year old son Dennis, whom Jack had never met, for further news of his status.

Jack was not transferred to Canada until January 1945. When he phoned Joyce from the Deer Lodge Veteran's Hospital in Winnipeg, it was Dennis who answered the phone. They both shared the excitement of that first "Hello Daddy!" Kemp had not heard his son's voice before.

The family was re-united, but the next two years would be trying. Jack underwent a succession of surgeries which sent him back to the hospital for up to four months at a time. After two years, he was ready to resume a more regular life.

Jack was welcomed back to the *Lloydminster Times* in 1946. He never left his military past far behind though. From 1953 – 1966, he joined and helped out the local militia. He remains an active member of the Royal Canadian Legion. He has been a key organizer of the Remembrance Day ceremonies for several years. He is proud of the service of his generation and has worked hard to ensure that their contribution is remembered and appreciated by the succeeding generations.

For more on Mr. Kemp's career after he left the service, see Chapter Six - Education, Page 72

Above and below: Jack Kemp inspects the Lloydminster Air Cadet Squadron in 2000, 60 years after donning his uniform for the first time.

Photos by Don Whiting

Photos courtesy of Keith McKoy

Prairie boys often make good sailors. Above: Keith McKoy who served in the Royal Canadian Navy from 1947-1952, including service on the destroyer HMCS Cayuga (inset) during the Korean War.

In recent years, Canadians have been involved extensively in peace keeping missions. Below: On one of the first missions, to Egypt, Peace Keeper Tom McKeachy tests out the local transportation.

Photo courtesy of Tom McKeachy

There was more hell ahead for Private Lafoy. Despite screaming artillery shells overhead and whizzing machine bullets around him, it was time to get to work. Lafoy was a member of an infantry transport company and it was their job to keep the ammunition and fuel moving forward and carry the dead and wounded back to a hastily established field hospital. By the end of the day a beachhead had been secured but it was only the beginning.

There was hard fighting still to be done - through France, Belgium and Holland. By the time they heard the cheers of the crowds in liberated Amsterdam, only six of the original company of 180 were still in active service.

Lafoy was next assigned to the Canadian contingent moving into Germany and on April 15, 1945 he saw first-hand that World War II was about issues of consequence. He was one of those who liberated the infamous Nazi death camp of Belsen. There were 40,000 sick and starving people inside clinging to life but even more shocking were the 10,000 unburied bodies stacked along a barbed wire fence.

"They were piled like cordwood," Lafoy recalled, "for a block and a half, as high as you could reach. It was the saddest thing of the war. It really moved us guys." The sight brought home to him the realization of what the world would have been like had the other side won. "It had been worth every bit of it. If we hadn't gone, the world would have been a far different place."

In the years following the War, Bert Lafoy was active in Remembrance Day observances and often visited schools to try to keep the appreciation for the war effort alive. He travelled back to Europe on three different occasions for military reunions. His last visit was to Holland in May of 2000. The outpouring of gratitude from the Dutch after so many years was overwhelming. The Queen of the Netherlands personally thanked once Private Lafoy and everywhere he went, Canadians were being honoured. In Holland he was a hero. Back in Lloydminster, he was simply Bert Lafoy.

Below: Bert Lafoy poses beside a modern tank while attending a Remembrance Day reunion in Holland where more than 7,000 Canadian soldiers are buried.

Photo courtesy of Bert Lafoy

They came from Lloydminster!

(Clockwise from top left): Ray Nelson is shown receiving an Honourary Doctor of Laws degree from the University of Alberta. In December 1999, at age 79, Mr. Nelson became the world's oldest heart transplant recipient, a key step in ending arbitrary discrimination based on age. Jonathon Fox (far right) is shown being inducted into the Canadian Agricultural Hall of Fame. He was only the second living person to be so honoured. Centre: Adios Pick sired more than 550 trotting horse winners from his home on Gunnholme Farm near Lloydminster. He was inducted into the Canadian Horse Racing Hall of Fame, an honour shared in 1981 with his owner, Dr. Brad Gunn (bottom right with wife Agnes.) Earlier in the century, Lloydminster's best known figure was probably Susan Gunn (third from left in bottom left photo). Mrs. Gunn was Vice-President and later President of the United Farm Women of Alberta and an executive member of the United Farmers of Alberta, the most powerful organization in the province from 1916 to 1934. She worked closely with Premier John E. Brownlee who appointed her to a number of provincial boards.

Photo credits: top left, Ray Nelson; top right; Jonathan Fox, centre and bottom left; Dr. Brad Gunn; bottom right and background by Don Whiting.

Alberta

Photo courtesy of BCHCC

Photo courtesy of Bud Miller

Above: Official opening of the Richard Larsen wing at the Barr Colony Heritage Cultural Centre. (l-r) Steve West (MLA), Richard Starke (City Council), Richard Larsen (long time advocate of preserving Lloydminster's history), Don Mazankowski (MP), Pat Gulak (Mayor) and Doug Cherry (MLA)

Bud Miller (above right) understood the unique character of Lloydminster – one city in two provinces. Bud spearheaded a variety of projects to benefit all of Lloydminster. He worked co-operatively with the many levels and branches of government to get things done.

The Meridian Bridge, the Stockade Building, the new Lloydminster Airport, a water line from the river, and a new hospital near completion all attested to his 15 years as an effective MLA. One of his biggest efforts was chairing the twelve-person board of representatives of Alberta, Saskatchewan, the Federal Government and Husky Oil which made the decisions about the creation of the Upgrader. The goal was to make the Upgrader as beneficial to Lloydminster as possible, providing local people and businesses with opportunities.

Another project Bud Miller facilitated was a regional park for Lloydminster. The park was designed for a variety of activities from hiking to swimming to fishing. Trails throughout the city lead to the park and it soon became our most popular facility. When it opened on June 19, 1986, the name chosen, Bud Miller All Seasons Park, seemed fitting and deserved recognition of the man who had contributed so much to our city.

Alberta Premier, Ralph Klein addresses a crowd of Lloydminster supporters in the Lakeland College gymnasium

Photo courtesy of Lakeland College

Photo courtesy of Lloydminster Regional Archives

Above: One time rural school teacher, Anders Aalborg represented the Lloydminster area for 23 years, 19 in cabinet (Minister of Education 1952-1964, Provincial Treasurer 1964-1971)

Saskatchewan

A Tale of Two Provinces

At no time does Lloydminster's bi-provincial existence seem more improbable than when discussing provincial politics. Alberta and Saskatchewan came into the world as twins on September 1, 1905. In the early days, thanks to the Federal Government, they both had Liberal regimes. However, by the time of the upset results of the Alberta and Federal elections of 1921, the two provinces were growing apart. With the advent of the CCF in Saskatchewan and Social Credit in Alberta in the 1930's it seemed the former twins were heading rapidly to the opposite extremes. By the 1950's, and on to the present, media and academic analysts have assured us that the two provinces are polar opposites of each other. Left wing Saskatchewan still holds on to democratic socialism while entrepreneurial Alberta embraces the "Alberta Advantage" of free market capitalism.

In Lloydminster, this difference is puzzling because we know that on most issues our neighbours across the road would echo our views, but in provincial politics, we're different. Or are we?

Photo courtesy of Gordon Harris

Above: Ron Harris (right) presents the Premier of Saskatchewan, Ross Thatcher, with a "Barr Colonist's Wagon" while shaking hands across the border

Below: Former Lloydminster Comprehensive High School teacher, Miro Kwasnica, served three terms in the Saskatchewan Legislature. (Note photo of former CCF Premier Tommy Douglas who once delivered a much rebroadcast Burns Supper speech in Lloydminster.)

Photo courtesy of the Saskatchewan Archives Board

Photo courtesy of Don Whiting

Members of the Legislative Assembly of Saskatchewan elected by constituencies containing Lloydminster:

1905 - Albert Champagne (Liberal)
1908 - Henry C. Lisle (Liberal)
1912 - John P. Lyle (Liberal)
1917 - Robert J. Gordon (Liberal)
1921 - Robert J. Gordon (Liberal)
1925 - Robert J. Gordon (Liberal)
1929 - Robert J. Gordon (Liberal)
1934 - A. J. McCauley (Farmer-Lab.)
1938 - William Roseland (Soc. Credit)
1944 - I. C. Nollet (CCF)
1948 - I. C. Nollet (CCF)
1952 - I. C. Nollet (CCF)
1956 - I. C. Nollet (CCF)
1960 - I. C. Nollet (CCF)
1964 - I. C. Nollet (NDP)
1967 - Miro Kwasnica (NDP)
1971 - Miro Kwasnica (NDP)
1975 - Miro Kwasnica (NDP)
1978 - Robert Long (NDP)
1982 - Michael Hopfner (PC)
1986 - Michael Hopfner (PC)
1991 - Violet Stanger (NDP)
1995 - Violet Stanger (NDP)
1999 - Milton Wakefield (SK Party)

Local physician Dr. Raffath Sayeed (left) makes a point with Saskatchewan Premier Roy Romanow.

Photo courtesy of the Saskatchewan Archives Board

Above: Bob Long found his youthful experience as a RM grader operator useful when he served as Minister of Highways. Later he was President of the Saskatchewan New Democratic Party.

Photo courtesy of Jack McGuffie

The Prime Minister Visits Lloydminster

Monday morning, August 8, 1910, was filled with excitement. This was the day that the Prime Minister of Canada, the silver haired orator, the leading statesman of the senior Dominion in the British empire, Sir Wilfrid Laurier was coming - here.

A special stand had been built complete with a carpeted walkway to it from the station platform. All had been decorated with evergreen boughs and colourful bunting and, of course, union jacks. Wagons and buggies had

Prime Minister Wilfrid Laurier (second from right) on the platform in Lloydminster displays the bouquet he had just received from Melitza Lynch (front right)

been streaming in from the surrounding countryside since before dawn. Hundreds of people, including a large delegation from Onion Lake, gathered, eagerly listening and looking east for the first signs of the special train. Soon the whistle of the steam locomotive answered their inquiries and quickly the great engine drivers were slowing and the gleaming luxury coaches were gliding across the border and halting in front of the station.

A few anxious minutes more and then loud cheers broke out as the official party alighted and strode quickly to the decorated stand. Never had Lloydminster seen such a bevy of dignitaries. Federal cabinet ministers and senators were mere by-standers. Both Walter Scott, premier of Saskatchewan and Arthur Sifton, premier of Alberta were present, as were our M.L.A.'s, H.C. Lisle (Saskatchewan) and A. Bramley-Moore (Alberta). Premier Sifton and Alberta political veterans Frank Oliver and C.W. Cross had come down from Edmonton in order to meet the Prime Minister as he entered Alberta.

Delegation from Onion Lake waits at Lloydminster's railway station for the arrival of Prime Minister Wilfrid Laurier, August 8, 1910.

Our local dignitaries also joined the platform party, among them Mayor J.P. Lyle of the Town of Lloydminster, Saskatchewan and Mayor R. W. Miller of the Village of Lloydminster, Alberta; as well as assorted local clergymen and presidents of local organizations. Mayor Lyle delivered the official address of welcome – an address that had been done in artful calligraphy by Mrs. Alice Rendell and which, after being read, was presented to the Prime Minister.

Photo courtesy of the Glenbow Archives - JA-1036-9

Photo courtesy of Ronald Rackham

There followed the reading of a number of petitions including the following: Mr. R. W. Miller presented a petition on behalf of the Board of Trade calling for better accommodation for the local Saskatchewan Light Horse regiment, and Mr. Stanley Rackham presented a petition on behalf of the Farmers Associations dealing with the construction of inland and Pacific coast terminal elevators, assistance to the chilled meat industry, and construction of the Hudson Bay Railway. Prime Minister Laurier (seated at left end of table) listens attentively as Stanley Rackham reads the petition. Mr. Rackham described the day as follows:

Entry in Stanley Rackham's diary for August 8, 1910:

Mon. 8<u>th</u> Sir Wilfrid Laurier, on his western tour, was to speak in town in the morning, so Smith and I went in early. We found a good many people in and numbers of farmers from different local associations for some distance around who had come in to support the presentation of the S.G.G.A. [Saskatchewan Grain Growers' Association] and U.F.A. [United Farmers of Alberta]. Laurier was due about 10 o'clock and before his arrival a farmers' meeting was held at which the petition was read over and discussed, and the question brought up as to who should read it. My name being mentioned it was suggested that I should give a preliminary reading at the meeting, and that being accomplished fairly satisfactorily I was appointed spokesman. A platform had been erected adjoining the station, on which Sir Wilfrid and his supporters were to sit and receive the various petitions, and a Guard of Honour of the Sask. Light Horse were drawn up at the station to receive him. A very fair crowd of people was present at his arrival, and he was well cheered as his party moved on to the platform. Two or three petitions as to customs, public buildings, etc. were presented, and then my turn arrived – and I think rather to the disgust of Sir Wilfrid's manager – I asked to be allowed to read the petition instead of just presenting it. The reading went off satisfactorily and was greeted with cheers at the close, and then Sir Wilfrid spoke for 10 minutes or so in reply. Following that a few people were presented to him and then the party boarded the train and left for the west. On our return to the farm, we continued our preparation for the Show [Lloydminster Agricultural Exhibition (Saskatchewan)] and in the afternoon took in the pigs and cattle.

Laurier's visit made headlines in the Lloydminster Times.

Robert Borden Visits Lloydminster During 1911 Election Campaign

According to the *Lloydminster Times*, "every last man – and woman – turned out to listen to Mr. R. L. Borden on Thursday evening". Borden's western tour was part of one of the most pivotal elections in Canadian history. The hot issue was "reciprocity", a term for "free trade" with the United States. Borden told Lloydminsterites "he was unalterably opposed to Reciprocity and would rather quit public life forever than consent to its culmination".

Borden's argument was that Reciprocity would start Canada down the slippery slope to commercial union with the United States and that would be decidedly anti-British and "unpatriotic". The *Times* declared "there was much flag waving and appeal to British sentiment".

The meeting was held in the Drill Hall, which "had been tastefully arranged for the occasion", and "Little Verna Miller presented Mr. Borden with a beautiful bouquet of flowers which was very gracefully received by the Opposition Leader".

The Conservatives would win the election; Laurier's 15 uninterrupted years as Prime Minister came to an end.

John Diefenbaker accepts a pair of western boots to take with him to Ottawa. Herb Sparrow and Ben Gulak (right) look on.

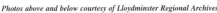
Photos above and below courtesy of Lloydminster Regional Archives

Prime Minister Lester B. Pearson poses with Lloydminster graduands of a federally sponsored business management short course in November 1964. Participants were identified in the Meridian Booster as follows:
(Standing, back row, l-r): David L. McCaw, Wayne Shortt, Amile Iwanic, Robert D. Noyes, R. Ernest Gillanders, Jack O. Handel, George M. Phillips, Donald Myers and E. W. Luther, instructor. Second row (l-r): John A. Berry, John W. Stevens, Harry J. Tymofichuk, William B. Noyes, Clifford V. McNeil, Alex Essar, Erd J. Fisher, Alfred Harris, Ray Germshied and James G. Young. (Seated l-r): Mrs. Rose Meyers, Mrs. Olinda Tindall, Mrs. Jeanne M. Holt, the Rt. Hon. L. B. Pearson, Mrs Joyce Essar, Miss Barbara Dobson, instructress, and Mrs. Verna Johnson. (Kneeling l-r): W. A. Bruchkowsky, President of the Chamber of Commerce, Ronald C. Harris, D. S. Congour, Federal Department of Labour, and W. Jack Crawford, a graduand and chairman of the Education Committee of the Chamber of Commerce.

"MAZ"

Certainly the most influential and effective Member of Parliament to represent Lloydminster was Don Mazankowski. Thoroughly in touch with his constituency, he attended countless functions in Lloydminster and area. He was a popular Member even before the Progressive Conservatives swept to power in 1984 under Brian Mulroney. Mr. Mazankowski will be best remembered locally for his central role in bringing the Upgrader to reality.

Above: Don Mazankowski liked to be involved in consituency activities.

Right: As Deputy Prime Minister, Maz literally worked shoulder to shoulder with Prime Minister Mulroney.

Below: Senior Ministers in the Mulroney Cabinet (l-r) Michael Wilson, Don Mazankowski, and Bill McKnight. Mr. McKnight represented the Saskatchewan side of Lloydminster, thus marking the only time in our history when Lloydminster had two federal Cabinet representatives.

Don Mazankowski was in cabinet throughout the Mulroney years in government occupying increasingly senior positions such as Minister of Finance and Deputy Prime Minister, unprecedented for an MP from Western Canada. By the end of the Mulroney period, in 1993, "Maz" was regarded as the most competent and influential Minister in cabinet.

All photos courtesy of Don Mazankowski

Photo courtesy of Paul Douglas

Joe Clark (left) poses with unidentified guest at the Wayside Inn just prior to Mr. Clark becoming Prime Minister in 1979.

Prime Minister Brian Mulroney made the final stop of his Charlottetown Accord campaign in Lloydminster on November 16, 1992. The result here was "No"

Other Prime Ministerial visits included an early morning whistle stop by W. L. M. King during the 1926 election campaign. The Lloydminster Times berated local Liberal organizers for not doing more to publicize the visit and bring out a crowd. In defense of the party faithful, Mr. King's train was scheduled to pause only briefly at 4:00 AM. Since it was more than an hour behind schedule, Mr. King did emerge to shake some hands.

Another visit of King was scheduled for the 1928 Lloydminster Fair when the 25th Anniversary of the arrival of the Barr Colonists was being celebrated. Apparently some believe he was here but the Minister of the Interior, Charles Stewart, filled in as King was chairing a League of Nations conference that week in Paris.

John Diefenbaker visited Lloydminster several times, both before and during his time as Prime Minister. Lester Pearson made a visit in 1964. Joe Clark stopped by in 1979 and Brian Mulroney in 1992.

As have other Canadians, Lloydminsterites have been caught up in the changing political climates and expressed their opinions for and against the issues of the day. Yet, on those few occasions when the Prime Minister has visited, Lloydminsterites have clearly expressed their pride in their community and love of Canada.

Photo courtesy of Don Mazankowski

BORDERING ON GREATNESS

The Royal Visit - July 31, 1978

Editor George Baynton of the Lloydminster Times described the visit under the headline:

A Lovely Kindly Queen

"...The account of her visit can be told quite simply. She arrived by special plane from Saskatoon; was greeted by Mayor and Mrs. Robertson at the airport; proceeded to Hallsholme and mingled with the Barr Colonists and pioneers; inspected Legion Colour Party and Old Log Church, listened to Mosaic Singers, signed the register, planted a pine tree and visited with the Mothers' Union at Weaver Park; greeted the dignitaries at the Centennial Civic Centre, signed the guest book, watched the Scottish, Indian and Ukrainian dancers, and mingled with the people; and then left by car for the airport and Edmonton - a short visit of slightly more than an hour. Prince Phillip and Prince Edward accompanied her."

To the Barr Colonists, steeped in the lore of the British Empire, it would have seemed a "dream beyond compare" for the monarch to visit their community in the wilds of Western Canada. Yet, despite all odds against it, more than a dozen Barr Colonists survived to be introduced to Queen Elizabeth II when she visited Lloydminster.

Photos courtesy of BCHCC

Above: Her Majesty chats with Joyce and Jack Kemp. Mr. Kemp had retired that day as Secretary-Treasurer of the Public School Board and thought it was very nice of the Queen to come to help him celebrate. Mayor Russ Robertson on the right.

Inset: (l-r) HRH Prince Phillip, Mrs. Anne Robertson, Her Majesty, and Mayor Russ Robertson.
Above: Queen Elizabeth II signs the City Guest Book outside the Civic Centre while excited Lloydminsterites look on.

Photos courtesy of the Barr Colony Heritage Cultural Centre

Afterword

We hope you enjoyed this overview of Lloydminster's first century. Obviously there are many more stories that could be told if space permitted. We anticipate many will come forward with stories and photos that they believe should have been included. If resources allow, we will include these, subject to editing for length and accuracy, on www.lloydminster.net where we will maintain a page of comments or updates to this publication.

Certainly, we who worked on this project have come to a better appreciation of the rich and unique character of Lloydminster's history. We have also been struck by how much of our history has already been lost and how much is on the threshold of passing away. It is for this reason that we advocate the continued development of a community archives where the written documents of our history can be collected, organized and preserved for future generations. Bishop Lloyd wrote in 1940 that he was donating his papers to the Lloydminster Archives. What he meant and where the papers went seems a mystery now. The Centennial Association worked hard in the late 1990's and secured a space and equipment for an archives. Since then, dedicated volunteers have been sorting and cataloguing a few donations but a professional archivist is needed to provide assistance and consistency. One is reminded that both the Lloydminster Public Library and the Barr Colony Heritage Cultural Centre began as volunteer operations. Eventually the community recognized they were important enough institutions that they deserved City support. We hope this book will stimulate enough interest in our history that citizens will press City Council to fund a Community Archives so that our history can be preserved in an organized way.

This does not mean just information about the earliest days. It means recording events on an ongoing basis and preserving records of them. As an example, we spent weeks verifying the identity of prominent individuals in a photo taken in 1985. This is how swiftly our history can be lost. We also had many instances where the recollections of "old-timers" proved inaccurate. One cannot do history by simply asking the nearest old-timer.

Another issue raised is why we need an Archives when we already have a museum. The two have quite different functions. Our BCHCC has some archival material simply because there was no archives. However, a museum is intended for objects (artifacts) while an archives preserves written documents such as newspapers, diaries, letters, pamphlets, and programs. Photographs are usually catalogued and preserved by an archives as well.

In compiling this book we looked at over 2000 photos. Sometimes we were fortunate to recover a rare or remarkable photo. More often photos that we know existed have now disappeared. On top of this, there are hundreds of photos with no identification as to who is in them, what event they portray or what date they were taken. An archives could help remedy all of these situations and make the job much easier for those who may write the history of Lloydminster's second century.

For those wanting to read more about Lloydminster's history, there are very few published sources available. This current volume is the first overall history of Lloydminster. *75 Years of Sport and Culture in Lloydminster*, compiled by the Lloydminster History of Recreation and Cultural Activities Committee, published by the Lloydminster Senior Citizens Society, and printed by the *Lloydminster Times* in 1979, contains useful information and interesting photos although, due to the technology and the budget at that time, most are reproduced in quite poor quality. There is the misleadingly titled *The Lloydminster Story* by David W. Paterson, published by the Lloydminster and District Agricultural Association Ltd. in 1966. It is actually an account of the background of the local co-operative. A more useful work on the same topic is *Reflections of 75 Years* by Wilma Groenen, published by the Lloydminster and District Co-operative Ltd. and printed by Meridian Printing Ltd. in 1990.

There were perhaps as many as two dozen first hand accounts by Barr Colonists. All are long out of print except Gully Farm by Mary Hiemstra reprinted by Fifth House Publishers in 1997. The others range from the humorous to the bitter. None are particularly useful as detailed histories in themselves. Only two professional histories relating to Lloydminster have been done previously. They are: Reid, Helen Evans, *All Silent All Damned: the Search for Isaac Barr*. Toronto: Ryerson, 1969; and Bowen, Lynne, *Muddling Through: The Remarkable Story of the Barr Colonists*. Vancouver: Douglas & McIntyre Ltd., 1992.

So, in conclusion, the recording of our history has only begun. We hope our efforts in this book will inspire others to build upon our work. To all of those who come after us, whether they are writing history or making history, we extend our sincere best wishes. We hope our pioneering effort takes its place in the history of a community - bordering on greatness.

Index

Photo courtesy of Carylanne Martin

Franklin Lloyd Foster
B.Ed., B.A., M.A., Ph.D.

Franklin Foster was born in Lloydminster and grew up on a family farm nearby. He graduated from Lloydminster Composite High School and received his first two degrees from the University of Alberta. He began his teaching career at Dewberry and Marwayne. Later he taught for the Department of National Defence and the Lakeland School Division before moving to Kingston, Ontario where he earned both a Masters and Doctoral degree, specializing in Canadian history.

During his student career, he received a number of academic awards, including: a University of Alberta First Class Standing Prize, an Ontario Graduate Studies Fellowship, a Samuel R. McLaughlin Scholarship, a Humanities and Social Sciences Research Council Scholarship and a Canada Council Scholarship.

Following completion of his Doctorate, he taught at Queen's University, Red Deer College and was in private business before returning to the Lloydminster area to accept the principalship of Tulliby Lake School. In 1989, Dr. Foster joined Lakeland College, establishing the History program in the University Transfer Department, in which he still teaches.

Dr. Foster has written extensively for a number of mediums. He is recognized for his expertise in the history of Western Canada. His best known previous publication was an account of the life of Alberta's fifth premier entitled: *John E. Brownlee: A Biography*.

Franklin lives in Lloydminster with his wife Dorothy and several teddy bears. His e-mail address is: franklin@fosterlearning.com.

A Word from the Author

The majority of my great-grandparents were in Western Canada before the 1885 Rebellion. Two of them, William and Margaret Hunter, were part of the group that established Saskatoon. Twenty years later, my great-grandmother baked bread, which my grandmother, then a teenager, delivered to the Barr Colonist camp in Saskatoon on horseback.

My parents, Ralph and Jean Foster, were likely the last folks to travel from Saskatoon to Lloydminster by horse and wagon – not as a hobby but out of necessity. They loaded all their household effects on one wagon, which my Mom drove while keeping an eye out for my seven year old brother. My Dad piloted another team pulling a wagon loaded with farm machinery. Two cows were towed behind and a foal and an old dog tagged along beside. They camped out along the way, arriving at their new farm in the Golden Valley district on March 30, 1945.

On the morning of July 17, my Mom felt the pangs of labour and, still without an automobile; my Dad walked a mile to the neighbour's for help. The husband was away, but the wife, the redoubtable Libbie Young, brought their car over and drove my Mom to the Lloydminster Hospital where that afternoon I was born. The first person I met was Dr. Smith. It's tempting to claim I discussed the state of medical care in Lloydminster with him but I have to admit that like so many I began life as a small child. My mother was determined to name me after her favourite political hero, the recently deceased Franklin Roosevelt, but my parents also wished to commemorate their arrival in the community so concluded that my middle name would be Lloyd.

Despite my middle name, I preferred life in the country to our visits to "town". Only in later years did I come to understand and appreciate the aroma of sulphurous asphalt. I attended Golden Valley School – same classroom, same teacher, for eight years, which may make me seem pretty slow but that's the way it was. When it came time to ride the school bus into town for grade nine, it seemed like a big adventure. We were supposed to be opening the new junior high school but it was still under construction so we crammed into the existing high school. One of the few people I knew, Charlie Bob Fox, and I, used to visit the construction site, once getting a guided tour out of the gymnasium before the roof was installed.

When I completed high school, I left Lloydminster and, except for visits to my parents, did not return for 25 years. When I came back, I was often asked if I knew a particular person – such as R.J.R. Noyes. Well, I knew the name but there hadn't been much opportunity for a rag tag country boy to do lunch with one of the town's movers and shakers.

I did have the good fortune to get to know Mr. Noyes, and many others, personally after returning. In fact, being away from Lloydminster helped me get a sense of its history in some ways better than if I had remained. I have come to appreciate that Lloydminster's story is an interesting and important one. We have done some pretty remarkable things over our first 100 years. The second 100 will likely be equally as "awesome". Best wishes to the group that tells that story. I hope they have more time, more money, but as much fun as we did putting together the story of Lloydminster's first century.

A Word from the Co-Author

If it were not for the paths that my family took, I might have never known this place. As a boy, my father, John, came to Lloydminster in 1952 from a farm near Brightsand, Saskatchewan. His stepfather was to start work at the new Sidney Roofing Plant. Dad attended the Meridian School and later the Lloydminster Composite High School. As an adult, he chose to make his life here, and went into business. My mother, Louise Fink, came from Paradise Hill, Saskatchewan in 1964 to attend Reeves Business College. Lloydminster, a thriving community, offered many job prospects for a young secretary and mom remained in the city after graduating. Eventually, my mother and father's paths crossed, and the two were married in 1967. After several years, they moved to an acreage a few miles east of Lloydminster where they raised their four children.

I arrived in the Border City via the Lloydminster Hospital in 1972. For twelve years, I stood at the edge of Highway 16 every morning waiting for the school bus to whisk me into town to school. On Tuesdays, I had soccer practice; Friday was Cub Night with the Lloydminster Boy Scouts. On Saturdays, I went to Lloyd with my mom to get the groceries. Sometimes, we would stop at Fisher's Department Store. When Fisher's installed their escalator, the only one in Lloydminster, I rode up and down it repeatedly while my mother went about shopping for shoes for my younger sister.

In 1978, I stood on tip-toes to catch a glimpse of Queen Elizabeth II, who had come on the occasion of the 75th anniversary of the Barr Colonists' arrival in Lloydminster. At the time I had little knowledge of who the Barr Colonists were and why the occasion was worth celebrating. What has become clearer over the past year of researching and writing Lloydminster's history is that the foundation of our community is based on a convergence of paths, reaching back to the the British settlers who journeyed here in 1903, to present day travellers who choose to make their homes here . It took me many years to realize it, but I have reached my destination. Lloydminster is my home. I hope that as you turned the pages of this volume of history, you too acquired a newfound or renewed connection with our community.

Special thanks to Dr. Franklin Foster and his wife Dorothy. The Fosters granted me a wonderful opportunity to take part in this important project, our history of Lloydminster. All of those who contributed to getting this book made must be graciously thanked. However, without the Fosters, this book would not exist. Their vision, dedication, persistence, financial contribution,and exhausting long hours of work have made Bordering on Greatness a reality.

In memory of a loving mother, Louise Griffith, 1946-2001

Mom, your belief in me allowed me to fulfill a dream.
Thank you for a lifetime of love, encouragement, and support.

Photo courtesy of Yi Jung-Soon

Alan Grant Griffith
B.Ed.

Raised on an acreage east of the city, Alan Griffith attended school in Lloydminster and took part in many local youth organizations including 4-H and the Boy Scouts.

Alan graduated from the Lloydminster Comprehensive High School and went on to the University of Saskatchewan where he received his Bachelor of Education Degree in 1994.

After teaching stints in Unity and North Battleford, Saskatchewan, Griffith packed his bags and moved to Seoul, Korea where he began teaching English as a Second Language to Korean elementary and middle years students. In the same year, he met his wife, Eun-Jung. Alan later took a job as an international school teacher, and the Griffiths welcomed their first child, Conor, into the world in September 1999.

In 2000, the Griffith family returned to Canada, and Alan's home, Lloydminster. After responding to a classified advertisement in the *Meridian Booster* calling for researchers, Alan found himself in contact with his former Lakeland College professor, Dr. Franklin Foster. What began as an assignment to research the history of education in Lloydminster soon became much more.

Currently, Griffith is a teacher at E.S. Laird Middle School in Lloydminster. In addition, he continues to work with Foster Learning Inc. By the time this book has been published, the Griffiths will have a new addition to their family.

Alan can be reached at his e-mail address:
alan@fosterlearning.com

The History of Lloydminster
You've only just begun...

Biographies ChapterCompanions KeywordSearches
LloydminsterLinks Submissions Photographs
ExpandedInformation UpdatesandCorrections
CentennialInfo HistoricalDocuments...

Your on-line companion to Bordering on Greatness

www.lloydminster.net

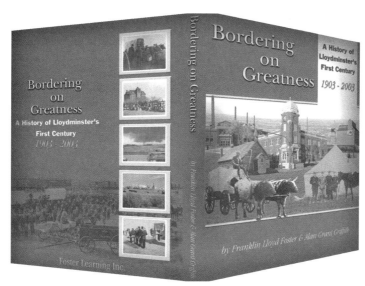

To order copies of

Bordering on Greatness: A History of Lloydminster's First Century
1903 - 2003
by Franklin Lloyd Foster & Alan Grant Griffith

Photocopy the form below, complete and mail to:

Bordering on Greatness Book Order
L.D.C.C.A.
Box 2003
Lloydminster, SK   S9V 1R5

Name: _____

Address: _____

_____ Postal Code _____

Telephone: _____ _____

$45.00 per copy	Number of books:
IF SHIPPING IS REQUIRED, ADD $5.00 FOR LOCATIONS IN ALBERTA OR SASKATCHEWAN, AND $10.00 FOR ALL OTHER POINTS.	Sub-Total: _____
PLEASE MAKE CHEQUES OR MONEY ORDERS PAYABLE TO: L.D.C.C.A.	Shipping (if required): _____
	Total: _____
G.S.T. and P.S.T. are not required *Offer good until December 31, 2003*	Signature: _____